THE COMPLETE
Fishing
MANUAL

THE COMPLETE
Fishing
MANUAL

Content previously published in *Eyewitness Companion Fishing*

Henry Gilbey

DK LONDON

Editorial Lead	Stephanie Farrow
Project Editor	Abigail Mitchell
US Editor	Heather Wilcox
Senior Art Editor	Gillian Andrews
Managing Editor	Gareth Jones
Senior Managing Art Editor	Lee Griffiths
Jacket Design Development Manager	Sophia MTT
Production Editor	George Nimmo
Senior Production Controller	Rachel Ng
Art Director	Karen Self
Associate Publishing Director	Liz Wheeler
Publishing Director	Jonathan Metcalf

DK DELHI

Senior Art Editor	Ira Sharma
Art Editor	Noopur Dalal
Senior Editor	Janashree Singha
Editor	Devangana Ojha
Managing Editor	Soma B. Chowdhury
Senior Managing Art Editor	Arunesh Talapatra
DTP Designers	Syed Md Farhan, Vijay Kandwal
Senior DTP Designer	Shanker Prasad
Senior Picture Researcher	Surya Sankash Sarangi
Picture Research Manager	Taiyaba Khatoon
Pre-production Manager	Balwant Singh
Production Manager	Pankaj Sharma
Editorial Head	Glenda Fernandes
Design Head	Malavika Talukder

This American Edition, 2021
First American Edition, 2011
Published in the United States by DK Publishing
1450 Broadway, Suite 801, New York, NY 10018
Copyright © 2011, 2021 Dorling Kindersley Limited

DK, a Division of Penguin Random House LLC
21 22 23 24 25 10 9 8 7 6 5 4 3 2 1
001–322623–May/2021

A catalog record for this book is available from the Library of Congress.

ISBN 978-0-7440-3416-5
Based on content previously published in
Eyewitness Companions: Fishing

DK books are available at special discounts when purchased in bulk for sales promotions,
premiums, fund-raising, or educational use. For details, contact: DK Publishing Special Markets,
1450 Broadway, Suite 801, New York, NY 10018 SpecialSales@dk.com

Printed and bound in China

For the curious
www.dk.com

Contents

Contents (continued)

World of Fishing 282

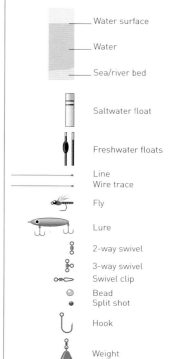

Key to rig diagrams
Standard symbols are used in this book to indicate different elements of fishing tackle. They are not intended to show, or to recommend, specific designs.

- Water surface
- Water
- Sea/river bed
- Saltwater float
- Freshwater floats
- Line
- Wire trace
- Fly
- Lure
- 2-way swivel
- 3-way swivel
- Swivel clip
- Bead
- Split shot
- Hook
- Weight

Never in a million years will I be able to fully explain why fishing has captured me so totally. The simple art of outwitting fish has become a burning passion for millions of people; I hope this book goes some way toward guiding you along the path to the exciting world of fishing.

Being lucky enough to work in and around fishing has given me a different outlook on the sport than I once held. While I was once obsessed about trying to catch bigger fish wherever I went, I am now excited by every aspect of fishing, to the extent that I believe I have come almost full circle. The places we visit, the people we meet, the fish (of course) that we might or might not catch, the quality of light, or the savagery of the weather—these are the things I have come to appreciate more fully over time. Fishing is about trying to outwit nature, and since our natural world is delightfully unpredictable, we, as anglers, are dealing with variables we simply cannot control, and we are always learning. Indeed, this new edition is full of updated information and is an excellent guide to get you started, but it is my hope that you will soon learn to think for yourself and to try different things. While the fishing strategies in this book will give you every chance of success, remember that there is nothing truly definite about the methods you can use in any scenario.

A key attribute of a naturally gifted angler is to strive to discover more and more information in the pursuit of the fish. Take a strategy and advance it to suit you,

and then feed the information you've discovered back into the food chain. Anglers are often extremely socially interactive—indeed, our sport is what we love to talk about (too much, some close to us might say), and information is continually passed around and then further adapted. This is how the sport of fishing grows and evolves, and it's informed this new edition of the book too.

As a teenager, I thought I knew everything about life, but when I reached my twenties it began to dawn on me that perhaps I had been a little hasty. Fishing is a little like that. Most anglers, at some point in their fishing, make the mistake of thinking that they have "gotten one over on" the fish, but nature always likes to give a little kick to remind us that we are but humans.

⏶ **Give me water**, wide open spaces and stunning fish to catch, and I will be a happy man.

Fishing is a sport that gives you the chance to learn something new every single time you practice it. If fishing becomes a lifelong pursuit for you—and I hope that it does—you will never stop learning.

Above all, I hope that this book brings you into a sport that is huge fun. We go fishing because we enjoy it. Whatever fishing is to you, hold on to the memory of the first fish you ever caught, and remember your beaming smile and shrieks of joy. Fishing offers a lifetime of simple fun, and if this book goes any way toward that, then my job is done. And I could not be happier.

Henry Gilbey

Fishing
Basics

Before you go fishing for the first time, it is really helpful to learn and understand more about fishing as a whole so that your initial experiences are successful and fulfilling. In time, fishing will become second nature, to the point where it becomes a part of your everyday life.

This section is designed to bring you to the point where you can go out fishing with a new set of skills and knowledge. Understanding the historical developments of the sport gives an insight into modern fishing tackle and techniques and their relevance today. Much of the tackle in use today is simply the next technological advance from more traditional equipment, but much older-style fishing tackle is still extremely useful. Time will never change the need for certain skills, even if fishing equipment has moved on. Tackle is now made from modern materials and can do things previously thought impossible. For example, a lightweight carbon-fiber pole allows amazing precision placement of a delicate float. Modern materials and engineering can give you better chances to catch more fish.

However, having the latest gear is not useful on its own—you need to know all about local

⚠ **Fresh baits** Learn about fishing baits, from a simple piece of bread to modern, high-protein commercial baits.

rules and regulations, or where to buy your bait and tackle. Meeting fellow anglers and learning about different fishing disciplines will help you develop your own fishing to better suit your situation. Keep an open mind, though; if you strive to learn more about all kinds of fishing, you will catch more fish. You will be amazed at the amount of crossover there is between the various disciplines; anglers can learn much from each other that they can then apply to their own fishing.

Having acquired all this knowledge, you need to learn how to reach the fish you want to catch. Casting your bait, lure, or fly is a fundamental part of fishing, and knowing how to cast properly, safely, and efficiently is vital to your success. Then you need to learn how to deal with that nerve-trembling moment when you finally get a bite. The techniques for landing a fish safely and humanely compose the final element of your basic fishing skills. Complete your introduction to fishing by learning about aquatic environments so that you know where fish are most likely to be.

◀◀ **Landing fish** However and wherever you go fishing, that moment of successfully catching a fish is such a thrill.

Getting started

Before you take to the water, spend some time learning about the rules and regulations associated with angling. Learn where to find up-to-date information and where to meet fellow anglers. Above all, spend time around water to pick up valuable advice from other anglers, which will help make your fishing experiences both pleasurable and safe. The more background knowledge you can acquire, the more kinds of fishing you can try.

Fishing today

The modern sport of fishing is practiced by millions of anglers around the world. Some people fish purely for sport, and try to return all fish to the water unharmed, whereas many anglers enjoy sport-fishing because it offers a unique mix of pleasure and food.

Categories of fishing

Angling is divided into three distinct disciplines: freshwater fishing; saltwater fishing; and fly-fishing. Traditionally, anglers would focus on a single discipline but, increasingly in modern sport-fishing, the boundaries are becoming less defined. Advanced fishing techniques and changing attitudes are bringing about novel ways to catch fish, opening up new areas to fish, and creating faster, more efficient ways of relaying information.

» **Modern reel** Much modern fishing tackle is far lighter and more efficient than in the past, enabling you to fish for large fish with surprisingly light gear.

Freshwater fishing

Freshwater fishing traditionally consists of fishing for freshwater species using either baits or lures. Coarse fishing is a largely English term applied to fishing for non-game species using baits and lures. In some parts of the world, anglers are accustomed to fishing for game species, such as salmon and trout, which are often targeted by fly-fishing, using baits or lures, and this is all part of freshwater fishing. Moreover, non-game freshwater species, such as pike, carp, and barbel, are increasingly being targeted with fly-fishing tackle.

Saltwater fishing

Saltwater fishing involves fishing for any saltwater species using baits and lures, from land or from a boat. This is arguably the most varied part of what is already an astonishingly wide-ranging sport, for the oceans contain many different species that respond to varying strategies. The most unpredictable waters to fish tend to be the oceans; tides, weather, and even the different phases of the moon can affect the way fish feed, move, and migrate, and whether anglers can access the waters in which they want to fish.

Fly-fishing

Fly-fishing has traditionally been the art of presenting artificial imitations of insects to predominantly game species such as salmon and trout, but fly-fishing today is a far broader discipline. While fly-fishing with dry flies on the carefully managed chalk streams of southern England might be considered the birth of modern fly-fishing, the sport has evolved to the point where fly-fishing methods are used in a wide range of environments. A fantastic array of freshwater species are fished for with modern fly-fishing tackle, and saltwater fly-fishing is becoming increasingly popular all over the world.

☒ **Saltwater fishing** The sea contains the fastest and largest fish, which often require the use of high-speed boats to fish successfully.

Pioneering fly-anglers have broken down stereotypes and worked on catching saltwater fish on fly-fishing tackle in a way that was once thought impossible. One only has to look at big-fish specialists targeting huge sharks, tarpon, and even blue marlin on fly-fishing tackle to see how far the sport has progressed. Fly-fishing for bonefish now seems as natural as fly-fishing for salmon. This means that the rigid categories that once defined fishing are now blending into what is simply known as the sport of fishing.

《 Fresh challenges
From the smallest rivers to the largest lakes, freshwater fishing offers a huge variety of species to catch and methods to use.

《 Skill and finesse
The graceful art of presenting artificial flies to fish requires great skill and finesse, whether in saltwater or freshwater. Many species of fish can be caught on the fly.

Fishing for the first time

Fishing is essentially a very simple activity. In its most basic form, it comprises no more than the attempt to fool a fish into taking a bait or artificial lure. Newcomers to the sport should not be daunted by the special terminology or the vast array of tackle choices available.

Getting hooked

An angler never forgets his or her first catch, whether it be a mackerel caught from a vacation pier or a largemouth bass in a warm Florida lake. Many novice anglers are lucky enough to catch a fish on their first fishing trip and become "hooked" for life.

The experience of outwitting both the wild animal and the environment that it inhabits lends an insight into what life might have been like for our prehistoric hunter-gatherer ancestors. Many of today's anglers will never eat the fish they catch, but the fact remains that humans first learned to fish in order to obtain food.

Going fishing for the first time is all about having fun. Although fishing is a serious sport, for many—especially for newcomers to the activity—it is, above all, a pastime or a hobby to be enjoyed.

Passing on knowledge

The best way to learn to fish is to go out with an experienced angler, whether a professional

»» Learning with an expert Nothing beats professional instruction, especially for fly-fishing, where casting is vital. All over the world you will find qualified instructors and guides.

»» Your first fish Few ever forget the thrill of their first catch, however modest its size. And even after years of fishing, an echo of that excitement is relived after every catch.

teacher or guide, or a willing friend or relative. One of the aspects of the sport of fishing that makes it so special is the fact that many experienced anglers are happy to impart their hard-earned knowledge to enthusiastic novices. Fishing as a sport is constantly evolving and this happens because each generation of anglers fishes in their own way, and then passes on their experience and knowledge to the next generation. However, the benefits of sharing fishing know-how are not all one-way. The sheer thrill of fishing and catching fish, that suddenly begins to seize the first-timer can be infectious. In this way, bringing a newcomer into the sport can often rekindle a dormant love for the activity in someone who has perhaps not been fishing for years. Nobody is ever going to care whether that first fish is a monster or a minnow, but nothing grabs the interest to the same degree as actually catching a fish.

Fishing safety

Fishing is about trying to outwit nature, and in so doing it requires proximity to perhaps the most unpredictable element: water. One of the first lessons the fishing novice must learn is to place safety above all else when planning a fishing trip— for example, by taking into account weather forecasts, or by wearing a buoyancy aid when on a boat. Shore-fishing, especially from rocks in tidal or potentially rough waters, requires constant vigilance for changes in the condition of the sea. In addition, one of the most vital safety precautions is not to fish near overhead power lines with long rods and not to fish when lightning is forecast. This is because modern fishing rods make excellent conductors of electricity.

Fishing with children When taking children on their first fishing trips, it is important to use the opportunity to teach basic safety. However, you also need to make the experience fun for them.

Fishing clubs and tackle shops

There are plenty of ways to meet fellow anglers, whether your aim is to get instruction, swap ideas, or simply access new waters. Fishing by its very nature is often a solitary pastime, but clubs, tackle shops, and Internet forums provide the opportunity for anglers to get together.

» Fishing with friends
Nothing beats a fishing expedition with a group of friends. Sharing the experience with those who love fishing as much as you do is what the sport is all about.

Local clubs

In most areas you can find a thriving fishing club. Ask in your local tackle shop, look in the local press, and search on the Internet for a fishing club that suits the kind of fishing you want to do. Most clubs have regular meetings, fishing days, and possibly even instructional sessions for beginners. Facilities can often be made accessible for different levels of mobility, with ramps, wide paths, and wheelchair-accessible pontoons to get anglers safely down to the water's edge. Roll-on, roll-off boats ensure wheelchair anglers are able to get out on the water too. Many also have access to stretches of waters that otherwise would not be available and/or for which the charges are far lower than to nonmembers.

Clubs often run competitions that can attract large numbers of anglers, and these might give you a taste of competitive fishing. Some clubs also organize fishing trips to waters farther afield, and even to other countries. But most of all, a fishing club provides a social center for the angler to spend time with other anglers and take part in the age-old traditions of talking, sharing fishing knowledge, and, of course, telling the tale of "the one that got away."

Tackle shops

Your local tackle shop is usually the busy hub of the local fishing scene. While there is a thriving network of discounted mail-order Internet shops, local stores can often give advice about baits and tackle that work in the area. Many people who work in tackle shops are themselves avid and skillful anglers. Local tackle shops are often like a kind of club where people stop to talk

⚏ **Getting advice**
A good local fishing-tackle shop will be able to offer plenty of up-to-date, reliable local fishing advice that is invaluable to the visiting or novice angler.

ONLINE FISHING RESOURCES

Increasingly the world of fishing is online, whether through various social media platforms, mobile phone apps, forums, or fishing tackle websites offering the complete online shopping experience. You can share fishing ideas and experiences online, ask fishing questions on a fishing forum, easily check local weather forecasts and conditions, post catch shots from your latest trip, and order fishing tackle from other countries.

and swap information. Whenever you go fishing away from home, anywhere in the world, be sure to take the opportunity to drop into the nearest tackle shop and spend time talking to the people there.

Specialist fishing instructors

There are plenty of fly-fishing instructors who are qualified to teach about fly-casting and the techniques involved in this discipline. You can find them by searching on the Internet or by asking in tackle shops. Many instructors also provide guiding services on local waters. Boat-fishing skippers and guides, especially in sea fishing, will always provide as much good advice as you are willing to ask for. The sensible traveling angler will always seek advice from the guide. There are plenty of fishing magazines that cover all the basic and more advanced skills, and these are useful resources. However, nothing beats actually getting out on the water and learning by trial and error. An instructor is there to help put you on the right path and teach you the fundamental skills that will allow you to progress in your own time.

⚏ **Ensuring accessibility**
Many local clubs can offer instruction and accessible facilities for a wide range of ages and levels of mobility.

Fishing licenses

While many waters are free to all for fishing, in many places an angler will require some kind of fishing license or permit. It is essential to check in advance the regulations that apply to the waters—whether freshwater or saltwater—that you intend to fish.

» **Buying your license** Many fishing lodges can obtain a license or permit for you if you ask. Carry it at all times when you are fishing; you might be asked to show it.

Licenses, permits, and tickets

In many countries, the angler is required to hold a license or permit that covers fishing, whether in freshwater or in the sea. Such regulations are usually administered by a governmental organization. The angler may have to buy an additional license that permits fishing for migratory species (usually salmon). Many lakes and rivers can be fished only by purchasing a ticket for the period in which you intend to fish; while others are available only to their owners or to club members. Be sure to find out (in local tackle shops or on the Internet) whether you must seek local permission or otherwise pay to fish the water.

Freshwater licenses

Most freshwater fishing requires that the angler purchases a license. Much of this money goes into restocking and water-management programs. A different license may be needed for fishing for game species, especially if you are targeting salmon. Be careful to check whether you may take fish home; fines for infringement are often very severe. Be aware that there are closed seasons for some species, often timed to protect breeding times. In addition, local, temporary closures can be imposed. Some regulations also govern fishing methods. Ask about local rules, such as those regarding the fishing methods permitted, the use of barbless hooks, if keep nets can be used, or whether or not you can use ground bait.

Saltwater licenses

Sea fishing in much of the world is free, but some countries require you to purchase a sea-fishing license. Be sure to check before going fishing; ignorance of the local regulations is unlikely to impress the fishing authorities. Licenses and permits are usually purchased in local tackle shops or online. Many species are closely protected and you will be allowed to take only a limited number of these to eat.

« **Freedom of the sea** Throughout much of the world you may fish the oceans for free. Always check for no-go zones and take limits for the fish you are targeting.

☑ Exclusive river fishing The licensing rules for general freshwater fishing and fly-fishing often differ. Many fly-only rivers are tightly controlled and access may be limited.

Developing your fishing

Choosing which fish to target depends on the local waters and the tackle and skills you possess. Many anglers choose to target a variety of fish in all sorts of environments—from rivers and lakes to beaches and oceans—using a range of methods. They are all-round anglers.

>> **Fishing on the rocks**
Standing on rocks among the breaking waves and casting a fly, although unconventional, is one of the most exhilarating forms of fly-fishing.

A varied sport

Fishing is such a varied sport that it can be very easy to remain within your chosen discipline and, for example, restrict your fishing to the use of only fly-fishing, freshwater, or saltwater gear. There is nothing wrong with this; many anglers love to fish in their own way for their favorite species all the time. There is enough to master within each fishing discipline to keep you enthralled for life.

However, many anglers find themselves drawn to different kinds of fishing that take them away from what they already know and do. This desire to stretch your boundaries and learn more about other kinds of fishing can also contribute to your usual type of fishing. After branching out into another kind of fishing, you can take back new insights that will help you catch more fish in your familiar area of fishing.

Fishing on the move

Anglers learn from each other, and anglers from all disciplines share knowledge and ideas, often without even realizing they are doing so. This "cross-fertilization" between the disciplines is how fishing develops as a sport.

It is hugely satisfying to be able to catch fish from all kinds of waters, using all kinds of techniques. The finest all-around anglers have a deep respect for the many skills required to do this. As an all-around angler, you are constantly on the lookout for insights and techniques that are being used by others in what may seem to be very different circumstances from those you are facing, but may open up new possibilities for you.

All-around enjoyment

People go fishing because they love it. One angler might like to pursue big fish to the exclusion of all else, while another might prefer to go fishing at a nearby lake when time allows and be happy to catch anything. Such anglers have in common an enjoyment of the activity of going fishing. Part of being an all-around angler is being open

◀ A proud moment
It is noticeable how a successful catch can make people smile, especially if the fish is an unfamiliar species, caught using new skills, possibly in waters that are far from home. Sharing the moment with a like-minded companion only increases the pleasure.

to making connections with other anglers from all walks of life and from all parts of the world. All-around anglers want to talk to other anglers and learn more about their sport and those who do it. Remaining open to the input of others invariably broadens your horizons and enriches your fishing.

◀ Freshwater fishing
Float-fishing for freshwater fish requires concentration, patience, and sensitivity that can usefully be applied to many other kinds of fishing.

Fishing tackle

There are many different items of fishing tackle, from a variety of rods for different types of fishing to intricate, high-tech gadgets—such as electronic bite alarms—that will increase your success. Learning about essential tackle items will enable you to equip yourself correctly to catch any number of fish species in a range of ways. Just wearing the right clothing can be the key to making fishing more comfortable and more effective.

Rod basics

Fishing rods are available in a wide variety of lengths, weights, uses, actions, and even colors. There are core "families" of rods that correspond to each of the main categories of fishing. Anglers choose a rod to suit the type of fishing they plan to undertake.

Rod choices

In its most basic form, a fishing rod is designed to cast or drop the lure, fly, or bait out to the fish and then act as a support to the line when playing the hooked fish. But there are huge differences in how rods are designed to achieve these functions, both in their construction and in what the individual angler wants from their rod. Rod preferences are personal and there will always be debate as to the merits of different actions, looks, prices, and feel. There are no rules with fishing rods, but when making your choice, get advice from an expert who knows your needs.

⊠ **Under pressure**
A rod acts as a shock absorber to protect the line and keep the hook in place as fish fight. An angler soon learns how much pressure to apply.

ROD ACTION

The action of a rod refers to how much of the rod bends when it is put under pressure, whether during casting or when playing fish. A rod with a fast action bends mainly in the top third of the rod, a medium- (or moderate-) action rod bends in the top half of the rod, and a slow- (or through-) action rod bends from the lower third of the rod through to the tip. Rods with more "forgiving" medium or slow actions are well-suited to beginners because they are easy to cast.

▣ **Fast action (top third)**

▣ **Medium action (middle-to-tip)**

▣ **Slow action (top two-thirds)**

Rod lengths

The length of a rod affects its performance: a long rod will cast farther than a shorter one for the same effort. However, a longer rod can be impractical. Rod length may also be a matter of national preference; for example, US anglers tend to favor spinning rods that are short with a fast action, but in the UK a longer rod with a slower action is usually preferred.

⌃ **Short rod** Often used on a boat, a short rod provides the huge lifting power needed to fight very large fish.

⌃ **Long rod** A long rod allows you to cast long distances from the shore, but can be heavy to hold.

Parts of a rod

All fishing rods share the same basic components. A rod "blank" is simply the bare rod, without any hardware attached. Many anglers buy blanks and build their own rods. Spinning and fly reels (*see* pp. 40–41) require a rod with the rings on the underside of the blank, whereas conventional reels are designed to be used with the rings on the top.

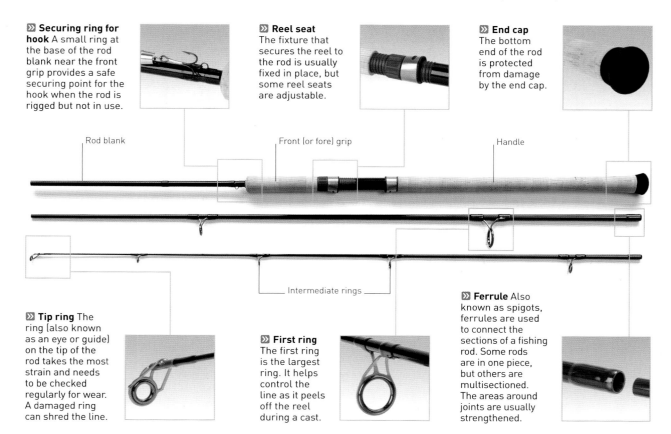

» **Securing ring for hook** A small ring at the base of the rod blank near the front grip provides a safe securing point for the hook when the rod is rigged but not in use.

» **Reel seat** The fixture that secures the reel to the rod is usually fixed in place, but some reel seats are adjustable.

» **End cap** The bottom end of the rod is protected from damage by the end cap.

Rod blank

Front (or fore) grip

Handle

Intermediate rings

» **Tip ring** The ring (also known as an eye or guide) on the tip of the rod takes the most strain and needs to be checked regularly for wear. A damaged ring can shred the line.

» **First ring** The first ring is the largest ring. It helps control the line as it peels off the reel during a cast.

» **Ferrule** Also known as spigots, ferrules are used to connect the sections of a fishing rod. Some rods are in one piece, but others are multisectioned. The areas around joints are usually strengthened.

Types of rods

Each type of rod is designed to enable the angler to cope with the demands of its intended use. For example, a float rod is typically delicate and sensitive, while a boat rod is short and robust to provide the lifting power required for fishing in deep water.

The right rod for the job

Most rods can be used for many different kinds of fishing. But the lighter, more delicate specialty designs, such as float rods, are best used for their intended purposes.

Although many rods can be used for both freshwater and saltwater fishing, rods intended primarily for freshwater fishing are not built to withstand the corrosive action of salt.

Ledger rods

Ledger, or feeder, rods are designed for fishing on the bottom with weights and swimfeeders. These rods often have highly sensitive, colored quivertips, which bend in response to the slightest movement of the line to provide bite indication.

Carbon-fiber
rod blank

Float rods

Although often used to target fish of a modest size, float rods have a relatively slow action and are strong enough to comfortably land big fish.

Extension
section

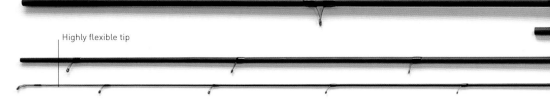

Highly flexible tip

Spinning rods

Spinning rods are designed to cast a variety of artificial lures. The term "spinning" refers to fishing with all kinds of artificial lures, both hard and soft. Look for a rod with an action that gives the flexibility you prefer.

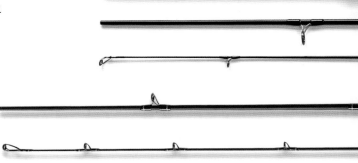

ROD RESTS AND BITE ALARMS

Many freshwater fishing methods require the rod to have a support system. Modern-day carp fishing, in particular, has become highly technical. Rods and reels are often set up on "pod" systems that hold everything steady and accessible. These pods may also incorporate bite alarms that alert you to a potential bite when you are not holding the rod (right). Long carbon-fiber poles also need rests or stands in order to be used effectively (see Pole-fishing, pp.116–117).

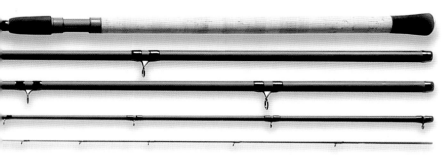

« 11–13-ft (3.4–4-m) feeder rod Suitable for rivers and lakes, this rod comes with four colored quivertips of different degrees of sensitivity for different needs.

Reel seat   Cork handle

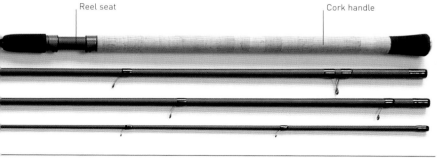

« 13–15-ft (4–4.6-m) float rod Long float rods are very sensitive, allowing the angler to cast light floats. This model comes with an optional extra section, if greater length is required, such as when river trotting (see pp.132–133).

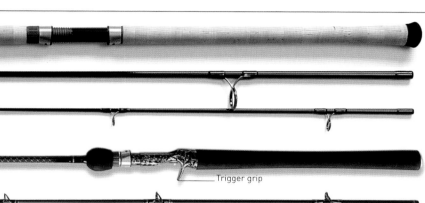

« 9-ft (2.7-m) spinning rod Used in freshwater and saltwater, this rod is rated to cast terminal tackle that weighs ½–1½ oz (15–45 g).

« 7-ft (2.1-m) spinning rod Ideal for catching European sea bass and pike, this rod is designed to be used with a conventional reel (see pp.38–41).

Trigger grip

Boat rods

Rods used on boats are shorter than other types. This gives increased lifting power for fishing beneath the boat, and a shorter rod is easier to use in a restricted space. Powerful boat rods, for catching large fish, often have a full set of roller guides to spread the strain on rod and line. Boat rods are rated by the line strength for which they are designed.

Surf-casting rods

Most surf-casting rods are long in order to help the angler to cast a long way, which is often necessary when fishing from the shore. Softer tipped rods are easier to cast and protect soft baits from damage during casting. Rock-fishing rods are special surf-casting rods that are specifically designed for fishing for hard-fighting quarry over rough ground.

Freshwater fly-fishing rods

Rod requirements for fly-fishing range from fishing with the tiniest flies on a small stream, through to fishing for salmon on large, fast-flowing rivers. Fly rods, lines, and reels are rated according to the AFTM code—for example, a #8 (8-weight) fly rod is rated to cast a #8 line.

Saltwater fly-fishing rods

Virtually all modern saltwater fly rods divide into at least four sections, making them easy to transport in bags. High-tech materials make these rods immensely strong and able to withstand the most extreme saltwater fly-fishing. For the more advanced fly-angler there are rods with a faster, stiffer action that produce faster line speeds and thus longer casts—a faster line also cuts through the wind and can give better fly presentation when this is needed. Rods with a more forgiving, slow action are better for beginners. Some heavier-class fly rods have an extra grip above the foregrip for fighting big fish.

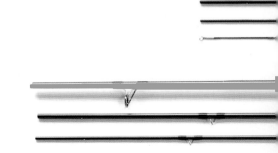

Ultra-slim rod blank to minimize wind resistance

Fast-action tip

« 20–30-lb (9–13-kg) boat rod
This rod is short and powerful
enough to fish for large species.

Short, strong
rod blank

Reducer

« 13-ft (4-m) rock rod Designed to
fish in rough ground, strong tides, and
choppy seas, this surf-casting rod has a
stiff tip designed to cast weights (terminal
tackle and bait) of 6 oz (170 g). It has an
adjustable reel seat.

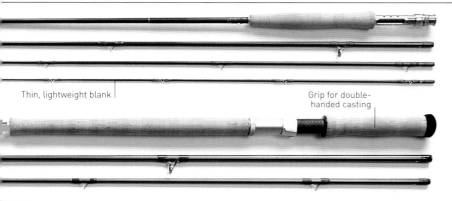

Thin, lightweight blank

Grip for double-
handed casting

« 10-ft (3-m) #5 river and lake fly rod
This general-purpose, four-piece fly rod is
easy to carry. It will handle a wide variety
of freshwater fly-fishing situations.

« Double-handed salmon rod This 14-ft
(4.3-m) #9 fly rod, built to facilitate double-
handed casting techniques, will handle big
rivers and tricky conditions, but remains
light and responsive.

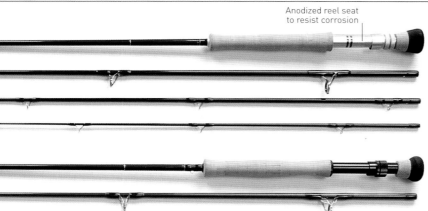

Anodized reel seat
to resist corrosion

« 9-ft (2.7-m) #12 saltwater fly rod This
powerful fly rod is able to handle heavy
lines, large flies, and big fish. It may be
harder to cast, but its greater strength is
necessary for more extreme fly-fishing.

« 9-ft (2.7-m) #8 saltwater fly rod
A good all-arounder, this precision-casting
saltwater fly rod is perfect for a variety of
applications, from catching bonefish on the
flats to bass fishing in northern Europe.

Reel basics

The primary function of a reel is to store line and enable the angler to cast it out to the fish and then retrieve it. Its secondary function is to help the angler to tire the hooked fish, by means of a drag system that can be adjusted to set the line tension as required.

Reel categories

There are three main types of reels: spinning, conventional, and fly. Fly reels and conventional reels have a revolving spool, turning the handle of which winches in the line. Spinning reels have a spool that stays stationary, and turning the handle causes line to be wrapped via a rotating arm, called the bail arm. The spool of a conventional reel revolves several times for each turn of the handle, which helps you reel in line quickly. Most modern reels have a drag or clutch system, to allow hooked fish to take the line at a tension set by the angler.

>> **Playing a fish on a fly reel** When fish want to run, the reel allows them to take line against the amount of tension provided by the drag system. This makes fish work for the line they take.

Attaching a fly reel

The simplest way to attach a fly reel to the rod is from the top, because it is easier to see what you are doing, although in fact fly reels are used below the rod (see above). When the reel is in use, be sure to check regularly that the reel seat and locking rings are tight.

1 **Hold the foregrip** on the rod firmly, and insert the reel foot into the groove at the bottom of the grip.

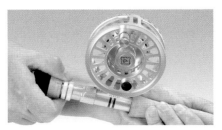

2 **Tighten the locking rings** against the reel foot, to secure the reel in place. They should be finger tight.

Attaching a conventional reel

A conventional reel is attached on top of the rod, and this is the position in which it is used during fishing. The reel seat on the rod has grooves, into which the foot of the reel is placed. It is secured in position with locking rings.

1 **Place the foot of the reel** into the grooves on the reel seat, while holding on tightly to the reel.

2 **Screw the locking rings** tightly into place, and make sure there is no play in the reel once they are tight.

Loading the line

Line loaded onto any reel must be laid under tight and even pressure. Under the strain produced by hard-fighting fish working against a tightly set drag, loose coils of line can bed down into the reel and may snap. Some reels have an automatic level-wind system (see below).

1 **Tie the line** around the spool with a secure knot, such as the blood or uni knot (see p.49 and p.50).

2 **Tighten the knot** close to the spool, and then trim the loose end with a pair of cutters.

3 **Wind the reel** to take up the line while holding it under tension. This is easier to do with a helper.

4 **Use your thumb** as a guide to spread the line evenly across the spool from one side to the other.

5 **Wind the line** on evenly. This will help with trouble-free casting, and will allow the fish to run.

6 **When you are filling** a reel for long-distance casting, make sure not to overfill it. Leave a ⅛-in (2-mm) gap at the top of the spool.

Line wound evenly across full width of the spool

LEVEL-WIND SYSTEM

Many conventional reels come with a level-wind system that spreads the line evenly over the spool. While this is by far the easiest, and often the most effective, way to wind line onto a conventional reel (especially when using thin-diameter braid), reels without a level wind offer longer casting.

Level-wind mechanism

Types of reels

There are three major types of fishing reels: spinning, conventional, and fly reel. Within each of these categories there are freshwater and saltwater fishing versions. A bait-casting reel is essentially a smaller conventional reel that is better suited to casting.

Freshwater reels

Spinning reels are most commonly used in freshwater fishing. This type of reel is easy to use and highly effective in many situations, and will work well with light lures and small baits. However, for casting larger lures, bait-casting reels are a popular choice. When used correctly, conventional reels can offer a more direct action and precision casting.

Large conventional reels are used in more demanding freshwater locations and for big fish, such as mahseer and Nile perch. These strong fish demand the use of powerful tackle.

⌃ **Spinning reel handle** Most spinning reels offer the angler the option of changing the handle to the left-hand or right-hand side.

Reel foot

⌃ **Small spinning reel** With the capacity to hold only a small amount of line, a small spinning reel is designed for taking smaller fish on a light rod.

Bale arm

Handle

⌃ **Medium spinning reel** A larger reel body, increased spool capacity, and stronger gearing allow for much larger fish to be landed on a reel like this.

Drag adjuster

⌃ **Low-profile bait caster** Designed to sit close to the rod, this small bait-casting reel is perfect for precision fishing with light lures. An internal braking system controls the spool during the cast.

Reinforced frame

⌃ **Round bait-casting reel** Performing a job similar to the low-profile bait caster (left), some bait-casting reels are strong enough to tackle big fish in freshwater or saltwater.

CENTERPIN REELS

Traditional centerpin reels are used mainly by specialist freshwater anglers for river- and lake-fishing at close range, or where sensitive control of trotting floats is required. They are not ideal for long-distance casting.

⌃ **Traditional centerpin reel**

Saltwater reels

Specialty saltwater reels are made from materials that incorporate resistance to corrosion from salt. They range from small spinning reels right through to the largest big-game fishing conventional reels, which are designed to hold huge quantities of heavy line and deal with hard-fighting fish. For this type of fishing, a heavy-duty reel that has an effective drag system enables the angler to play and land the largest specimens.

Spool-release lever

⏶ **Small conventional reel** Many smaller sized conventional and bait-casting reels have a braking mechanism that helps slow the spool down when you are casting. This prevents overruns and tangles.

Drag adjuster

⏶ **Medium conventional reel** A large line capacity and strong construction make these reels suitable for heavier fishing. Many also have a braking system (see left).

Reel foot

⏶ **Large conventional reel** Big conventional reels built for heavy-duty boat-fishing are very robust. Many have smooth lever-drag systems strong enough to deal with fast, powerful fish.

Reel stem

Body casing

⏶ **Medium spinning reel** Well suited to long, smooth casts with lures, this type of reel works well for spinning and light bait-fishing. It can be filled with monofilament or braid line.

Spool

⏶ **Large spinning reel** Modern spinning reels can cope with heavier lines and larger fish, and they are easier to use than conventional reels.

Fly reels

Modern fly-fishing reels appear to be intricately engineered, but inside they are usually simple. Large fly reels incorporate drag systems, but they are rarely geared in the same way as a conventional or spinning reel. The size of fly reel you choose is governed by the potential size of your quarry and the line weight you are using. They are usually rated according to the AFTM system used for fly rods and lines (see pp.36–37). Choose a reel that is compatible with the rod and the weight of line you wish to use.

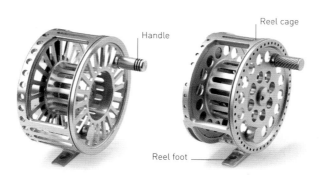

Handle

Reel cage

Reel foot

Ventilated spool lets water drain from the line

⏶ **Large saltwater fly reel** Designed to hold large quantities of line, this reel can be used to catch big fish. Reels of this type incorporate a drag system.

⏶ **Salmon-fishing fly reel** Modern salmon-fishing reels are more robust and larger than standard fly reels. They hold large quantities of line.

⏶ **Small-river fly reel** These reels are light but very strong. They are best for small rivers and lakes, where the targets are usually trout and grayling.

Hooks and weights

Hooks and weights are the main elements of what is collectively termed "terminal tackle." The hook is your final and crucial link with the fish, and usually, your line will not reach the fish without a weight. Spend time working out which types suit your fishing best.

Hook basics

The most widely used hook is the single J-hook, but many lures carry triple hooks, and some salmon flies are tied on double hooks. For freshwater fishing, a spade-end hook is sometimes used (a hook with no eye, just a flattened end), but most hooks have an eye through which you attach your trace or leader (see pp.48–49). The gauge refers to the diameter of the wire from which a hook is made. Heavier-gauge hooks are used for larger fish, and to help sink flies.

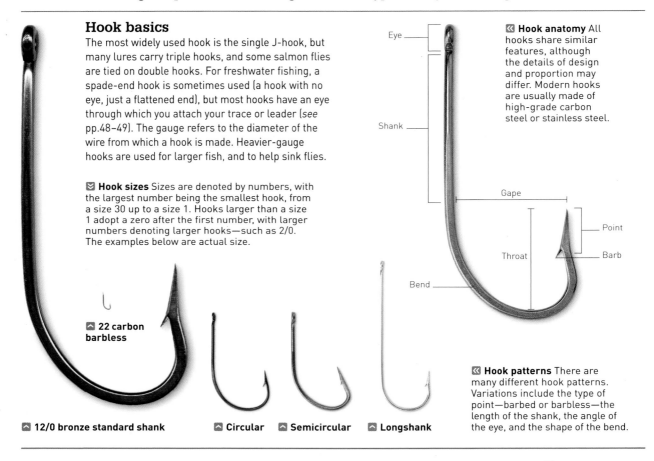

☑ **Hook sizes** Sizes are denoted by numbers, with the largest number being the smallest hook, from a size 30 up to a size 1. Hooks larger than a size 1 adopt a zero after the first number, with larger numbers denoting larger hooks—such as 2/0. The examples below are actual size.

Eye

Shank

☒ **Hook anatomy** All hooks share similar features, although the details of design and proportion may differ. Modern hooks are usually made of high-grade carbon steel or stainless steel.

Gape

Point

Throat

Barb

Bend

🔼 **22 carbon barbless**

🔼 **12/0 bronze standard shank**

🔼 **Circular** 🔼 **Semicircular** 🔼 **Longshank**

☒ **Hook patterns** There are many different hook patterns. Variations include the type of point—barbed or barbless—the length of the shank, the angle of the eye, and the shape of the bend.

Saltwater hooks

Hooks used in saltwater fishing need to have some corrosion resistance, whether this is a coating applied to the hook or the use of a material such as stainless steel. Points are often chemically sharpened, to provide efficient hooking. Choose a size and shape that will cope with your target. For sea fishing, these often need to be immensely powerful to deal with big fish that fight hard. Circle hooks hugely reduce the chances of deep hooking, and weedless hooks reduce the risk of snagging up.

➡ **Specialist hooks** Circle hooks generally have very solid hook-up rates, while weedless hooks help to keep the hook point away from snags when fishing with soft plastics.

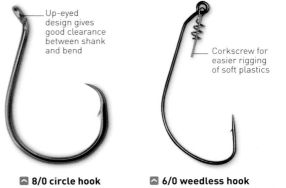

Up-eyed design gives good clearance between shank and bend

Corkscrew for easier rigging of soft plastics

🔼 **8/0 circle hook** 🔼 **6/0 weedless hook**

Freshwater hooks

Many freshwater hooks are small, but can deal with surprisingly large fish, and there is a range of shapes for bait-, lure-, and fly-fishing. Fly-fishing hooks vary widely, to cater to fly patterns requiring different styles of hooks (*see* pp.60–61).

☑ **Carp hooks** There are numerous hooks available for carp fishing, in different shapes, sizes, and gauges, for a variety of conditions.

 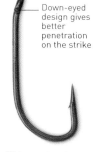

Down-eyed design gives better penetration on the strike

Fine-gauge wire

⬆ **Wide-gape carp hook**   ⬆ **Longshank carp hook**

BARBLESS HOOKS

The barb holds the hook in place when a fish is caught, and sometimes they can make a hook difficult to remove. A barbless hook slips out very easily. Many anglers choose to use this design for that reason, and many fisheries have regulations that specify the use of barbless hooks, especially where there is a catch-and-release policy.

⏩ **Treble hooks** A treble hook has three points and is usually encountered as part of a lure in which a standard hook could be obscured. Many lures only work when used with treble hooks. They can be hard to remove.

Treble hook

⬆ **A typical surface lure**

Weights

Weights on a fishing rig are used for many tasks, from anchoring a bait on the bottom, to setting the depth (known as "cocking") of a float. Other functions of weights include keeping baits at the desired depth, helping them roll around in the tide or current, and helping lures go deeper. Different shapes of weight perform different tasks.

☑ **Leads** Large weights, or leads, help to put baits down in fast currents and deep water. Certain shapes cast and sink better than others.

⬆ **Split shot** These small weights are crimped onto the line. They are mainly used to cock floats and to add weight to a rig.

⏩ **Grip lead with a bait clip** A grip lead has spikes to anchor it to the seabed. When you come to retrieve, the spikes break out of the bottom and the lead comes in. A bait clip behind the hook helps protect baits during the cast, and improves aerodynamics.

Additional terminal tackle

The main function of terminal tackle, which is attached to the end of your line, is to present your baits, or to work your lures, more efficiently. Your link to the fish will be weakened by poorly chosen terminal tackle. Use the best-quality components you can afford.

Swivels and crimps

Use swivels to join lines that do not have to pass through rod rings. They come in various sizes, and the eyes rotate in the swivel body to help prevent line twist when casting. Three-way swivels are often weak, but used correctly they can tie a dropper off the trace.

Use crimps to secure heavy mono line or wire that cannot be tied. Pass line through the crimp, through the eye of the swivel or hook, and then back through the crimp. Squeeze the crimp closed with pliers or a crimping tool.

⌃ **Swivels** Two-way swivels (right) come in barrel and stronger, ball-bearing types (shown). Three-way swivels are usually barrel-type, and have a larger size-to-strength ratio.

⌃ **Crimps** Crimps can be used to stop and trap swivels on a trace, for making long dropper rigs.

Booms

In its most basic form, a boom is used to spread the trace out from the mainline, to prevent tangles, and to provide extra coverage for the bait. Some lures are also fished from long booms, such as on a flying collar, and most booms are not designed to be cast far. They come in varied shapes and sizes, so choose a boom that provides the spread and anti-tangle capabilities that you desire.

» **Zip slider** A small, tough zip-slider boom, which runs along the mainline, before the trace, is used to hang a heavy lead. Usually part of a simple running-ledger rig, a zip slider helps prevent your lead from tangling around the line.

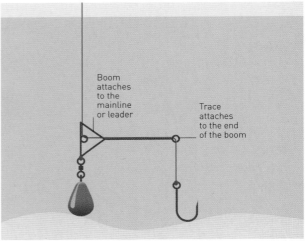

Boom attaches to the mainline or leader

Trace attaches to the end of the boom

⌃ **How a boom works** A boom helps spread the trace away from the mainline. This prevents tangles, but also restricts casting. Often booms are used at close range or off boats and they are good for creating multi-hook rigs.

Trace attachment

⌃ **French boom** An old-style French boom still has lots of uses, especially in a flying-collar rig where a long trace carrying a sand-eel type lure needs to be held away from the mainline to prevent tangles in the current.

Swimfeeders

For freshwater ledgering, a swimfeeder is a convenient way of presenting either ground bait, or further samples of the hook bait, close to where your baited hook lies. A swimfeeder is weighted, so it replaces any other weight, but once loaded with bait it may become so heavy that your rod cannot cast it. The method feeder is a weighted frame around which you pack your groundbait into a solid ball, and is fished in-line. The mainline threads right through the feeder.

Block-end feeder Large holes allow bait, such as maggots, to crawl out to attract fish. The ends come off for filling.

2-way swivel

Weight

Open-ended feeder A cage feeder allows faster groundbait dispersal. The water washes through to flush it out.

Bait clips

Clips are used in saltwater fishing to tuck bait close to the trace when distance casting; they release on impact with the sea. Clips reduce wind resistance, so the rig will cast farther. They also protect soft baits, especially worms, that may become damaged in distance casting. Clipping the bait down also makes it easier to cast long traces, because the extra line cannot flap around.

Breakaway clip The bait clips behind the plastic dome. When it hits the water, the impact drives the dome up and away from the leader, which ejects the baited hook.

A simple rig

The rig is the collective term used for terminal tackle: the weights, hooks, swivels, swimfeeders, and other components that you tie on to catch the fish. Lure set-ups tend not to be called part of a rig, whereas anything involving a baited hook is. Some rigs are intricate, to aid bait presentation and casting, and some include up to three hooks.

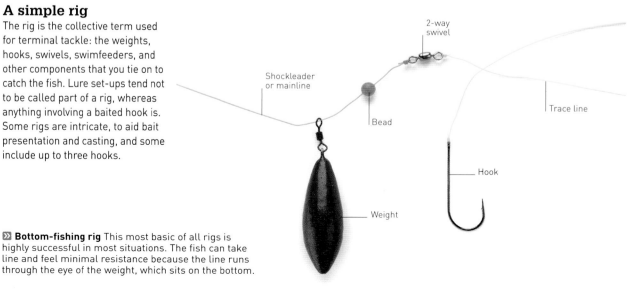

2-way swivel

Shockleader or mainline

Trace line

Bead

Hook

Weight

Bottom-fishing rig This most basic of all rigs is highly successful in most situations. The fish can take line and feel minimal resistance because the line runs through the eye of the weight, which sits on the bottom.

Floats

There is a huge range of floats on the market, each designed to work in a specific type of water. To choose a float, read the notes on the packaging, or ask in the tackle shop for the floats most suitable to your fishing. Carry a selection in a crushproof box.

⟩⟩ Rigging a float Most floats sit above the trace, fixed or sliding into place via weighted stops that fish the bait at the required depth. The weight cocks the float upright.

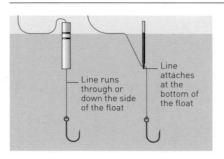

Line runs through or down the side of the float

Line attaches at the bottom of the float

The function of floats

A float is a means by which you can suspend a bait at a specific depth—either on the surface, somewhere beneath the surface, or right on the bottom. It also provides a visual indication when a fish hits your bait. If the float twitches erratically, shoots under, or comes up suddenly and lies flat on the surface, you have a bite. Most floats will need some kind of weighting to get them to cock properly, but some are self-weighted or require no weight because the bait is heavy enough to make it work.

Using saltwater floats

Floats will help get your baits (and lures at times) to places where you could not possibly cast. Saltwater floats are generally larger, and less varied, than freshwater floats because they have to support large baits. Floats that are round in shape will support larger baits, such as crabs and fish for tarpon bait, and many specialist floats cock purely from the weight of the bait. Balloons are used to great effect as floats for shark fishing, when the bait may be very large indeed. Aim to drift your float in the current when possible, to cover more ground where the fish might be.

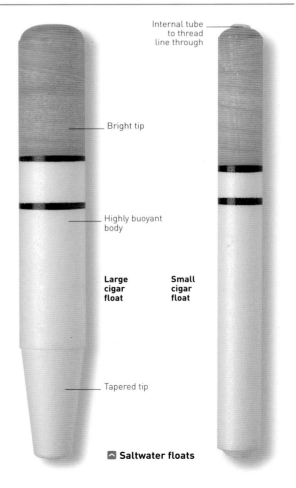

Internal tube to thread line through

Bright tip

Highly buoyant body

Large cigar float

Small cigar float

Tapered tip

⟨ Saltwater floats

⟩⟩ Saltwater float-fishing A large float needs more weight to make it cock properly (sit upright) and, when required, can be cast fairly long distances. Big, bright tops on the floats are easy to see on the surface of the water.

Using freshwater floats

Sometimes you will want your float to remain in one position on a lake, perhaps over ground bait, whereas on a river it is usual to let the float work with the current to cover more ground. It is helpful to place two or three of the required split shot close to the bottom of the float, and then put the rest closer to the hook to help the float fish correctly.

▽ **Types of freshwater floats** A range of floats are used to cover river and lake fishing. A key feature that distinguishes peacock floats from others is their weighted end, which provides additional stability in turbulent waters.

CHOOSING THE RIGHT FRESHWATER FLOAT

The float you choose depends on the kind of water you are fishing, and the types of bait you will use for your target species—for example, stick floats are for river-fishing in a current, pole floats are small and precise, and are suited to fishing with long poles, and wagglers can be used in most freshwater conditions.

Float type	Uses
Carp float	Surface fishing
Drift beater	Still water, strong winds
Loafer	Swift, turbulent water
Big stick	Smooth-flowing swims, fished close in
Peacock	Turbulent water, sensitive to bites
Loaded giant crystal	Weighted base for casting farther
Peacock waggler	Still water, slow- to medium-pace rivers

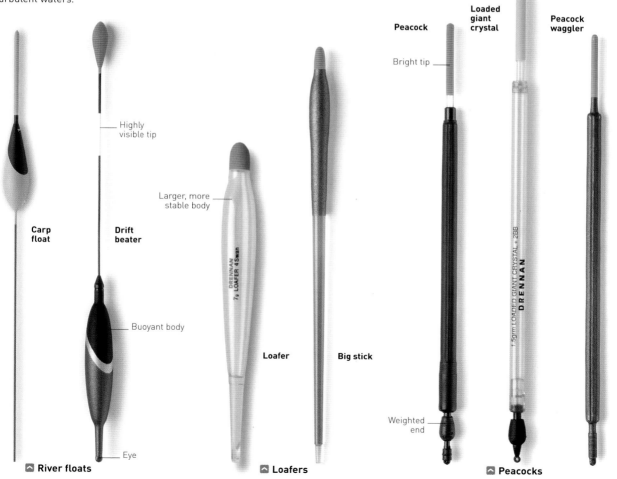

Carp float

Drift beater

Highly visible tip

Larger, more stable body

Buoyant body

Eye

DRENNAN 7g LOAFER 4Swan

Loafer

Big stick

Peacock

Loaded giant crystal

Peacock waggler

Bright tip

1·5grm LOADED GIANT CRYSTAL + 2BG   DRENNAN

Weighted end

△ **River floats**

△ **Loafers**

△ **Peacocks**

Lines and knots

Line is the main element that connects you to the fish you hook. Mainline is the bulk line on your reel, and your leader (or shockleader) is tied to the end of it. A trace (or hooklength) is the shorter line tied to the hook. Fly lines are different, and must have a leader attached that holds the fly.

Types of mainline

The principal types of mainlines are mono (monofilament), braided, and fly lines. For fly-fishing, light flies need a weighted fly line to impart momentum, or casting weight, to get the fly out onto or into the water. The relatively short main fly line is then joined to a long length of backing line (braid or specialty backing material).

>> **Mono lines** Used for freshwater and sea fishing, monofilament line is good for long casting, and its inherent stretch gives shock-absorbency for landing fish.

>> **Fly lines** A fly line consists of an insert line and a coating. Some are designed to float, some to sink slowly (intermediate), some to sink quickly, and some to sink at different speeds, from medium to ultra-fast.

>> **Braided lines** Braids have a high strength-to-diameter ratio, allowing thinner, lighter lines to be used to cut through tide and wind. Care must be taken as they do not stretch like mono. The lack of stretch provides a very direct contact with hooked fish.

↗ **Line choices** Mono and braided lines are available in a range of strengths and are rated by breaking strain and line diameter. Heavier lines, which are often used as shockleaders (*see* p.50), tend to come in shorter lengths and on smaller spools than mono and braid mainlines. Fly lines are rated according to the AFTM code, where a line is given a specific weight, such as #8.

THREADING FLY LINE

A useful trick for threading fly line onto the rod is to double the line over and then push it through the rod rings. This will drag the leader behind the fly line, pulling it through the rings. Mono and braid lines will be damaged if doubled over, and must be threaded through in a single strand.

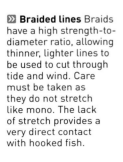

↑ **Fly line pushed through ring**

Wire traces

Wire mainline used to be popular in deep water and fast tides, where its small diameter could cut through the water with little resistance. Braided lines now perform this function, and wire is now used mainly for wires for fish with sharp teeth. Some wire traces can be tied almost as easily as mono. Heavier wires require either crimping or a special knot.

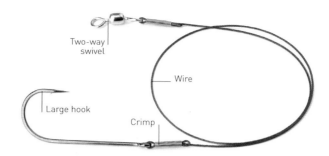

Two-way swivel

Wire

Large hook

Crimp

◀ **Shark trace** A typical shark-type trace consists of a big hook and a swivel, joined by a durable wire trace that is crimped at both ends.

Blood knot

Also called the half-blood knot, this is the most basic of fishing knots, used to tie line to items such as hooks, swivels, and lures. It is also commonly used to tie together two lines of similar diameter. It will work effectively for many fishing applications. Most anglers will quickly learn a variety of knots.

△ **A hook joined to a line** The blood knot provides a neat way of securing a hook to a line. It is secure under tension.

Make five turns

1 **Take the line** through the eye of the hook, swivel, or lure, and then loop the end around the line at least five times.

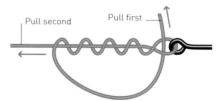

Pull second

Pull first

3 **Lubricate the whole knot** by applying saliva. Pull the short end through (but not tightly), and then pull steadily on the other end.

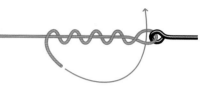

2 **Pass the end** that has been looped around the line back through the gap that is left between the eye and the first loop.

Trim tag end

4 **Ease the coils down** with a steady, non jerky pull, to form the knot. Trim the end close to the knot, but leave a tag sticking out.

Surgeon's knot

This alternative knot for joining two lines that are of unequal diameter is especially useful in fly-fishing, where you may need to join lines of different breaking strains.

△ **Surgeon's knot**

1 **Lay both lines** side-by-side with the tag ends facing in opposite directions. Keeping the lines together, form a loop. Pass both lines through the loop twice.

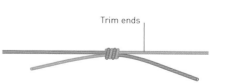

Trim ends

2 **Moisten and pull the knot** tight by pulling both ends simultaneously. Trim the tag ends short with a pair of scissors or sharp clippers.

Shockleader knot

When casting with heavy lures and weights, use a strong knot to join a length of stronger line, known as a shockleader, to your weaker mainline. The shockleader protects the mainline from the shock of the cast. Also known as a hooklength, or trace, a leader is generally shorter, and is used to provide protection against rough-skinned fish and fish with powerful teeth.

◀ **Shockleader knot**
The shockleader knot is useful for joining thick shockleaders and thin mainlines. The knot has a low profile that will pass easily through the rod rings.

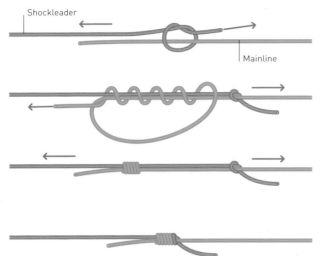

Shockleader

Mainline

1 **Make a loose overhand knot** in the shockleader. Pull a length of mainline through the middle of the overhand knot.

2 **Loop the mainline** over and around the shockleader to form a uni knot (see below). Ensure that the turns enclose both lines.

3 **Moisten both knots.** Tighten the overhand knot in the shockleader, and ease the coils of the uni knot together by pulling the tag end.

4 **Ease the knots together** (moisten the knots again if necessary) and then trim the knots very close to leave very small tag ends.

Uni knot

An extremely versatile and strong knot, the uni knot is simple to tie and has a range of uses. When fully tightened, it can be used as an alternative to the blood knot. It can also be used as a loop knot by pulling the tag tight just before the knot pulls all the way down. Joining one uni knot to another is a great way to join two lines of similar diameter, but be sure to ease each knot gently into place.

◀ **Joining line to a swivel** One of the main applications of this multipurpose knot is to join line securely to a swivel or hook. Be sure to trim the tag end neatly.

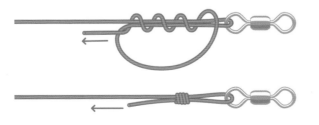

Trim tag end

1 **Take the line** through the eye of the swivel and form a loop by bringing it back toward the eye. Make several turns inside the loop and around both strands of line.

2 **Gently pull the tag end** of the line so that the knot closes but is not tight. This will form the knot a little way from the eye of the swivel.

3 **Ease the knot** (moisten with saliva if necessary) close to the eye of the swivel and then pull both ends until the knot is tight. Trim the tag end close to the eye.

Blood loop

Also known as a dropper loop, this knot creates a fixed loop at right angles to your line onto which you can attach a lure or hook. While there are stronger variations, the basic knot described below is easy to tie and works well for many fishing applications.

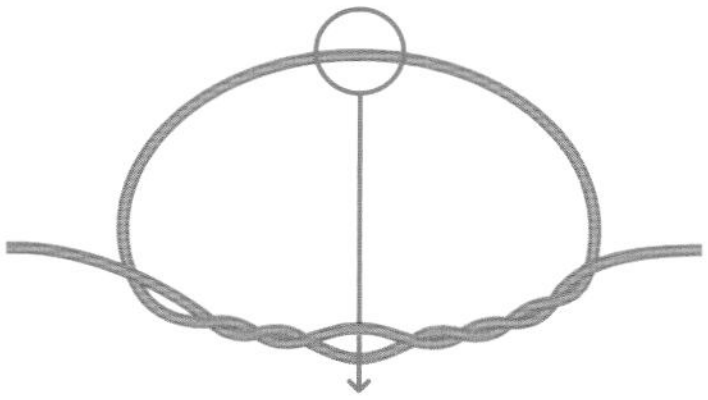

1 **Make a loop** in your line of approximately the required size of the finished loop. Then wrap the loop around itself several times. Take the middle of the loop through the center section of the coils that you have created.

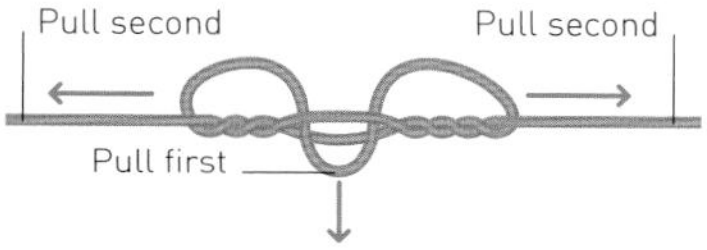

2 **Pull the loop** through to form a new loop. Moisten the knot and then pull both ends of the line gently.

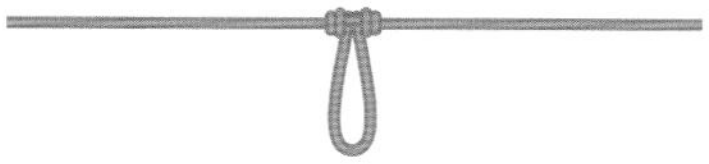

3 **Ease the coils together** tightly to secure the finished loop.

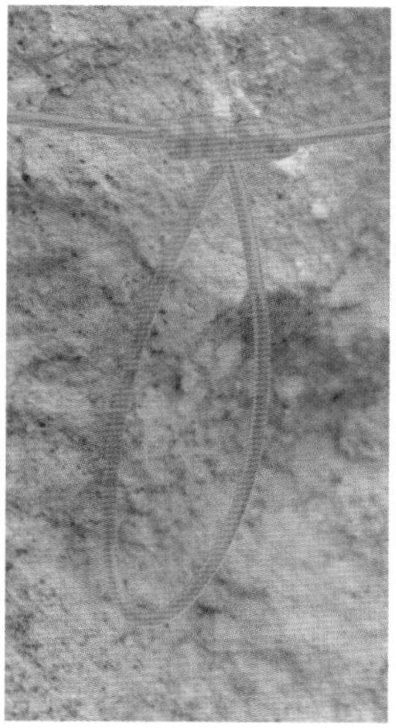

Using a blood loop
Thread the hook or lure onto the loop, or cut the loop and attach the item with a blood or uni knot.

Rapala knot

The Rapala knot is an effective method of forming a loop for the lure, hook, or fly, allowing it to move more freely and naturally than if secured by a knot that is tight to the eye. Make the initial loop large enough to allow the knot to be formed well away from the eye. Remember to ease the knot up slowly, and moisten it before doing so. The Perfection Look and Nonslip Mono knots can also be used for this purpose.

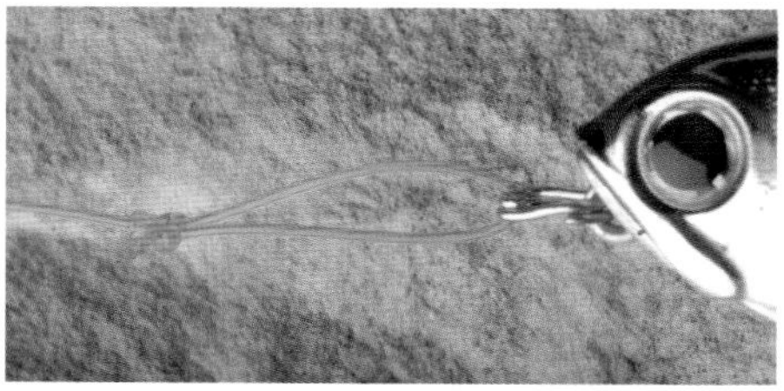

Attaching a lure
Many lures fish more effectively when attached to a line with a Rapala knot. This type of knot gives the lure more freedom of movement in the water.

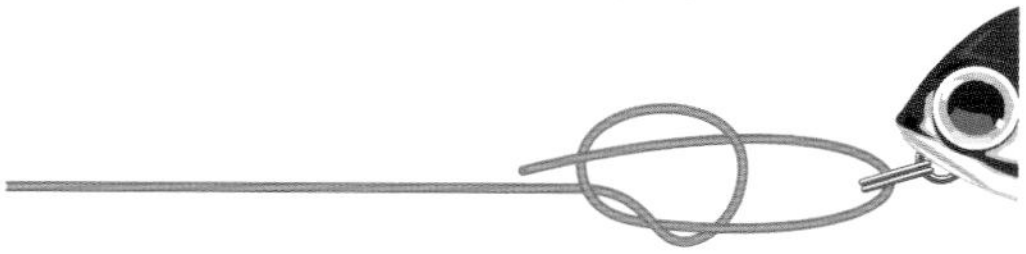

1 **Tie a loose overhand knot** in the line and pull the free end through it and the lure eye, and back through the knot.

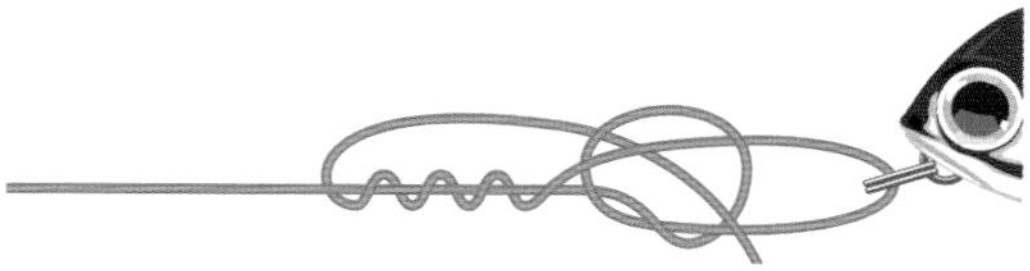

2 **Wrap the free end** three times around the line and take it back through the original overhand loop.

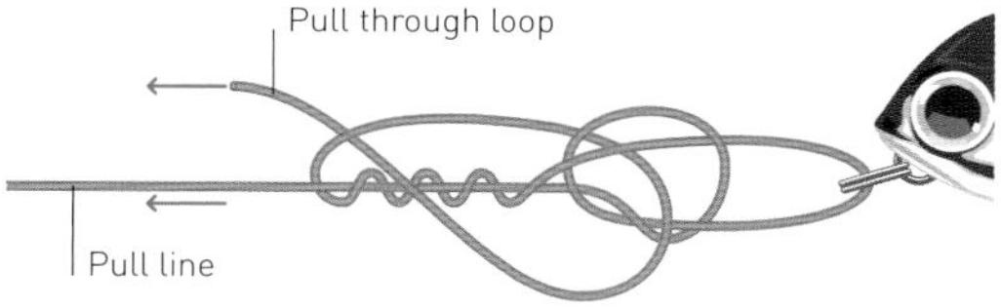

3 **Feed the free end** through the loop that has been formed from the previous step. Tighten the knot.

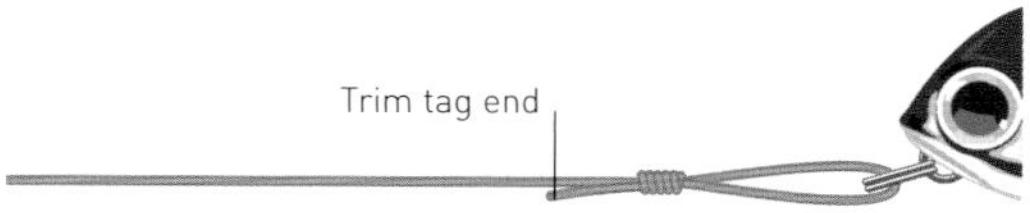

4 **When you have pulled** the knot tight, trim the tag end neatly.

Freshwater baits

The range of baits available to freshwater anglers is huge, from the everyday food that a fish would eat naturally, to the high-tech, high-protein baits full of added flavors, colors, and scents. Take time to choose the correct bait for the type of fishing you intend to do.

Natural baits

Natural baits are often freely available if you are prepared to collect your own—most anglers dig for worms at some time. Tackle shops usually stock plenty of the popular freshwater baits, such as maggots, worms, casters (pupated maggots), and pinkies (greenbottle-fly larvae), and various frozen baits for predatory species like pike and perch.

Many freshwater baits can be stored in the refrigerator in bait boxes that have perforated lids to allow air in. When you remove them from the refrigerator, protect them against extreme temperatures by using a cooler.

Natural baits work best where the fish have not experienced serious angling pressure, but are worth trying anywhere if all else fails. Some fish become wise to natural baits (especially big carp), but they may still be successful.

Carry a selection of natural baits and take enough to enable you to throw in offerings (little and often). This is like using ground bait, a mixture designed to spread out in the water and attract the fish to you via its scent and visual appeal.

⌃ **Maggots** Often dyed to enhance their appeal to a wide range of species, maggots are generally used on small hooks.

⌃ **Worms** Lugworms (earthworms) are frequently used to great effect. They are usually stored in some damp soil and will keep for a long time. Make sure to hook the worm a few times to aid hooking the fish.

☑ Organisation Permanent fishing pegs help with keeping the tackle and bait you need close to hand and easily accessible.

Processed baits

Baits that are not part of a fish's natural diet are often made from our own foods, such as bread, corn, cheese, and processed meats, as well as dog biscuits, seeds, and grains. However, high-protein baits have recently become much more widely used. These specialty baits were originally made solely for carp fishing, but they are proving successful in a variety of everyday freshwater angling.

High-protein baits are manufactured from a mixture of animal proteins, soy flour, eggs, flavorings, and colorings, and their various smells and flavors are incredible. They are commonly used as a malleable paste that can be secured around hooks, or as "boilies"—balls of mixture that are usually boiled, hence the name. The resulting hard outer coating helps them resist the attentions of smaller, unwanted fish.

PUTTING BAIT ON A HOOK

When "baiting up," match the hook size to the bait and the fish. Most baits are hooked without burying the point of the hook within the bait, especially when using hard baits. However, for some specialty applications, such as using luncheon meat for barbel, the hook is masked by the bait. Boilies are often attached separately via a "hair rig," which, theoretically, allows wary fish to pick up the bait without feeling the hook.

« **Boilies** Made in different sizes, colors, and flavors, boilies and paste baits can be very successful.

« **Dog biscuits** Soft dog biscuits or the dry variety (presoaked in water) are great for carp fishing on the surface.

« **Corn** Canned corn works well for many species. Flavored and colored varieties are available.

Ground baiting with a catapult

There are plenty of times when you need to cast out your float or weight beyond your natural throwing range, and this is when a bait catapult is useful. This can be an accurate way of getting ground bait to where the fish are, in order to attract them, and keep them feeding. A mixture of ground bait and hook bait works well in a catapult. Use a catapult only for placing ground bait; be aware of safety at all times.

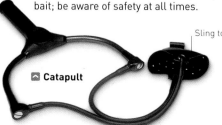

Sling to hold bait

⌃ **Catapult**

⟫ **Using a bait catapult** Aim the front of the catapult out over the water, pull back the cup, and let it go.

Saltwater baits

With most saltwater baits, the aim is to put as much scent into the water as possible, to get the fish to come to you. The most effective way of doing this is to use good-quality fresh baits. Many anglers collect and store their own, but tackle shops always have a selection.

>> **Sand eels and rag worms** Sand eels (left) are used for bottom-fishing, beneath a float, or for spinning. Rag worms (right) are often used with other baits. Beware of their sharp pincers.

Choosing baits

There are four basic categories of saltwater bait: fish (whole fish, sections, fillets, and strips), worms, crustaceans (crabs, shrimp, and so on), and live bait (various species of fish), as well as regional specialties. Some areas have regulations against using certain baits—ask in your tackle shop and check the Internet for up-to-date advice.

Research the fish you are targeting—knowing what they feed on will increase your catch rates, especially as different fish species show marked preferences for particular baits, often varying according to the time of year.

Base the sizes of your baits on the size of your prey and the size of its mouth, and on how far you need to cast the bait. Big baits may catch big fish, but so can small baits, and they also catch lots of smaller fish.

>> **Hooking a mackerel** Mackerel is a versatile bait—few species will not eat it. One of the best ways to hook whole mackerel is to insert the hook up through the jaw and out between the eyes. Many fish hit baits at the head end, and by having the hook there you stand the best chance of connecting with them.

Caring for and using baits

Take care of your baits at home and when you go fishing. Do not let frozen baits defrost unless you are about to use them; defrosting and refreezing make them far less appealing and they will lose their fresh smell. As you want a pleasant natural scent coming from the baits, be careful of taking them out in hot conditions. Invest in a cooler to keep them as cold as possible, and keep them out of direct sunlight. Bait scent is gradually washed away, so change baits often, even if you are not getting any bites. Softer baits, such as worms, need changing more frequently. Putting a juicy scent trail into the water via your baits is like ground baiting; chum (see p.162) and other free offerings are also often used.

>> **Peelers** Crabs that are about to shed their shells are known as "peelers," and they make excellent bait. Look for splits in the shell, and new soft shell beneath. Peeler crabs often hide under rocks and weeds.

>> **Lugworm** "Lug" burrow in sand and mud, leaving distinctive casts, which gives you a clue where to dig for them. These worms work particularly well for cod and European sea bass. Store them in newspaper in the refrigerator, and sort through them daily and remove any dead worms if you are going to keep them for longer than a few hours.

⏫ **Cocktail baits** Baits are often combined in "cocktails." Calamari squid are among the various baits used, including rag worms, to attract a number of fish species.

⏮ **Live mackerel** Feather rigs are used to catch mackerel for fresh bait. They may be used for live bait, but are hard to keep alive. Frozen mackerel are a good alternative to fresh ones.

Lures

A lure is an imitation of a baitfish, designed to provoke an attack from a predatory fish. There are many lures available, so seek advice and consider what will appeal to your target fish, taking into account the lure's color, size, the depth at which it works, and the way it moves.

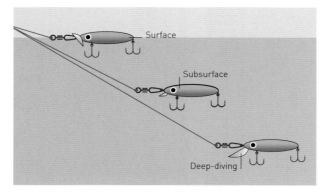

Surface

Subsurface

Deep-diving

How lures work

Lures are usually made of metal, plastic, or wood, but modern designs made of soft plastic are also popular. Lures are designed to work in different ways, but it is the angler who, by constantly working the line, must impart "life" to them. Without this, they remain an inert and uninteresting imitation that will not appeal to any fish. One of the great attractions of lure-fishing is that the angler is always active and is therefore highly involved in the process of fishing.

« **Lure depths** Lures swim at particular depths to appeal to specific predators. The design of the vane, or blade, of the lure often determines the depth at which it works.

Types of freshwater lures

As with all types of lures, freshwater lures mimic the appearance and swimming patterns of various freshwater baitfish. Some lures are designed to imitate healthy baitfish swimming normally, whereas others are intended to mimic distressed or injured prey, to make them even more attractive to a predator. To use lures successfully, it is important to learn as much as you can about the species you are targeting, and to discover what will make them most likely to want to charge into your lure.

» **Surface lures** Some surface lures work on the water surface, where the predator will spy them from below, and cannot sink. Others are designed to float until the angler begins to retrieve, at which point they will dive down to a specific depth.

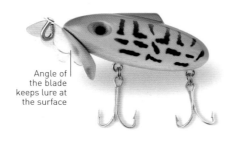

Angle of the blade keeps lure at the surface

⌃ **Bass-a-Rooney**

⌃ **Fat T-Tail Minnow**

⌃ **Soft plastic lures** Soft lures, or soft plastics, as they tend to be known, offer anglers many different choices of shapes and sizes, and the rigging options are almost endless. Many anglers carry a good selection of hard and soft lures.

» **Subsurface lures** Designed to swim under the surface, most subsurface lures do not dive very deep. Some work most effectively on a steady retrieval, while others demand a twitched, jerky retrieval that gets them moving erratically.

⌃ **Zalt Zam**

Choosing a lure

Without doubt, many lures are designed more to attract the angler than the fish, but over time you will learn which lures work best for which fish, and under which conditions. Some fish show a marked preference for certain colors; for example, barracuda like a red and white combination. Dark lures often work best in dull conditions and bright lures work better when the light is brighter. If a fish swirls at your lure but does not connect, stop the retrieval for a second and see if the fish comes back. If it does not, aim to cover the same area with your next cast. Give a lure plenty of time to work and do not change it too hastily. Your confidence in the lure you have selected is all-important.

≪ Making a selection
Anglers usually carry all manner of different lures, but will tend to return to the one with which they have had most success in the past.

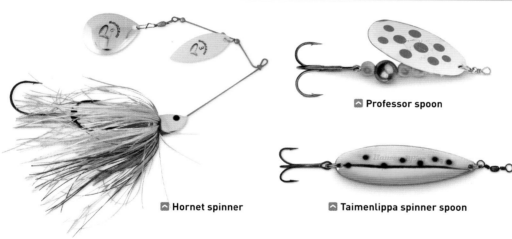

⌃ Hornet spinner

⌃ Professor spoon

⌃ Taimenlippa spinner spoon

≪ Spinners and spoons
These lures are often made of metal. A spinner is designed to spin in the water when retrieved; light often bounces off its shiny sides to further entice a predator. When using a spinner, make sure you have a swivel in your trace because this will help counteract line twist. Spoons are very similar to spinners, but they usually wobble and jerk erratically when retrieved, rather than simply spin.

≫ Jerkbait lures Available in both hard and soft materials, and in surface and subsurface designs, jerkbait lures are cast out and twitched back. A short, strong rod is needed to cope with the large lure and its jerky movements.

⌃ 3D Roach Shine Glider

» Hooked perfectly
A small lure known as a jig is worked along the bottom, often acting like a moving shrimp. A jig has successfully hooked this fish.

Saltwater fishing with lures

From the shallowest inshore waters to the blue depths offshore where the biggest species roam, the oceans contain plenty of predatory fish that will readily take lures. It is the variety in saltwater lure-fishing that makes it so special. Whereas bait-fishing is about casting or dropping your bait and waiting for the fish to come to you (sight-fishing excepted), lure-fishing involves working your lures to fool the fish. Among the most exciting moments you can experience in angling is the sudden jolt as a fish hits your sinking lure or the great swirl of water as a fish charges your surface lure.

» Surface lures
Surface lures come in a variety of shapes and sizes and are all designed to create a degree of water-surface disturbance, which sends out what appear to be distress signals to hungry predators. Poppers have an incurving front that can be made to spit water to imitate an injured baitfish. Others are weighted in such a way as to enable the angler to "walk" them across the surface by moving the rod tip back and forth—known as "walking the dog."

Types of saltwater lure

Like freshwater lures, saltwater lures are designed to work at different depths, although many of the big predators are happy to hit surface lures too. Top-water angling is popular, especially in warmer tropical seas, because they contain the most species to fish for using this approach. Surface and just subsurface lures are also excellent for rough ground, where a deep-diving lure would get snagged. European sea bass can be caught using these lures, as can some big-game species, such as marlin and tuna, which are often caught just under or very near the surface on trolled lures.

Slim
profile

Realistic
baitfish color

⌃ **Sand Eel Surf Walker 125**

Concave
face promotes
popping action

Treble hook

⌃ **3D Minnow Pop Walker**

Bib to make
the lure dive

Hard plastic
lure body

⌃ Sand Eel Jerk Minnow

« Subsurface lures These attract a variety of fish, even the big-game species. Be aware that they can pick up weeds or floating debris, which kills their action. With practice you will know when the lure is not working.

Two split rings

⌃ Surf Seeker 35g

Aerodynamic body
for long casts

« Metal lures From spinners to speed jigs, there are many different metal lures and they cover almost the whole water column.

Squidlike plastic
tentacles

Hard face
to disturb
water surface

⌃ Marlin Super Shaker

⌃ Rocket Jet Head

« Trolling lures Designed primarily for the big-game species, such as marlin, these often big and colorful lures are trolled in particular patterns on outriggers behind boats. Many are intended to be fished with live or dead bait that sits behind the lure's "head," often on a pair of large hooks.

Attachment point

⌃ 3D TPE Minnow

« Soft plastics Many natural baits have been imitated by these flexible, sometimes scented lures. These designs vibrate and make realistic movements, which appeal to a wide range of fish. The famous jellyworm and shad patterns are used with and without weights.

⌃ 3D Needlefish Pulse Tail

⌃ Savage Gear Sand Eel

Fly basics

Flies are made from a variety of natural and synthetic materials, to create an illusion of life that fools the fish. When fly-fishing, you need to carry a selection of fly designs, or patterns, that will entice the fish, chosen according to the habitat and diet of the target species.

Attractors and deceivers

Flies are often categorized as either attractors or deceivers. Attractors are usually brightly colored, with lots of mobility arousing an aggressive feeding instinct in the fish. Deceivers work by imitating a specific food item that will interest the fish. When stocking a fly box, be sure to add a variety of flies designed to both attract and deceive.

⌃ **Squid pink** This pattern has the outline of a squid, but its bright pink coloring does not resemble the natural creature, so it is classified as an attractor.

⏩ **Fish fry** Flies do not always imitate airborne food items. The Surf Candy fly (right) is designed to look just like a small baitfish, and would be used when fly-fishing for saltwater species, such as European sea bass.

⏩ **Daddy longlegs** Trout love the crane flies that hatch in large numbers during the fall. The artificial daddy longlegs fly mimics the delicate wings and gangly legs of the natural fly perfectly, and is a great example of a fly designed to deceive.

⏩ **Mayflies** Fly anglers look forward to the seasonal hatch of mayflies, which often triggers a gluttonous response from species such as trout. Mayfly fly patterns mimic the key features of the natural insect, such as the long tail, barred abdomen, and characteristic wings.

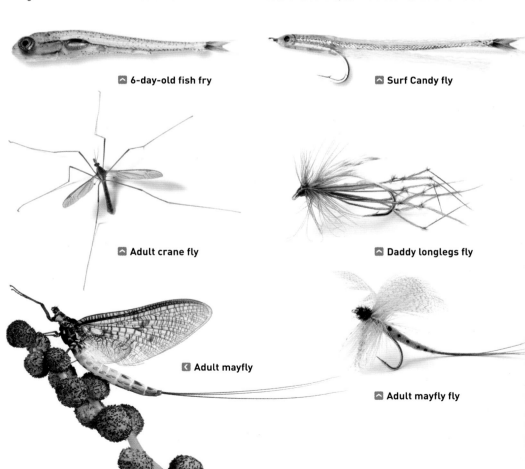

⌃ **6-day-old fish fry**

⌃ **Surf Candy fly**

⌃ **Adult crane fly**

⌃ **Daddy longlegs fly**

◀ **Adult mayfly**

⌃ **Adult mayfly fly**

Tying your own flies

There is something deeply satisfying about tying your own flies, and it saves money—professionally tied flies can be expensive. Examples of basic materials include pheasant tail feathers, rabbit fur, and thin wire. There are many companies that offer fly-tying resources for sale; for a beginner, it is worth investing in a basic kit incorporating a number of useful materials, hooks, and a few fly patterns with instructions on how to tie them. Practice tying flies at a well-lit table, and tie several of the same pattern until you master it. Don't worry if your first attempts are a bit scruffy and not like the pictures shown; the fish will probably accept them.

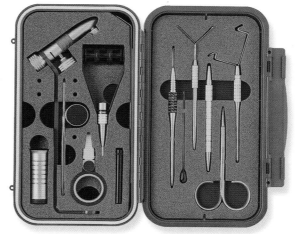

Fly-tying kit You will need a number of tools to tie flies, including a vise to clamp the hook, a bobbin to hold your tying thread, and a pair of sharp scissors to cut materials.

Anatomy of a fly
Fly patterns incorporate a number of features; some flies have all the features, while others possess only a few. Learn the techniques required to tie each part of the pattern shown here, and you will be well equipped to create a wide-ranging supply of artificial flies for your box. In general, flies are constructed from the bend of the hook toward the eye, and completed at the head.

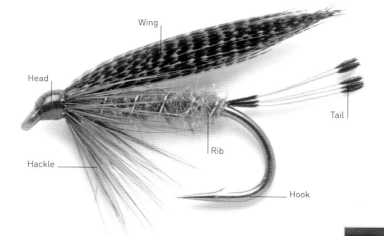

Wing

Head

Tail

Rib

Hackle

Hook

A saltwater fly
The pattern being made here will imitate a saltwater shrimp. The body is spun fur, bound on to the hook using a process known as "dubbing."

Tying a fly Fly tying requires concentration, a steady hand, and good lighting. The fly-tying vise should be set at a comfortable height, and sharp scissors are essential for success.

Types of flies

When you choose a fly, take into account the depth at which the fish are usually located and the food upon which they generally feed. Artificial flies are split into two groups: subsurface patterns, which are called wet flies, and surface patterns, which are known as dry flies.

Freshwater wet flies

Wet flies are intended to imitate a range of fish food found under water, such as the pupae of flies ascending to the surface, or nymphs and larvae often found near the bed of lakes or rivers. Some wet flies are designed to look very much like small fish and even various crustaceans, such as shrimp.

Wet flies often incorporate some kind of weight to assist their descent. A sinking fly line is used to fish them at a variety of depths. When using a wet fly you will often be unable to see the fly while fishing, and will, therefore, need to feel for a take or watch the fly line for signs of a fish. You can also try fishing a group of wet flies together on a leader. This tactic will allow you to position the patterns at a range of depths, increasing your chance of success.

△ **Damsel Nymph (medium olive)** Trout rarely take the adult damsel but cannot resist the nymph, which moves with an enticing wiggle. Olive is a favored color.

△ **Dabbler (claret)** Traditional wet flies, such as the Dabbler, imitate semihatched or drowning flies, and often have a feathery outline called a hackle.

△ **Super Buzzer Supreme (olive)** Much of the trout's diet consists of midges (also known as "buzzers"). The Super Buzzer imitates the midge pupae.

△ **Depth Charge Czech Mate** This fast-sinking artificial fly, which was designed by Czech anglers, will fool fish feeding deep down on caddis-fly larvae.

△ **Hare's-Ear Nymph** This versatile design is almost guaranteed to catch fish that feed on a variety of insects and crustaceans all year round.

Freshwater dry flies

Dry flies can be used to attract the fish either by imitating a natural fly or by disturbing the surface of the water. They are tied on lightweight hooks and incorporate features that will assist their buoyancy. Among the enormous variety of top-of-the-water patterns, some mimic insects as they hatch and others resemble those that are stranded on the surface after hatching. There are also designs that mimic a fly that has reproduced and has now fallen into the water.

If your dry fly starts to sink, retrieve it and dry it with tissue paper and apply some floatant. This can be purchased at a tackle shop in the form of a liquid, spray, or gel.

Observe your surroundings carefully when fishing with dry flies. In particular, look for insects on the water, hiding in vegetation, and flying in the air. Try to match these findings by choosing fly patterns that are similar in appearance. Fish feeding at the surface are often selective and may refuse a fly that does not mimic their chosen prey.

Chernobyl Ant The Chernobyl Ant is an excellent example of an artificial fly with a strong silhouette. It can be fished in rough water, or down and across a river, where it will create an enticing wake.

Adam's Parachute This famous and effective fly is justly popular and will catch fish on both moving and still water. It is a good general dry fly pattern.

Dad's Demoiselle Fish rarely take adult damsel flies, as great energy is needed to catch them. However, it is worth having a copy in case you find an energetic fish!

Klinkhammer Caddis (Green) This is another essential dry fly that sits perfectly in the surface film and imitates an adult caddis- or sedge-fly in the process of hatching out.

Humpy The Humpy is particularly useful in rough water as the stiff feather hackle and deer-hair body provide superb buoyancy and a strong silhouette.

F-fly This is a simple yet deadly pattern, often called an emerger. The body sits just below the surface and is made buoyant by a duck-feather wing laced with oil.

Freshwater fly-fishing Freshwater fish live on a diet of the various stages of development of insects and bugs, which lend themselves to imitation with artificial fly patterns.

Saltwater flies

In saltwater fly-fishing, the "fly" patterns that are used to outwit saltwater species take the form of anything but insects. Saltwater "flies" have to mimic a variety of food items including crabs, shrimp, and small fish. To be successful it is important to arm yourself with patterns that replicate the diet of your target. Take into account the depth to be fished and remember that saltwater habitats vary enormously, so carry flies in a range of sizes, colors, and weights.

Choose appropriate rods and lines, too. Saltwater patterns can be heavy and may require rods rated above line #8 to cope with their weight and create high line speeds to counteract air resistance.

Imitative patterns

Whenever you are purchasing or tying flies that aim directly to imitate the quarry's diet, make sure the artificial pattern reproduces all the essential elements of the natural food because it is these that can trigger a hit. Fish species that inhabit tropical saltwater flats, such as the bonefish, feed heavily on crustaceans, including shrimp.

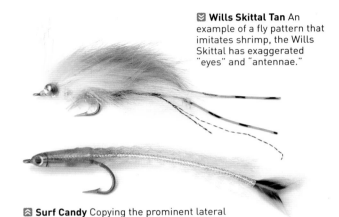

◙ **Wills Skittal Tan** An example of a fly pattern that imitates shrimp, the Wills Skittal has exaggerated "eyes" and "antennae."

⌃ **Squid White** Imitating its namesake, the Squid White has feathers that mimic tentacles and conspicuous "eyes," features that may provoke a feeding response.

⌃ **Surf Candy** Copying the prominent lateral line and forked tail of many juvenile fish, the Surf Candy is highly realistic.

Baitfish patterns

Numerous predators—including European sea bass and tuna—are attracted to baitfish patterns, and the result is often hectic sport. Simple, lightweight patterns are easy to cast, while lending themselves to many color variations and sizes that imitate an extensive range of baitfish. For success with baitfish patterns, look for signs of feeding activity, such as diving gulls, and head swiftly to the area, as the frenzied activity can be brief.

⌃ **Gummy Minnow** The translucent artificial materials used in the Gummy Minnow produce a highly successful pattern.

⌃ **Clouser Minnow** Incorporating the two-tone livery displayed by many baitfish, the Clouser Minnow's weighted "eyes" ensure that it fishes upside down and clear of snags.

≪ **Bass Grizzle** An example of a simple lightweight pattern, the Bass Grizzle is a popular and reliable fly.

Surface patterns

Commonly known as poppers, surface patterns are designed to create disturbance in the water surface when retrieved. When you choose them, take into account the conditions to be fished, as well as the size of your quarry. The commotion and stream of bubbles that surface patterns produce is particularly attractive to predatory saltwater fish, which home in on them.

Piwi Popper A classic example of an all-around hardworking lure, the Piwi Popper has rubber "legs," which create plenty of movement and a strong silhouette.

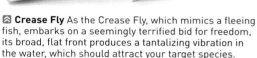

Crease Fly As the Crease Fly, which mimics a fleeing fish, embarks on a seemingly terrified bid for freedom, its broad, flat front produces a tantalizing vibration in the water, which should attract your target species.

Bobs Banger A large, cylindrical fly, Bobs Banger is particularly suitable for using on the surface of rough water, where it creates the desired disturbance.

Unusual flies

Flies are not always designed to be thought of as natural food by the target species. Many are intended to arouse an aggressive response, rather than a feeding instinct, while others are tied to copy long-established ground baits, such as corn or even bread. Some people dislike this break with tradition, but many modern-day anglers want to push fly-fishing boundaries to the limit, and this calls for a whole host of unusual flies aimed at a variety of species.

Whatever your target, always carry a range of flies because it is often the case that when one species is proving difficult, another is more amenable, so long as you have the right mix of fur and feather.

Temple Dog Tube flies, such as the Temple Dog, have a mobile three-dimensional dressing that is attractive to salmon and sea trout.

Cactus Booby (orange) Perhaps one of the most unusual fly patterns, the very buoyant eyes of the Booby give it its name. It is often used with a fast-sinking line popped up off the lake bed.

Bonio Carp love the very buoyant Bonio fly, which is constructed from spun deer hair and designed to resemble dog biscuits, which are proven carp bait.

Cold-weather clothing

Wearing the right clothing when fishing in cold weather will keep you warm, dry, and—most important—safe. Modern fishing clothing is easy to wear and offers levels of protection that will enable you to keep fishing in almost any weather.

On land

Clothing requirements in cold weather are the same for freshwater and saltwater. The outer layer needs to be waterproof, to keep you dry and to cut wind chill. Chest waders are a good choice, but in cold weather you must wear some warm layers underneath. A large proportion of body heat is lost through the head, so wear a warm hat, and a scarf or neck warmer. Gloves keep hands warm. Choose fingerless gloves or types that convert between full coverage and fingerless. Footwear depends on where you are fishing, and whether you need to get into the water. Standard rubber boots offer the best waterproofing, but they need to be lined with thermal socks, and they do not offer a good grip. Fully lined, thermal boots are the best option for really cold weather. Waterproof hiking boots are great for fishing.

>> **Layering** Under waterproofs, build up layers of clothing, for layers both trap the heat and allow your skin to "breathe." It is easier to adjust thinner layers than if you wear big, bulky items. The final layer before your waterproofs is often a fleece jacket, which can be your outer layer if the weather is dry.

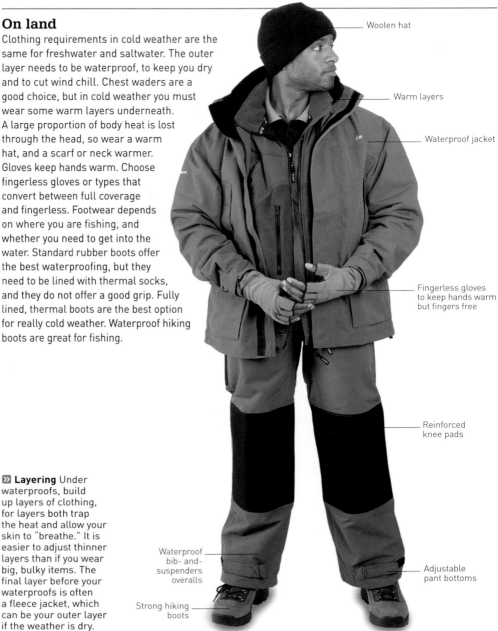

Woolen hat

Warm layers

Waterproof jacket

Fingerless gloves to keep hands warm but fingers free

Reinforced knee pads

Waterproof bib- and- suspenders overalls

Strong hiking boots

Adjustable pant bottoms

On a boat

Wear a life jacket or buoyancy aid when boat-fishing; on many fly-fishing lakes and reservoirs this is a regulation. A life jacket will keep your head above water, faceup; a buoyancy aid gives the wearer a degree of buoyancy only, and will not keep you afloat faceup if you are unconscious. Fishing from boats in cold weather requires the same clothing as fishing on land, but because you cannot move around as much, you need to wear extra layers to keep warm. The more protection you have against the elements, the better you will fish.

◀ Life jacket A modern life jacket is designed for comfortable wear over long periods. A small gas canister automatically inflates the life jacket if you fall in the water.

At sea

When you are fishing on a boat out at sea, there is little shelter from the weather, and it will always feel colder than on land. Never go fishing on a boat without a life jacket on board for every person, a minimum safety requirement. Wear layered clothing underneath waterproofs, and bib-and-suspenders waterproof overalls. Choose bright colors so you can be easily spotted if you fall overboard.

⌃ Whistle A whistle is one of the ways of attracting attention if you fall into the water. Most flotation suits have a whistle included.

NEOPRENE CHEST WADERS

Neoprene chest waders are warm, and are ideal for land-based fishing. They combine well with layers, and are available with various sole materials on the underside of the boots. Some have a stocking foot that allows you to wear wading boots. It is not advisable to wear chest waders when boat-fishing.

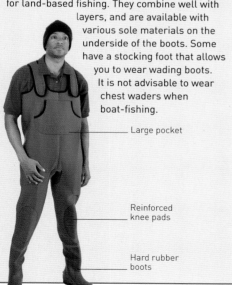

Large pocket

Reinforced knee pads

Hard rubber boots

⯮ Flotation suit Useful for boat-fishing at sea and shore-fishing, a flotation suit is warm and waterproof for fishing, and also helps keep you afloat if you fall overboard. Reflective tape shines when picked up in lights.

Thermal boots

Warm-weather clothing

When fishing in hot weather, protect yourself against sun and energy-sapping heat. Special fishing clothes, made from modern fabrics, will keep you fishing safely and comfortably in the hottest conditions. If you travel for your fishing, research beforehand what clothes to take.

Preparation for the sun

Check vaccination requirements for your destination, and take insect repellent. Anglers spend long hours with the direct sun overhead and water reflecting the sun's rays; take care in these conditions, and always wear waterproof sunscreen with high UV protection on any exposed skin. Above all, drink plenty of water to keep fully hydrated—drink before you get thirsty, avoiding alcohol and sugary drinks.

Wide-brimmed hat for protection from the sun

Polarized sunglasses

Lightweight cotton shirt

≫ Pockets Zipped and vented pockets store anything from clippers and sunglasses to spare flies.

⌃ Sleeve button Tropical fishing shirts can be worn long- or short-sleeved. When sleeves are rolled up, they are held in place with buttons or loops.

Sun gloves

Lightweight, quick-drying pants

⌃ Flats pants Ultra-lightweight pants (often called flats pants) are good for warm-weather fishing, with zip-off legs for anglers who prefer shorts. Play it safe with the sun when wearing shorts.

Flats boots

≪ Tropical gear A classic tropical fishing outfit offers a high degree of sun protection, but allows the angler unrestricted movement. Back-vented shirts are cool, and modern, breathable materials wick sweat away from the skin. The clothes are made slightly larger than normal to allow for unhindered movement.

Additional equipment

The clothing you take depends on where you will be fishing. In the tropics, carry a lightweight waterproof jacket when fishing, ready for sudden downpours. Some warm-weather fishing may be fine with bare feet and, if that is the case, keep applying sunscreen to them because water and sand wash it off far faster than from the rest of your body. Lightweight boat shoes work well for boat-based fishing, but if you are going to be walking on the flats, always wear flats boots—they help protect you against rocks, coral, stingray barbs, or poisonous, spiny fish buried in the sand. Wrap gravel guards around the tops of your boots to keep sand out. Sun gloves protect your hands. Carry extra fishing tackle in a waterproof boat bag, or a small backpack or fanny pack, and try not to carry unnecessary gear.

SUNGLASSES

Polarized sunglasses serve several distinct purposes. Primarily they serve as fish-spotting tools, to help you see more clearly into the water—polarizing technology works by cutting out glare from the surface of the water, which allows you to see underneath the surface. This is invaluable for spotting fish, and for understanding what lies in front of you. Sunglasses also help protect your eyes from long periods in sunny conditions, and they act as a barrier against a fly hitting you directly in the eye during a cast.

《 Face protection
Always wear a hat, to protect your head and shade your eyes. A neck protector or a drop-down back to your hat will protect your neck. In extreme sun you may need to cover your lower face.

Drinking-water pipe

Gravel guards (or long socks turned down)

《 Flats boots
Invaluable for wading the flats, these lightweight boots are designed to drain off water when you take your foot out. Hard soles protect the bottoms of your feet from cuts or spikes, and ankle supports help when walking and wading long distances.

Fly-fishing clothing

The clothing usually worn for fly-fishing reflects the sport's highly mobile nature. Choose lightweight fabrics, while ensuring that you are prepared for all weather and water conditions. Comfortable anglers enjoy their fishing far more than those at the mercy of the elements!

Clothing for wading

Fly-fishing frequently calls for wading, especially in running water. Breathable chest waders provide a durable, lightweight, and waterproof layer that allows freedom of movement and produces minimal perspiration. Waders are available as a boot connected to a pant leg, but the stocking-foot versions, worn with separate footwear, are more versatile and comfortable. Wear a hat to retain warmth; caps with a bill are popular because they reduce glare. Polarized glasses are compulsory fly-fishing attire, protecting your eyes from wayward hooks and assisting with subsurface observation. Consider the terrain to be negotiated when choosing a boot sole.

>> **Chest waders and jacket** The essential items for fly-anglers who want the option of wading include a pair of chest waders and a waterproof jacket.

>> **Gravel guard** Worn over waders with separate boots, gravel guards prevent stones from entering the boot and causing discomfort.

>> **Felt soles** Choose wading boots with felt soles to provide a secure foothold when fishing in rocky rivers.

Polarized sunglasses

Waterproof pocket

Waterproof, lightweight jacket

Waterproof, breathable chest waders

Gravel guard

Felt-soled wading boots

Boat and bank fly-fishing

As when wading, you will need a roomy, wind-resistant, and waterproof jacket that permits freedom of movement. It is important that any jacket you choose has plenty of pockets. Pick a long jacket when fishing from a boat to protect your back from the wind; a decent hood is highly desirable because there is nothing like cold water running down your neck to ruin the day. Waterproof overalls are well worth having; if possible, purchase the bib-and-suspenders variety. Multilayering with thermal underwear and fleeces will help retain body heat in cold weather.

THIGH WADERS

Thigh waders attach to a belt with a strap and are ideal when wading in shallow rivers, or when bank-fishing on a lake. Be careful, however, not to wade too deep or your thigh waders will fill with water.

Quick-release clip for ease of removal

Integral rubber boot

Waterproof, lightweight short jacket with hood

Large pockets Pick a garment that has plenty of generous pockets to carry a variety of vital accessories, such as fly boxes and leader material.

Retractable clips
Handy clips enable you to keep all your essential angling tools, such as line snips and forceps, convenient and safe at all times.

Lightweight, waterproof pants with pockets

Knee reinforcement for extra protection and reduced wear

Ankle reinforcement to reduce friction damage

Hiking boots

Fly-fishing footwear Comfortable waterproof hiking boots are ideal for angling from the bank. A nonslip sole is essential when fishing from a boat.

"BE PATIENT AND CALM—FOR NO ONE
CAN CATCH A FISH IN ANGER."

Herbert Hoover

Shelters

Long fishing sessions by lake, river, or seashore become more manageable with the use of special shelters. These provide refuge from wind and rain, dry equipment storage, and a place to sleep when night fishing. Many anglers use umbrellas as shelter for short sessions.

Freshwater shelters

Small shelters are designed to store just enough fishing gear for the day, and to keep you dry in a rain shower or out of the hot sun. Larger shelters are more like tents. Shelters designed for the carp-fishing market are easy to erect, and include useful features that help make long fishing sessions comfortable and dry. Many carp anglers spend days, even weeks, by big-carp waters, and the more room and comfort they can have within a waterproof shelter, the better. Colors are usually muted, to blend in with the surroundings and to avoid spooking cruising fish. Some freshwater shelters are simply big umbrellas. Make sure your chosen shelter is easy to put up and take down, and that it is big enough to store your clothes and tackle out of any rain.

≫ **Rod strap** The more organized you are, the easier it is to fish with more than one rod. When you are baiting up, hold your rod in place and keep it from sliding off the shelter with a Velcro rod strap.

≫ **A carp shelter** Commonly known as a bivvy, a good carp-fishing shelter can serve as an angler's home through long periods spent chasing big fish. Lay your tackle and gear out so that you can get to it conveniently but it remains dry.

Beach shelters

Shelters designed for fishing on the beach often have to withstand strong winds and rain, so they are generally smaller than freshwater equivalents, with increased rigidity and stability. Beach sessions are never as long as carp-fishing sessions, so the shelters are basic—just keeping you and as much of your gear as possible out of the rain. Set up the shelter so that the opening faces away from the wind. It is possible to stay warm and dry in these shelters, even during extreme cold and rain. Rock-fishing is not really suited to erecting shelters because uneven surfaces and an often mobile approach simply do not call for a shelter.

UMBRELLAS

A big fishing umbrella, perhaps with special extended flaps, is perfect for freshwater fishing when you will not be camping overnight. Set up close to the river or lake and draw the umbrella around you and your fishing tackle so that everything is easily reached. An umbrella helps protect you and your bait from sun and rain. It is quick to erect, and creates little extra weight to carry.

⏏ **Snug beach-fishing**
For fixed-position beach-fishing, a beach shelter provides enough space to remain warm and dry for long periods. It is light enough to carry with other gear.

Carrying your equipment

Anglers always tend to carry a lot of gear, trying to cover as many eventualities as possible. Choosing versatile and convenient ways to transport your equipment is important, as is bearing in mind how far you have to walk or travel to fish when you are packing.

Fishing bags

Fishing bags take on all shapes and sizes, from the voluminous, which can hold a wide range of gear, to the very simple, which are designed for specific jobs such as transporting bait or reels. Rod holdalls are popular and extremely useful for carrying numbers of rods. Some carp-rod bags carry the rods with the reels attached, and offer excellent protection against damage as well. Buckets and fishing boxes offer a waterproof solution for your equipment, but many bags are water-resistant, too. If you need to access your fishing spot on foot, select bags that are easy to carry; if you do not and you need a lot of tackle around, choose a bag that opens easily and lets you arrange the items neatly inside.

》 Holdall Designed to be crammed full of fishing equipment, holdalls usually have internal dividers that enable you to organize everything neatly for a day's fishing. They are particularly useful for fly-fishing on a boat.

Large pockets

》 Cool compartment With the addition of a frozen cool block, this compartment is perfect for storing your baits.

》 Fishing bag This alternative to a holdall has side pockets to keep items available. It is water-resistant and will carry all the gear you need.

⌃ Rod bag Rod bags or holdalls carry your rods safely and efficiently. Many will also take bank sticks, landing net handles, and even small shelters.

Hands-free carrying

A backpack is ideal for transporting your fishing equipment over greater distances, especially if you plan to move around. Choose one that is comfortable to wear for long periods. Chest packs and fanny packs are light and handy for smaller items. Quiver-type rod holdalls are ideal for carrying rods when walking.

CARP BARROWS

Chasing big carp on tough waters can call for a serious amount of equipment, especially if you are fishing long sessions that involve camping out. A carp barrow is a modern take on a wheelbarrow. It allows you to pile all your gear on top, strap it down, and then push it to your swim. The barrows are light and easily maneuverable, but increase the temptation to carry a little bit too much gear.

⏵⏵ Back and chest pack An integrated backpack and chest pack system is especially useful for fly- and lure-fishing. The chest pack unclips so that you can use the backpack separately if you prefer.

⏴ Fanny pack Very useful for carrying limited equipment over long distances, fanny packs can be worn on the front or back. The various pockets hold a surprising amount of gear, often plenty for a day's fishing.

Wide webbing spreads load on shoulders

⏶ Fly box This fly vest incorporates a drop-down fly box. Others have pockets to store small fly boxes. Both are ideal for carrying a selection of flies from your collection.

Rigid casings protect flies

⏴ Fly vest Most fly vests allow you to store essentials, such as flies, leader material, snips, and disgorgers, on the front for easy access. Many have an optional backpack.

Essential skills

Unless you are fishing from a boat and can drop your lure or bait directly down into the water, reaching the fish usually involves casting—which requires certain fundamental skills that you need to learn to get started. Hooking, playing, and landing fish are what you do every time a fish bites, and you need to know how to release your catch to enable it to swim away unharmed. Understanding the waters you fish will also pay dividends.

Simple casting

Casting is the means by which anglers propel the bait, lure, or fly to the fish, whether they are close to shore or farther out. There are many variations on casting, but—in both freshwater and saltwater fishing— virtually all are based on the overhead cast.

Getting your bait or lure where you want it

Whenever fish are feeding farther out than the length of your fishing rod, a cast is needed to reach them. Your cast will usually require a combination of controlled power and accuracy, and, with practice, this will enable you to place your baits or lures almost exactly where you want them to go.

Casting relies on momentum. It works by compressing the fishing rod to build up power, then releasing the power during the cast, which straightens out or "unwinds" the rod, catapulting your bait or lure out onto the water. You hold the fishing line in place on the reel until the point of release (see step 4, opposite) and by then letting go, you allow your bait or lure to fly out, dragging the main line behind it. Close-range casts—consisting of little more than a quick overhead, sideways, or even underhand flick—are also often needed.

There is no right or wrong way to cast, but make sure you are comfortable and relaxed and be ready to apply power, while staying steady on your feet. Aim for a smooth buildup of power, then release the line.

》 Speed and precision
The overhead cast can be fast or slow to regulate the power. Many casters look at the rod as it comes through, then turn their head as it "unwinds."

Making an overhead cast

The overhead cast consists of placing the rod behind you with the lure or weight dangling off the end (have a drop of at least 24 in/60 cm), turning to look at where you want to release, and then bringing the rod around under pressure to bend it and cast. The faster you bring the rod around and the harder you "punch and pull," the farther you cast.

>> **Easy casting** A spinning reel makes for fuss-free casting. Place the line over your forefinger before casting and then release as the rod comes around.

1 **Stand comfortably** with the rod behind you. With your top hand held behind you on the rod, hold the line on the reel with your thumb (conventional or bait-casting reel) or index finger (spinning reel, *see* p.113).

2 **"Punch" the rod** through its arc with your top hand, and "pull" the butt down into your chest or stomach with the lower hand. Keep looking up and aim to really compress (bend) the rod.

3 **The acute bend** in the rod unwinds very suddenly as the rod moves through its arc, and catapults the lead or lure out to the fish. Try to keep your head relatively still through the cast, looking up at about 45 degrees. Remain firm in your stance, with your front leg holding you in position, straightening it if necessary.

4 **As the rod reaches** an angle of about 45 degrees in front, its compression will rapidly unwind. Stay in position, your bottom hand keeping the rod butt down into your chest or stomach, with the top hand holding firm. Lift your thumb or index finger to release line from the reel.

Roll casting

The roll cast is the principal casting method for novice fly-anglers. It is a relatively simple cast that must be learned in order to handle a range of everyday fly-fishing situations. Practice your technique regularly because this relatively simple technique has a multitude of uses.

Using the roll cast

When casting a fly, it is imperative that the line is straight at all times to ensure that tension is placed on the rod, and to avoid slack line developing, which can lead to the fly striking a part of your anatomy. The roll cast is the perfect answer to these problems, and is primarily used to straighten the line sharply before making an overhead cast (see pp.84–85). The roll cast is also ideal for casting in enclosed situations because very little line passes behind the angler during its execution. Finally, a roll cast can be used as a safety technique to pull sinking lines to the surface prior to re-casting, which reduces the water tension placed on the line.

⏫ **The grip** Place your thumb on top of the cork handle and imagine that you are gently holding a screwdriver to achieve a comfortable, well-balanced grip. Ensure that your grip is relaxed at all times.

1 **Begin with the tip** of the rod low to the water and two rod-lengths of fly line on the water's surface, your elbow tucked into your side, and your arm relaxed. Imagine a clock face at your side with your rod as the hour hand and 12 o'clock above your head. This sequence shows a right-handed cast; if you are left-handed, alter the "times" accordingly—for example, 11 o'clock will be 1 o'clock.

2 **Raise the rod tip** smoothly to 11 o'clock, using your elbow, not your wrist. This action will gradually peel the line from the water so that it slides across the surface in readiness for the back-cast.

3 **Tip your arm** slightly away from your body and slowly move the rod back to 1 o'clock. The fly line should fall behind the rod, creating a distinct "D" shape. Check that your thumb is almost upright and located in your peripheral vision. Make sure that a short section of line remains in the water, prior to starting the forward cast.

4 **From the 1 o'clock position,** smoothly accelerate the rod forward, following the direction of the line. Note the bend in the rod created by the line dragging against the water, a process known as "loading the rod."

5 **Stop the rod's forward movement** abruptly between 11 and 10 o'clock. Watch the line creating a narrow sausage shape as it extends, known as a casting loop.

Overhead casting

The overhead cast is the most common of all fly casts, and is most effective when used with the roll cast. It is not a difficult technique to grasp, but requires a little hand-eye coordination and timing. Practice overhead casts in a safe, wide-open space such as a playing field.

Using the overhead cast

Although the overhead cast does not have as many uses as the roll cast, it is an essential fly-fishing skill. The technique eliminates the pressure placed on the line by the water, and this results in substantial line speed and, consequently, a "loaded" rod (see step 4). Once unloaded, the line achieves distances unobtainable with a roll cast. If fishing with a dry fly, use the overhead cast to pass air through the feathers to aid buoyancy. The overhead cast can also be used in most stillwater fly-fishing situations. It involves an extension of line behind the angler, so it is unsuitable for enclosed environments.

1 **Start off with your rod** close to the water's surface, as for the roll cast. Keep your grip on the rod relaxed and your arm relaxed and tucked into your side. Imagine the clock face once again. This sequence shows and describes a right-handed cast; if you are casting with your left hand, alter the "times" accordingly—for example, 11 o'clock will be 1 o'clock and vice versa.

2 **Smoothly raise the rod tip** to 11 o'clock, using your elbow, not your wrist. This will gradually peel the line from the water and create a bend in the rod, in readiness for the back-cast.

3 **Bring the rod back,** accelerating smoothly, until your thumb is adjacent to your eye with its nail in a near-vertical position and the rod tip at 1 o'clock. To create the right amount of speed, imagine you are gently flicking mud from the rod tip. Ensure that the rod remains motionless once the movement has been completed, to allow a loop to form.

4 **As the line extends** behind you, pause while saying "WAIT" or "TICK," which permits the loop to completely unroll and place tension on the rod. This process is known as "loading," and is critical to a successful cast. If you do not pause, slack line will create an audible "crack," which can break the leader.

5 **Accelerate the rod forward,** ensuring that your elbow stays tucked at your side. Look straight ahead. Do not look into the sky or down at the ground as this will create a casting angle that makes it difficult to land the fly line gently in the water at the end of the cast.

6 **Bring the rod to a halt** between 11 and 10 o'clock, saying "PUSH" or "TOCK." The line will pass over the tip of the rod, forming a loop. Ensure that the upper part of the loop passes close to the lower part, as this will create a tight, wind-resistant loop.

7 **Allow the fly line** to straighten out above the water as the rod gently falls back to the start position. Try to land the fly line gently on the surface with as little disturbance to the water as possible.

Double-hauling

The double-haul is not so much a cast in its own right, but rather a series of coordinated hand movements applied to the overhead cast to create more tension within the rod. A well-executed double-haul will attain optimum line speeds and help achieve a tight, aerodynamic loop.

Using the double-haul

The double-haul technique should be used when you are fishing with flies at long range, to help you achieve maximum distance with minimal effort. Large, artificial patterns have a great deal of air resistance and may be heavy—casting them with the double-haul combats both these problems because the line effectively slices through the air. The double-haul is also highly effective in windy conditions. Furthermore, it can be used to present the fly accurately, as the rapidly moving line is more likely to reach its target. Only attempt double-hauling once you are proficient at overhead casting.

1 **Assume the low rod position** and relaxed grip that are used for roll and overhead casting. Take the fly line in your free hand, which is known as the line-control hand. Your two hands should be 4–12 in (10–30 cm) apart. Begin the back-cast, ensuring that you do not release your grip on the line with your line-control hand until required in the forward-cast phase of the sequence.

2 **As the rod accelerates** backward, make a short, smooth pull downward with your line-control hand. Imagine bouncing a ball on the ground as you make this movement, and say "HAUL" as you do so.

3 **Allow the line-control hand** to begin moving toward its original starting position as the line extends fully into the back-cast. Say "FEED" during this movement and ensure that you make it smooth and unhurried.

Double-hauling in saltwater

Use the double-haul on tropical saltwater flats to shoot rapid, accurate presentations to species such as bonefish and permit. It greatly increases your chances of catching these nervous fish, and is effective for casting the heavy crab and shrimp patterns often required. It is also handy when fly-fishing for fast-moving species, such as European sea bass, that require baitfish patterns to be constantly strip-retrieved.

《 High-speed double-haul
Incorporating a double-haul into an overhead cast will cause the line to blur at high speed toward its target. This is a particularly useful technique for fly-fishing on tropical saltwater flats.

4 **Pause, allowing the line** to extend behind you while your line-control hand returns to its original starting position, ready for the next stage.

5 **Begin the forward-cast** with your rod hand, while also hauling with your line-control hand as you did in step 2, and saying "HAUL."

6 **As you complete** the forward-cast, say "FEED" and release the line, or repeat the steps to extend the line and achieve more distance.

Spey casting

Spey casting was invented in Scotland and is named after the famous river. Perhaps the most elegant of all casting techniques, Spey casts are often carried out with a double-handed rod, and can be used in many situations to target species such as salmon, sea trout, or steelhead.

When to use Spey casts

Spey casts are roll casts (see pp.82–83) with a large change of direction, making them perfect for use in rivers where there is little space available for a back-cast. Salmon fishing, for example, calls for an artificial lure to be cast across stream and allowed to drift down the river, which eventually results in the line arriving below the angler. In this situation, it would be impossible to make a standard roll cast without the line becoming tangled. A Spey cast allows you to place the line in the right position, ready for delivery back across the river without snagging the fly in vegetation.

1 **Allow the line** to fish across the river until it rests below you. Strip in the remaining line and trap this against the butt of the rod, using your lower hand if you are using a double-handed rod. You are now ready to begin the cast. The cast demonstrated here is known as the single Spey cast, and should be used when the wind is blowing upstream.

2 **If you are using a double-handed rod,** for the single Spey cast, place your right hand at the front of the handle when fishing from the left bank. Place the left hand at the front of the handle, when fishing from the right bank.

3 **Lift the rod smoothly,** gently peeling the line from the water so that the resistance begins to place a bend in the rod.

4 **Gently dip the rod,** drawing a shape in midair that resembles a smiling face.

5 **As the line moves** across your body, smoothly accelerate and begin lifting the rod into the back-cast.

6 **A large "D" shape** will form on the rod side of you. The moment the line touches the water and the "D" has fully extended, apply power by pulling on the rod butt with your lower hand.

7 **Aim the rod high.** This results in a sausage-shaped loop and the line then skips off over the water. Do not force the tip toward the water or the cast will collapse.

Striking, playing, and landing fish

When a fish has finally taken your lure, fly, or bait, you need to know just when to strike to set the hook, and how to fight or play it. This is not an exact science—your instinct will always be important. Landing fish follows basic rules that apply to most species.

A rapid strike The fish has taken the fly so fast that there is still loose line to clear as the angler strikes and sets the hook. Keep clear of loose line as the fish runs.

When to strike

Sometimes the fish will hit your lure, fly, or bait so hard that it ends up hooking itself. Lifting the rod into the fighting fish will then keep the line straight so the hook does not work loose and fall out. But some species fiddle around with baits for a while before taking them properly, so you need to understand when to strike, sweeping the rod back or sideways to set the hook in the fish's mouth.

While you are watching for a visual sign of a bite, such as a float dipping, a dry fly being taken, or your rod tip bouncing, try to gauge when to strike by what you can feel through the line and rod. Have patience, and wait until the fish has picked up the bait, or taken the fly properly. Some fish have hard mouths and require that you strike hard and repeatedly, but for most species, you need not make exaggerated movements.

Playing a fish

When a fish is small, it can be wound in without playing. For larger fish, the drag on your reel should be set so that the fish can take line when it runs, with just enough resistance to tire the fish without risking a broken line. You will lose fewer fish with a tight line. While you are playing a fish, use one hand to hold the foregrip of the rod, and the other to turn the reel handle.

Keeping the line tight The rod is not working against the fish unless there is bend in it, and the more strain you can put on the fish, the sooner it will tire.

Landing your catch

As you play the fish, you will begin to feel it tire. The runs and lunges may become shorter and less powerful, or the fish may come to the surface and be easier to pull in. Landing techniques vary; some fish are easily captured in a landing net, while others are too large and powerful for this. If you can, netting is always the safest way to land a fish.

Other methods include lifting it out with the rod; pulling the line up, and grabbing the fish by the tail or another accessible part (only take hold of the mouth if you know the fish does not have sharp teeth); unhooking it in the water with a disgorger or T-bar; or beaching it. To beach a fish on a seashore, let the waves wash it onto

the beach until you can safely grab it. If you are on a river or lake, you may be able to steer a fish close to the edge of the water. When landing fish, watch the water conditions, and do not go out too far into the water and get into difficulties.

TAILING

Play the fish out, and then carefully grab it by the "wrist" of the tail. The shape of the tail prevents the fish from slipping out of your hand. Some species, such as trevally, have a sharp ridge on the tail wrist, so be sure to wear protective gloves to tail them. You need to be close to or in the water to tail a fish; be sure to play it safe.

Netting a fish
Hold the head of the net underwater and steer your catch over it with the rod and line. Then scoop up the fish and gently bring it ashore.

Landing with two
For big, heavy fish, you need an extra pair of hands to net your catch. The angler can use two hands for the rod, while a companion wades in with the net.

Unhooking and releasing fish

Taking fish for eating requires that you dispatch them quickly and humanely. Check if local regulations permit catch-and-release. If you can return fish to the water, you need to unhook them, care for them, and release them in a way that ensures full recovery.

>> **Unhooking safely**
There are many different ways to safely and humanely unhook fish. Make sure the fish is not flapping around and use a pair of forceps on smaller hooks and flies especially.

Unhooking a fish

It may be possible to take the hook out with your fingers, especially when using a small, barbless hook. For fish with teeth, or when the hook is deeper inside the mouth, use a special tool, such as long-nosed pliers, a disgorger, or a T-bar. Keep the fish's time out of the water to a minimum, unhooking it either in, or very close to, the water. Wear protective gloves when unhooking a fish with sharp teeth, or a big, powerful fish, because it may move suddenly while you are unhooking. If a big fish, like a shark, has taken a bait down beyond its mouth, cut the wire trace as close to the hook-eye as possible; the acidic stomach juices of the shark, plus the saltwater, will soon rust the hook out. Make sure that the fish is fully supported when you unhook it, to prevent distress; big freshwater fish like carp should be laid out on a wetted mat.

Caring for fish

A fish will be tired after a fight. Unless it is dispatched quickly for eating, you need to take care of the fish to enable it to recover. Many fish that have come in quickly can be unhooked and released immediately because they have expended little energy. But if a fish has fought hard, or has been hooked deeper than the mouth, take time to revive it.

Cradle the fish to support its weight in the water, face into any current to allow well-oxygenated water to run through the gills, and allow the fish to regain its strength while in your hands. If it is big, consider holding it by the tail either over the side of the boat or by wading out in the water with the fish held as best you can.

>> **Stay close to water**
Most people value a photograph of their hard-won catch. Remove the fish from the water for as short a time as possible. Hold the fish close to the water for the photograph, cradling it gently to support its weight while it is out of the water.

Releasing fish

As soon as a fish is strong enough to swim away with enough energy to survive, it is time to release it. If you take time to revive a fish that has fought hard, you will feel when it is ready to be released. When the fish starts to kick hard, and tries to swim away, remove your hands and allow it to move off. Watch as it swims away, in case you need to grab it and help it for a while longer. Fish caught in deep water and affected by pressure change, such as pollack and cod, should be humanely dispatched as quickly as possible. These species are badly affected by rapid changes in depth, and their swim bladders distend so much that they are unable to swim back down. Really large fish like sharks and marlin are released at the side of the boat.

MEASURING AND WEIGHING FISH

Most anglers want to know how much their fish weighs, and there are different types of weighing scales and slings to safely hold a fish while you weigh it. Many anglers choose to simply measure their fish these days, and it can often be done with the fish still in the water and held securely. Weighing or measuring fish can easily be done without causing the fish harm or distress. With experience, it is possible to estimate the weight of fish fairly accurately.

❯ **Measuring a fish**

◀ **Holding into the current** Wait until the fish feels really strong and is almost kicking in your hands before you release it. It is a great feeling to watch a healthy fish swim away, unharmed by the experience.

Freshwater watercraft

Good watercraft skills enable an angler to observe a location carefully and decipher as many features as possible that may attract fish. All fish require food, shelter, and oxygen, so examining the water with these factors in mind will lead you to the fish-holding areas.

Reading freshwater

Rivers and lakes offer many clues to help you find your quarry. All fish require food, in the form of insects or small fish, depending on species and location. These food items are attracted to weed beds, rocks, and similar features, so the likelihood is that the fish that feed on them will not be far away. Overhanging bushes and trees provide a natural pantry, while also acting as a shelter to the fish when threatened by a predator. Protection may also be provided by rocks, tree roots, and other natural "obstacles." Most important of all, however, fish need good levels of oxygen to survive—turbulent water is highly sought after by many species.

Moving water This stretch of river is a perfect fish habitat, with a good flow, and plenty of cover. It is also a sensible location, with sufficient space, to make a cast.

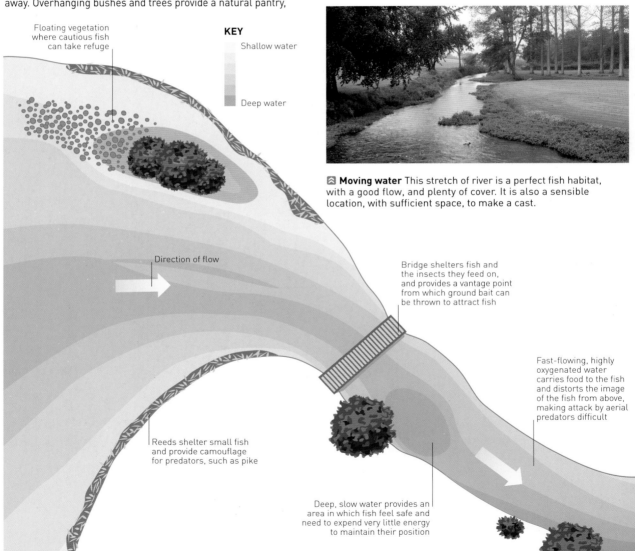

KEY

Shallow water

Deep water

Floating vegetation where cautious fish can take refuge

Direction of flow

Bridge shelters fish and the insects they feed on, and provides a vantage point from which ground bait can be thrown to attract fish

Fast-flowing, highly oxygenated water carries food to the fish and distorts the image of the fish from above, making attack by aerial predators difficult

Reeds shelter small fish and provide camouflage for predators, such as pike

Deep, slow water provides an area in which fish feel safe and need to expend very little energy to maintain their position

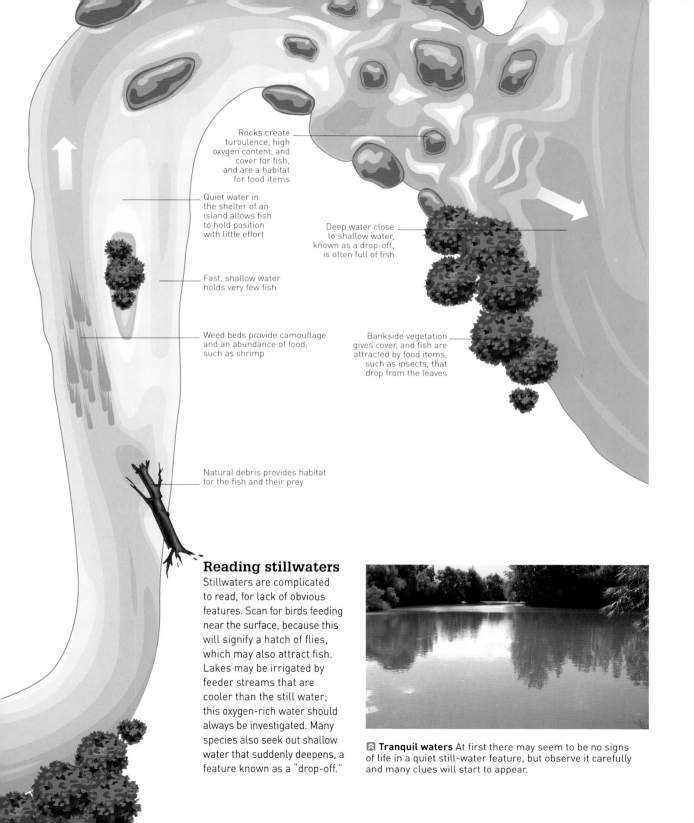

Rocks create turbulence, high oxygen content, and cover for fish, and are a habitat for food items

Quiet water in the shelter of an island allows fish to hold position with little effort

Deep water close to shallow water, known as a drop-off, is often full of fish

Fast, shallow water holds very few fish

Weed beds provide camouflage and an abundance of food, such as shrimp

Bankside vegetation gives cover, and fish are attracted by food items, such as insects, that drop from the leaves

Natural debris provides habitat for the fish and their prey

Reading stillwaters

Stillwaters are complicated to read, for lack of obvious features. Scan for birds feeding near the surface, because this will signify a hatch of flies, which may also attract fish. Lakes may be irrigated by feeder streams that are cooler than the still water; this oxygen-rich water should always be investigated. Many species also seek out shallow water that suddenly deepens, a feature known as a "drop-off."

⬢ **Tranquil waters** At first there may seem to be no signs of life in a quiet still-water feature, but observe it carefully and many clues will start to appear.

Saltwater watercraft

The ability to "read" the water, understanding where various species are likely to be, allows you to spend more time fishing the right water. Knowing about feeding habits, timings, and likely locations is as important as being able to pick the right tackle and fishing strategy.

Reading rocky coastal waters

Waters close to a rocky coast tend to contain abundant large fish attracted by the shelter and food items that these waters often provide. Rocky areas offer a complete food chain in a concentrated area. Some species inhabit the rocky terrain; others turn up when conditions suit their feeding habits. Shallow water over rocky ground may be turbulent, churning up the bottom and dislodging food that brings in fish. Reef systems lying offshore hold lots of fish, with a greater range of species living in the direct vicinity. Many bottom-dwelling fish are territorial, feeding over limited areas, whereas free-swimming fish feed over wide areas. A wrecked ship will become a haven for marine life; small fish and creatures use the wreck as a refuge, and larger predators are attracted by this ready food source.

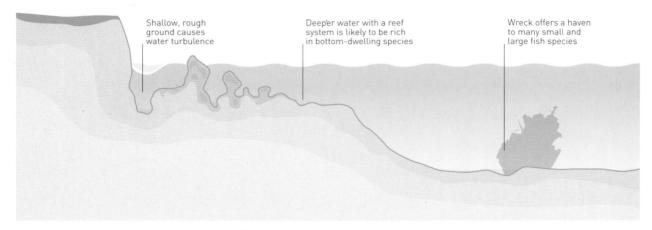

Shallow, rough ground causes water turbulence

Deeper water with a reef system is likely to be rich in bottom-dwelling species

Wreck offers a haven to many small and large fish species

⚠ Cross-section of a rocky coast
Rocky coastlines produce great fishing for anglers who are prepared to walk and explore. Boat-anglers often fish over reefs and rocks out at sea.

≫ Rocky coast A jagged and seemingly inaccessible coastline can be a highly inviting area to fish. There are often many different places you could fish within a comparatively small area.

Reading sandy coastal waters

Fish will generally only come close inshore to feed when conditions suit. Cod, for example, come inshore after a storm, to mop up the food that turbulent seas have dislodged from the bottom. The seabed is shaped and influenced by waves and currents, so many beaches change shape constantly as the sand and gravel shift around. By looking at the ways the waves break, and where the currents run, you can tell what lies beneath the surface. Fish look for food and shelter, and in time you will recognize signs that indicate holes, gullies, sandbanks, and the flatter areas.

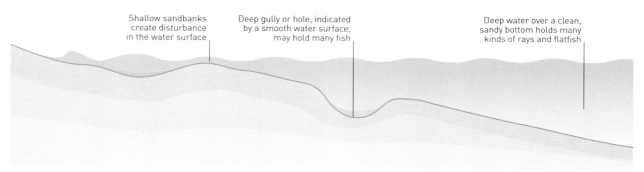

Shallow sandbanks create disturbance in the water surface

Deep gully or hole, indicated by a smooth water surface, may hold many fish

Deep water over a clean, sandy bottom holds many kinds of rays and flatfish

Cross-section of a beach A shelving beach runs out gradually to deeper water farther offshore. The movement of the sea provides clues to the underwater features that hold fish.

Reading beaches A beach offers plenty of fish-holding features. Understanding what species are likely to be around them is an essential part of beach-fishing. A short, choppy sea may disturb the bottom, providing food for larger fish, while many species like to move in the gullies and holes, even those close to the shoreline.

Reading tropical flats

Flats are areas of very shallow, warm water, often known as "skinny" water, with a hard sand or coral bottom. Certain tropical species thrive in these waters, including bonefish, rays, milkfish, some sharks, and permit. Tarpon, barracuda, various trevally, and jacks also pass through some flats areas. Flats may be extensive, and most fish are sight-fished— the angler or guide finds fish visually. Many flats drop off into deeper water, which holds predatory fish waiting for the tide to allow them up on to the flats to hunt.

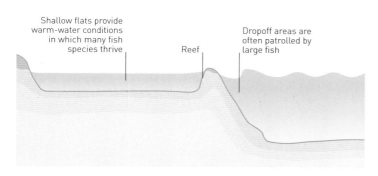

Shallow flats provide warm-water conditions in which many fish species thrive

Reef

Dropoff areas are often patrolled by large fish

Cross section of tropical water Many inshore tropical waters consist of extensive flats systems that stretch out to natural, protective reefs. Beyond, there is often a deepwater dropoff.

Color changes on the flats The color of the water reveals the depth and nature of the sea bed. The bluer water is deeper.

Fishing
Strategies

Once you have learned the basics of tackle, and the essential techniques of casting and landing fish, the time has come to put your skills into practice. Casting for the first time might seem daunting, but absorbing the useful information in this section will give you a valuable head start.

While it is possible to put you on the right road to dealing with a huge number of worldwide fishing situations, in reality, fishing is never perfected. That is the beauty of the sport—its sheer unpredictability.

The strategies in this section will go a long way toward helping you catch lots of fish, but always remember that there are numerous ways of approaching each fishing situation. Fishing is a sport that is developing all the time, but by reading these logical, easy-to-follow, step-by-step guides, you will gain a deep understanding of how to actually go fishing. It is entirely expected and hoped that over time you will adapt and refine some of these strategies to suit the particular challenges posed in your local fishing waters. If fishing comes naturally to you, you will be able to question, adapt, and refine established strategies to better suit "your" style of fishing much more quickly.

⬆ **Choosing tackle** The right choice of tackle is one of the keys to success. Using a simple metal lure works well in many situations.

It is very important to understand that many of these strategies will also work well for other species, in other waters. By improving your understanding of how to tackle waters and fishing situations, you will begin to better comprehend how the strategies you have learned about—and put into practice—can be further applied. While there might be fundamental differences between freshwater and saltwater fishing, for example, many of the strategies bear remarkable similarities. Lure-fishing for European sea bass can be similar to lure-fishing for pike, for instance. The steps involved are concerned simply with putting your lures in front of hungry fish.

Holding baits tight to the bottom requires techniques that will work for all kinds of fish, big and small, in freshwater and in saltwater. While fly-fishing may seem to be in a world of its own, an understanding of fish behavior and patterns is helpful in all situations. The more you learn about core fishing strategies, the easier and more logical this fascinating sport will become.

◀◀ **Concentration** Different fishing strategies demand different approaches, but careful planning and intelligent thinking will help you catch plenty of fish.

Freshwater bait and lure

Freshwater bait- and lure-fishing provides a variety of opportunities for the adventurous angler. Much of what you learn in freshwater with baits and artificial lures is also applicable to saltwater, and to fly-fishing. Starting with baits and lures is a logical way of approaching many types of water and many species. Using the strategies in this chapter, you will be able to put your new skills into practice.

Drop-shot fishing for perch

Drop-shot fishing, or "drop-shotting," is a light lure-fishing technique that can be particularly effective when targeting perch, especially when the water is colder and the fish are therfore less active. Minimal tackle is needed, so you can stay mobile and cover a lot of water efficiently.

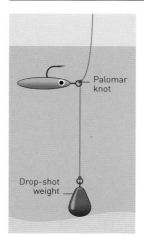

Palomar knot

Drop-shot weight

Rod and rig set-up

Drop-shot rods for perch-fishing are generally short, with plenty of power in the butt sections and very sensitive tips for feeling the gentlest of bites. Match a small, light spinning reel with this rod. Drop-shot lures are soft plastics, and the drop-shotting technique is based around fishing these lures above a weight that is either worked slowly along the bottom or almost held in place and moved subtly up and down by the angler.

《 Drop-shot rig
All you need is a weight, hook, and lure. The soft plastic lure is rigged above the weight.

》 Soft plastics
Mostly, small lures are used for perch-fishing. Many different styles and colors are available, with the type of tail really affecting how the lure moves.

Light lure-fishing

This is an enjoyable and involved way to fish, thanks to its mobile nature and the opportunity to finesse your approach. Perch are inquisitive and sometimes aggressive fish, and they respond well to lure techniques. The beauty of such a light-tackle lure-fishing approach is how modern, technical, and unrestricted it is. A thin braid main line will improve sensitivity between lure and rod tip, with a length of fluorocarbon tied to the end of the braid to make the actual drop-shot rig. Fluorocarbon is more invisible than monofilament underwater.

1 **Think out of the box,** as predatory freshwater species such as perch, pike, and zander respond very well to various lure-fishing techniques. As the water temperature drops in winter, drop-shot fishing and deliberate, subtle working of smaller lures close to the bottom can really appeal to bigger, more lethargic perch.

2 **Use the thin braid main line** to help you feel what is going on with your lure, where it is, and what the fish are doing. Light lure-fishing is all about feel; the more you can feel, the greater the success rate.

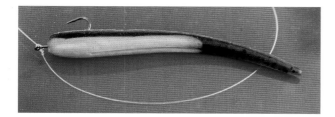

3 **Use a palomar knot,** as this allows for enough line to attach the weight, which sits below the lure, and allows the hook to sit at 90 degrees to the leader. An easy alternative is to buy a simple but specialist drop-shot kit, which will comprise a weight, a hook, and some lures.

4 **Cast your drop-shot rig out,** let it hit the bottom, and while maintaining contact with the bottom, start to vary how your lure moves. You can gently bump the weight back along the bottom, and using a sensitive rod really helps to impart subtle movements to your lure.

Precision fishing

Drop-shot fishing is about precision: for example, when working very tight areas of cover. When the weight is on the bottom, you can literally hold it in place but subtly move your rod tip to impart action to the lure, which helps to keep the lure in the same place and draw inquisitive fish from cover. The technique works well in canals, for example, because conventional lure-fishing tactics do not really allow for such precision placement and deliberate fishing of lures for slower-moving fish, especially in colder water.

Lure- and fly-fishing for pike

Pike fishing is popular in many parts of the world. These hard-fighting predators can be caught on both baits and lures, and they provide one of the ultimate freshwater challenges—taking them using light-tackle lure-fishing techniques is incredibly exciting.

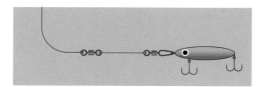

» **Pike-fishing rig** Use braid line and a wire biting trace. Mono will not withstand a pike's teeth. Many fishing waters demand the use of barbless hooks.

» **Subsurface lure** Pike respond to lures at all depths and in various designs, from a wobbling type of shallow diver to a heavy jerkbait.

Rod and rig set-up

Small lure rods enable you to fish for long periods. They have plenty of power to deal with large pike, but find out what size fish you might encounter and tailor your tackle accordingly. Longer, heavier pike rods, better suited to bait-fishing, can work for lures, although from a boat it is best to use a spinning or casting rod under 10 ft (3 m) in length and rated to cast the lure weights you will be using. As for reels, it's a matter of whether you prefer a small bait-casting reel or a small to medium spinning reel.

Preparing for pike

The real trick to catching pike is to find the kind of habitat they like to lurk around and feed in. An electronic fish finder can also be useful in locating them. In addition to showing the fish, it reveals the configuration of the bottom, allowing you to identify fish-holding features such as underwater islands, lumps of rock, sunken trees, and holes. Begin by fishing your lures in and around these sites as well as close to the bank, particularly where there are large reed beds or overhanging or dead trees.

Carry a selection of lures to cover a range of depths, from tight to the bottom to on the surface. There is a good chance that your lure will pass close to the pike many times before they decide to hit it, so work the water systematically. Move quietly around the boat because sound carries through water and may spook the fish.

A big landing net is essential, as is a glove for protecting your hands when unhooking. Many anglers like to unhook pike on a wetted carp mat on the bottom of the boat, but it is often possible to safely remove the hooks from the fish in the net at the side of the boat.

1 **When casting from your boat,** adopt a steady stance because movement is always exaggerated when a boat is rocking slightly. Anchoring will allow you to place the boat to give maximum lure coverage, but if the wind is light, consider slowly drifting through the area.

2 **Takes can be savage.** The pike often engulfs the lure before you register that you need to strike. Maintain a bend in the rod during the fight and, as far as possible, keep the fish's head toward you to prevent it from reaching sanctuary.

USING FISH BAIT

Baits are an excellent way to catch pike, using long, powerful rods that enable you to cast heavy weights. Bottom-fished dead baits work well close to structures, and are often fished carp-style with bait alarms, but one of the most enjoyable methods is to fish dead and live-baits under floats (check local regulations on live-baits). Use a fairly large, buoyant float to support the bait at the required depth, and use a wire trace. Make the most of the current on a river, or the breeze on a lake, to steer your float, and keep an eye on its movements. Do not strike until the pike pulls the float under hard.

3 **Position the net** just below the water surface. As the pike tires, draw it over the net's mouth and lift the net. It is possible to "glove" a pike (grab it at the bottom of the gills where it is bony and will not be damaged) for unhooking, but this requires experience.

4 **Hold the pike** by the bony part of the lower gill area and unhook using long-nosed pliers or a special unhooking implement. Wear a glove and do not put your fingers near the fish's jaws. A pike's teeth are numerous and sharp and are designed to grab prey and not let go.

"ALWAYS HAVE YOUR HOOK BAITED;
IN THE POOL YOU LEAST THINK,
THERE WILL BE A FISH."

Ovid

Lake-fishing for largemouth bass

Among both pleasure and competition anglers, the largemouth bass is one of the most popular freshwater species in the US. Many lakes in the southern US hold large numbers, and anglers usually fish for them from fast boats that have a shallow draft for access to all areas.

Rod and rig set-up

Bass rods are usually short—which is preferable on a boat—and powerful to assist in setting the hook in the bass's bony mouth and for keeping these strong fish away from snags. Small baitcasting reels are the most popular reels because they offer good control when fishing lures and baits in tight areas, but spinning reels also work well.

≪ **Largemouth bass rig** Use a simple float set-up for fishing with live baits. Lures can also be used for bass fishing. Braid mainlines are increasingly popular because they give direct, accurate fishing.

⌃ **Small baitcaster** The demands of bass fishing have led to developments in small baitcasting conventional reels, such as electronic braking systems.

High-speed boat fishing

Like many other species, largemouth bass thrive around areas of cover and shelter. Because their feeding habits vary according to atmospheric pressure and water temperature, boats are used to provide access to the ever-changing bass-holding areas. High-speed boats are popular because the faster you can travel, the more fishing time you will have. Special bass boats are usually equipped with big engines, fish finders, and live-bait wells. Many have seats on the bow to sit on and cast from, and a separate, foot-controlled, electric motor for a quiet final approach to the fish.

1 **Accurate casting is vital** because the fish are often hidden, and fishing with either lures or live baits requires precision. The more good ground you cover with a lure, the greater your chances of hooking up; the closer you cast live bait to a likely spot, the more likely a bass is to come out and hit it.

CHOOSING LURES

There are an enormous number of freshwater bass lures. Soft plastics are popular for fishing at all depths, and are cheap enough to replace if ripped up by the fish. All manner of hard plastic lures work well, including shallow-diving ones.

2 **Strike the fish hard** and start winding almost in one motion, particularly when you are close to an underwater structure. It is vital to turn the bass away from potential danger as quickly as possible, and then play it out in the clear water closer to the boat.

3 **Using a net** is the safest and most efficient way to land your catch. The easiest way to land the fish is to have the net's mouth under the water and bring the fish over it. The person with the net then scoops it up.

4 **Hold the fish** by its bottom jaw and be careful not to cause it any distress. Keep its time out of the water to an absolute minimum.

Lake bottom-fishing

Many freshwater fish feed on or close to the bottom, and the best way to catch them is to bottom-fish with various baits. The weight that takes the bait down also ensures that it stays in place. Accurate use of ground bait helps draw the fish to you, much like chumming (*see* pp.162–163) in saltwater.

Rig and rod set-up

It is important to fish with as much finesse as possible. Bottom-fishing rods are around 12 ft (3.6 m) in length and slightly more powerful than a float rod, to cope with weights and swimfeeders. However, the tips are sensitive so you can tell when you have a bite. Specialized tip sections are available for many bottom-fishing rods. These are designed to work with different weights and in a variety of conditions.

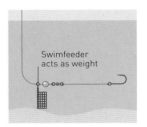

Swimfeeder acts as weight

« Freshwater rig
Most rigs are a variation on a basic bottom-fishing set-up, with the mainline running through the weight or swimfeeder.

» Small spinning reel Use this type of reel with either a rear or front drag, set to use light main lines. Relatively big fish can be caught on a light line.

Preparing and fishing the lake

Start by finding a good swim (place to fish)—look for signs of fish moving around, or choose somewhere that has potential fish-holding features.

Like specialty carp fishing, bottom-fishing entails getting the fish to come to you. Do this by using ground bait: introduce limited quantities to get the fish feeding and to keep them there while you fish. The secret is to put out just enough to tempt the fish, but not to overfeed them; this skill comes with practice. Do

not simply turn up at the lake and throw in all your ground bait and expect the fish to come running. Various ground-bait mixes can be purchased and are designed to appeal to different species; it is always worth including a little of your hook bait in with your mixture as well.

1 **Mix your ground bait** with the lake water in a bucket to create a sticky consistency that begins to break down when it enters the water. Test this by throwing in samples beside you.

2 **Use a catapult** to introduce some hook bait into the same areas as your ground bait. With practice, you will become very accurate at this. Remember to feed little and often.

3 **Fill the swimfeeder** with a mix of ground bait and some of your hook bait. Your baited hook will lie on the bottom in an irresistible cloud of ground bait from the swimfeeder.

4 **Mold some flavored paste** around your hook. These high-protein baits release a lot of scent into the water and different flavors are designed to appeal to different species.

≪ **Holding the line**
Before casting, open the bale arm, slip your index finger over the line so it is tight to the spool, take the rod back for the cast, and release the line from your finger as the rod comes around.

TRYING DIFFERENT BAITS

A wide range of baits are successful for bottom-fishing on lakes. Many unprocessed baits, such as worms, corn, and bread, can nearly always be relied upon for catching fish; indeed, few fish refuse them. But modern high-protein processed baits, such as paste and boilies, are well worth the extra expense, especially where the fish are hard to catch. This is when you need to have something special to give you an edge.

△ **Corn**

△ **Boilie**

△ **Bread**

5 **Make an accurate and controlled overhead cast** (see pp.80–81) to the areas you have ground-baited. Get comfortable before casting and remember to look up into the sky to the point where you will release the line. Cast lower when the wind is in your face, and cast sideways to reach under overhanging trees.

6 **Set the reel** so line can be taken off by a fish, but is tight enough to prevent overruns. Before striking, tighten the reel back up, or use a baitrunner system, which automatically snaps the reel back into your preset drag mode.

Float-fishing lake margins

Many freshwater species feed close to the margins of a lake, near overhanging trees and reed beds. Because they offer accessible fish-holding spots that can be ground-baited and fished with no need for distance casting, these areas are ideal for float-fishing techniques.

Rod and rig set-up

Use a light float rod, about 12 ft (3.6 m) long, that feels balanced in your hand when a reel is attached. Choose a basic reel; there is no current to pull the float, and consequently no need to pay out line. Rig a small hook and light float so that the bait either sinks quickly or drops slowly to its set depth. Many freshwater fish will hit a bait "on the drop."

⬆ **Centerpin reel** The classic centerpin reel (above) is popular with many anglers, but a small spinning reel will work just as well, and is easier to use.

◀ **Float rig** Weight the float with split shot so that only a small part of it sticks out of the water. This is known as cocking the float.

Preparing to fish the lake margins

Look around the lake for spots where this simple method is likely to work. Species such as carp, tench, bream, and roach all respond to light float-fishing tactics. Fish love some kind of cover, so concentrate on overhanging trees, overgrown banks, and reed beds. Tench, especially, like to feed at first light, right up close to reed beds, and you can often see bubbles breaking on the surface from their feeding activity down on the bottom. Look for features that give the fish reason to feed in close, then ground-bait these areas, either to attract the fish or to hold them there while you fish for them.

1 **Mix ground bait to attract** your target, including some hook baits. Canned corn (the hook bait), hempseed, and pellets make up this mixture.

2 **Catapult or throw** some ground bait out in a fairly tight area where you can fish your float effectively. Also throw in some hook baits from time to time around your float. Occasionally, walk away from your fish and gently ground-bait a different area. This will give you options if your fish stops swimming.

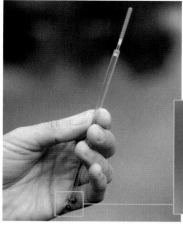

⊠ **Float stops** Set the float to fish at the desired depth with dedicated float stops or easy-to-change split shot.

3 **Take the line through** the eye at the bottom of a simple float, which will then cock at the right angle with the correct weight of split shot.

⊠ **Braking the reel** A centerpin reel requires manual braking, to prevent a tangle. Use either your thumb or one of your forefingers to stop the reel.

4 **Aim to cast accurately** to where your ground bait lies, or where you judge the fish will be. Often a simple underhand cast will put your float where you want it.

5 **Concentrate hard** on your bite indicator, the float. Watch for every bite-signaling twitch and movement, for your float shows you what is going on beneath the surface.

Striking, playing, and landing fish

When the float disappears, or comes up and lies flat on the surface, be sure to strike and set the hook in the fish's mouth. There is no need for a large movement—instead, sweep the rod back until the line goes tight and the tip of the rod bends over.

You can play really big fish on very light line, because a long, through-action float rod helps to protect the line and cushion against the lunges of the fish. Small fish can simply be swung into your hand for unhooking. Make sure you have a soft-mesh landing net ready for dealing with larger fish. Pull the fish over the net and scoop it up. Unhook your catch carefully, and then gently slip it back into the water.

Many anglers retain their fish in keepnets until they are done fishing, and then release all the fish together. Make sure to check any local rules to do with the use of keepnets. Never overfill a keepnet, which can distress the fish through lack of space and oxygen.

Pole-fishing

Pole-fishing is a specialized method of float-fishing that involves the use of a long pole with no reel. The poles, usually made of carbon fiber, are 20–60 ft (6–18 m) in length, which allows for great precision with the presentation of your float because your line is directly above it.

Pole and rig set-up

Attach the line directly to the tip of the pole or, for greater shock absorption when playing larger fish, via a piece of elastic secured inside the tip. Since the float is placed, not cast, it requires little weight and is purely a visual bite indicator. Choose carbon-fiber floats for greater sensitivity. Precision is key and the direct contact over the float is a clear connection to what is going on below the surface.

◀ **Light rig** Cock the float with small weights, and set the hook at an appropriate depth.

▶ **Pole-fishing kit** A tackle-box seat with legs, which can be set up in shallow water and has easily accessible bait and tackle compartments, is ideal.

Pole- and match-fishing

Set up your base, or swim, so everything you need is close at hand, allowing you to fish efficiently. Match-fishing (competitive pole-fishing) calls for particularly fast work. Holding and fishing with a long pole takes practice, but it is perfect for float-fishing for a number of species and, in time, it will come to feel natural. Precision placing of the float also demands careful placing of ground bait. Most poles have several sections that slide into each other to create the length required. Add sections to place your float, and remove them to bring larger fish to the net. Smaller fish can be swung straight to hand. Have a soft-mesh keepnet close by.

1 **In windy conditions,** choose a body-up float (with the "bulb" near the top) for stability. Body-down floats are more useful when the water is calm. The thinner the float profile, the better it is for smaller species.

2 **Add sections to the pole** to place your float exactly. Have one hand on the butt of the pole behind you and the other on the underside of the pole in front of you, positioned to balance the rod. Store spare sections behind you, and bring them forward to join them onto the pole in front of you.

3 **Make sure you can** deal with the pole, bait the hook, land fish, and introduce ground bait all from the seat on your tackle box. If you get a bite, set the fine wire hook in the fish's mouth by tilting the pole into the air. Do this by pushing down with the hand on the butt section of the pole, which lifts the tip of the pole.

4 **As your pole bends,** if the fish is small, you can swing the pole out of the water and straight into your hand in one simple movement; a larger fish will require some playing out. Keep gentle pressure on the fish to avoid breaking the light line or pulling the small hook out of its mouth.

5 **Draw the fish over** a long-handled landing net that is in the water. Unhook the fish and place it gently in the keepnet. It is vital not to overcrowd your keepnet. Many freshwater competitions are fished for via a "bag-weight" system, whereby the angler with the heaviest total weight of fish is the winner. Once weighed in the net, the fish are released unharmed.

Lake-fishing for carp

Fishing for big carp on large expanses of water is an increasingly popular form of angling. Special lakes exist throughout Europe, and with large numbers of big wild carp in North America, anglers in the US and Canada are starting to take notice of this prized fish.

Rig set-up

In well-fished waters, the carp become wise to certain baits and rigs over time. To keep pace with this, big technological advances have taken place within carp fishing. The usual rig is a bottom-fishing set-up with a hair-rig arrangement (below). Weight, line, and trace are in camouflage coloring, so that these wary fish are not spooked. The weighted line sits on the bottom.

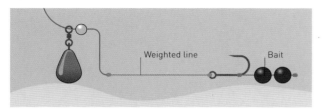

Weighted line   Bait

» Big-pit reel Large spinning reels for carp fishing (known as big-pit reels) come with high-capacity, wide spools that make it easier for you to load the line evenly. The more smoothly line comes off the reel during a cast, the farther the baited rig will fly.

« Hair rig The bait is attached to the hook on a fine line. The fish sucks up the bait without feeling the hook.

Oversize handle

Setting up and preparing your swim

Carp anglers spend long periods on the water and therefore need equipment to remain comfortable—this may include a shelter for night-fishing, a bed, a sleeping bag, and thermal clothing for cold weather. It is common to set up at least three rods, to enable you to cover as much water as possible.

Carp prefer to feed near some form of cover, so look to place your baits near islands, reed beds, visible sand bars, sunken trees, and drop-offs. Many lakes have favored swims (fishing areas) where carp are caught frequently. Throw or catapult ground bait into your chosen swim, to encourage the carp to come into the area. Cast your rig into this area, and carp may pick it up while feeding. A hooked carp often runs for cover, hence the need for a large reel, strong main line, and a powerful, through-action carp rod that absorbs shocks and provides power to turn fish away from snags.

1 **Spend time looking** for signs of fish before setting up. Keep an eye out for carp rolling on the surface, reeds moving around because carp are knocking them, and water visibly stirred up by carp feeding in the shallows.

2 **Secure extra ground bait** to your rig, in a PVA net bag, held in place by foam, before casting. The bag dissolves quickly, to leave your baited rig surrounded by tempting morsels.

3 **Cast accurately** to where your ground bait lies, using a simple overhead cast, and looking up at the sky at about 45 degrees when releasing. Carp rods have a forgiving through action that enables smooth long-range casting.

⟪ Stopping the reel
Spinning reels require the angler to use a forefinger to secure the line during the cast. Release the line at the end of the cast.

4 **Place each rod** on a rod rest and into an electronic bite alarm. This will produce sounds and light indicators on the receiver when a fish picks up your bait.

5 **Watch patiently for a bite.** Fishing for big carp is all about putting in the time. Some waters may produce few fish, but the longer your baits are fishing in the right areas, the greater your chances of hooking a monster carp.

Tent

Bite-alarm indicator

Baits

Multiple rods on rod rest with bite alarms

Carp bed on which to place your catch

Stalking for carp

Seeking out feeding carp and then perhaps entering the water to fish for them is an exciting way to target these large freshwater fish. Any kind of sight-fishing, which involves seeing the fish you are hoping to catch, adds an extra edge to your enjoyment of the sport.

Rod and rig set-up

A standard 12-ft (3.7-m) carp rod is a good choice, but many anglers prefer shorter stalking rods for fishing in confined areas. Mono line has a degree of stretch for safety when hooking fish at close range, but it sinks, whereas braid is sensitive and floats, which is useful for surface fishing. Travel light; the more mobile you are, the closer you'll be able to get to the fish.

›› Surface rig A float such as a carp controller will enable you to cast to the fish. If they are close, you may be able to freeline bait.

Surface-fishing float

›› Spinning reel A large-capacity spinning reel copes well with stalking. It is worth carrying a smaller, lighter reel if you do a lot of mobile sight-fishing.

Finding and fishing for carp

Stalking for carp is all about finding the fish, which is best done by walking and looking. Move stealthily and do not let the fish see you first. Dawn and dusk are good times of day to spot them. The quieter the water, the greater the chance of sight-fishing; fish shy away from noise and vibrations.

Carp suck bait rather than charge in and engulf it, so hesitate for a split second before striking when you see a fish take your bait. Initially, watch them feeding to learn their habits, and build up their confidence before introducing baited hooks into the area.

1 **Find an elevated vantage point** from which to look for fish—even carefully climbing a sturdy tree, if necessary. Wear polarized sunglasses to cut glare and enable you to see into the water. In order not to spook the fish, dress in dull-colored clothing, remain quiet, and do not break natural horizons.

2 **Pre-bait your chosen spots** with ground bait of bread or dog biscuits and regularly check these areas. If the carp come up for the ground bait, use it for hook bait too. Lightweight chest waders are useful. Step carefully and do not go out too deep.

3 **Keep as still as possible** when carp are feeding very close to you. It can get exciting, but you must be stealthy. Fish are naturally wary of foreign objects in the water and on the bank, and their eyesight is very acute, so once in position, make sure you make as little disturbance as possible when moving. Carry some bait with you so that there is no need to leave the water to rebait the hook.

4 **Land your carp** with a large, soft-mesh landing net, and unhook and weigh it on a wetted carp mat or in a sling that will not damage the natural protective slime. Keep the fish near the water and make sure its time out is short to reduce stress.

Freelining and light bottom-fishing

To freeline, use only the bait for weight and let it move with the current to find natural holding areas. For light bottom-fishing, a small weight holds the bait in place. Both these fishing methods keep the angler constantly in touch with the bait, feeling for bites all the time.

Rod and rig set-up

No rod rests or bite alarms are used for freelining or light bottom-fishing—it is just you, the water, and the fish. You will be holding your rod for long periods, so look for the lightest, most responsive set-up you can find. There will be no casting heavy weights, so choose a rod around 10 ft (3 m) long, and match it with a small, fixed-spool reel. A light tip on the rod helps give visual indications of any interest from the fish, and allows you to cast freelined baits a little if need be. These styles of fishing are more about feel than about high-tech gear.

◀◀ Freeline rig For freelining, just tie a hook on your line. For light bottom-fishing, add a small weight.

▶▶ Spinning reel A small spinning reel holds plenty of line for these styles of fishing, but use one with a good front- or rear-drag system, since big fish require careful playing on light lines.

Freelining on lakes and rivers

On a river, use the current to work freelined baits gently downstream. Putting light weights on the line gives the possibility of precision casting, and allows you to hold the bait in a specific area. On lakes, use these methods when fish are feeding close to the banks, or if there are overhanging trees or weed and reed beds. Look for a breeze on a lake that will float surface-fished, freelined baits right under overhanging trees.

1 **Use naturally floating** bread flakes for surface-fishing. To fish close to or on the bottom, use a small weight to sink the bait. Alternatively, squeeze the bread around the hook to remove all the air, and it will sink naturally. High-protein baits also work well.

2 **Look at where** you want to place your bait, and cast gently and precisely. Your bait and tackle should be accessible, because the less you move around on the bank, the less the fish will be spooked. Kneeling down helps you stay concealed below the fish's natural horizon.

3 **Hold the line constantly** in your fingers so that you can feel when to strike and set the hook. If you are fishing close to cover, work the fish hard during the fight and use the bend of the rod to try to keep fish away from snags, and to protect the light main line. Apply extra drag to the reel by palming the front of the spool.

4 **Have the landing net close at hand,** in case you hook a fish suddenly and cannot move to grab your net. Sink the head of the net under the water, so that it does not spook the hooked fish, then pull the fish toward you and over the net. Lift the net and scoop in the fish.

FISHING FOR BARBEL

Barbel feed in a way that makes freelining and light bottom-fishing the perfect methods to fish for them. To catch barbel requires a stealthy, refined approach because they move around in clear, shallow water—but hold on hard when you hook one: they are powerful fighters that will find any snags.

5 **Keep stress to a minimum.** A fish that fights hard needs careful treatment before releasing. Keep it close to or in the water, or on a wetted carp mat, while you take the hook out. Gently support the fish as you take it back to the water and continue to cradle it in the water to make sure it is breathing strongly. As strength kicks through its body, allow it to swim off through your hands.

River-fishing for giant catfish

The most accessible and consistent catfish fishing is in the Ebro River in Spain. Avid anglers journey to this river to fish for the huge catfish, often with professional guides who can offer all the necessary tackle and knowledge to mount a serious challenge for these powerful fish.

Rod and rig set-up

Catfish are potentially huge, sometimes weighing more than 200 lb (90 kg), and call for extremely powerful tackle. Rods should be fairly short and very strong, to provide leverage against the fish; there are some on the market that are designed purely for catfish fishing. Mainlines should be at least 30 lb (13.5 kg).

◄ **Catfish rig** Use live bait with a large saltwater hook or a special catfish pattern. Tie the baited rig to a float, which is previously secured by a weight on the riverbed.

◢ **Large reels** Use a big spinning reel or conventional reel to hold a lot of heavy line. A strong drag and comfortable handle are essential.

How to fish for catfish

Targeting these monsters is a waiting game. Catfish are true predators and prefer to hunt mainly during low light, either in the evening or at night. They come close to the surface to feed, and are often to be found crashing into unsuspecting fish right next to the banks as the sun goes down.

Generally, anglers fish from the bank with live baits that are tethered out in the river, but some people take to a boat in the evening and work the margins for the catfish that are out on the prowl. Fishing for catfish from the riverbanks is much like a bigger version of carp fishing—so set yourself up to fish long sessions with a tent, bed-chair, and bite alarms. Often you will be woken from your sleep by the sound of a bite alarm as a catfish takes one of the baits and starts running off. The rush to figure out what is going on, and then make the strike at the appropriate time, takes a bit of getting used to, but the result could be a freshwater fish of incredible size.

1 **Stand on the bank** or in the shallows, and feed out line from your reel as your guide or companion takes a small boat out to the floats already anchored firmly to the bottom of the river. Your guide will attach the baited rig to a float via a weak link of line that is easily broken when a catfish hits the bait. The anchored float will hold the heavy bait where it needs to be.

Using a rod pod

A rod pod, or tripod, holds multiple rod and reel set-ups in place at the same time, often together with bite alarms and various other forms of bite indicators. A rod pod will hold rods rock-steady for long fishing sessions, but it is important to place them so that the lines coming out of the tips are in the right order, and are not crossing one another. Place the rod pod or tripod in an accessible position to enable you to strike fast-running bites, but also so that there is sufficient clearance for you to be able to walk around. As close to the water as possible is often the best place.

2 **Fix the rods** in a rod pod as each bait is put out. Secure them with elastic cord in case a reel jams when a catfish hits, or the rod could fly out of the pod and into the river. Have more rods rigged in the back of the boat for fishing the margins until dark. Make yourself comfortable to fish a long session.

3 **Land a catfish carefully;** your guide will go into the river and put the fish on a stringer— a soft rope that passes through the mouth and gills—while it recovers.

Saltwater bait and lure

Your first taste of saltwater angling could easily lead to a lifelong passion, because some of the most varied and exciting fishing exists in the oceans of the world. So much water, so many fish to catch, and so much to learn about how to catch them. You will see how both saltwater and freshwater fishing borrow and learn from each other through the strategies in this chapter.

Estuary fishing for mullet

Many fish species, including small fish and predators, gather in the calm waters of estuaries. The thick-lipped gray mullet is a fish that is highly adaptable and is found in many saltwater environments, but estuaries are a good place in which to fish for them.

Rod and rig set-up

For estuary mullet fishing you will need a 12–13-ft (3.7–4-m) feeder rod (*see* pp.36–37) or a carp rod of a similar length. This should be matched with a spinning reel, and the line should be either 8-lb (3.6-kg) mono or 15–20-lb (6.8–9.1-kg) braid (*see* p.48). Keep the set-up simple, and use your time learning where, when, and how these clever fish feed.

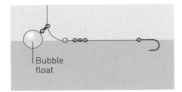

Bubble float

Surface-fishing rig A rig incorporating a bubble float enables you to cast your bait (usually bread) a long way. Squeeze the bread around the hook so that some air is trapped to help it float.

Spinning reel A small- to medium-size spinning reel allows effective casting and works well with the light weights and small baits that are used for mullet fishing in estuaries.

Techniques and tips

Mullet are mysterious fish, often seeming to wander at random and turning up anywhere, but the more you fish for them, the more you will find that distinct patterns of behavior emerge. Many fish, including mullet, switch into feeding mode at different stages of the tidal cycle, and this explains why certain locations fish well at different stages of the tide. Mullet love to move in on mud flats that are being submerged by the incoming tide, especially when the ground has been warmed by the sun. You can often see where mullet have been feeding by the telltale scrapes in the mud. Look also for fish moving around; they are often to be found around boats, moorings, and structures such as piers and breakwaters.

1 **Wear polarized sunglasses,** which allow you to see into the water and observe the fish moving around. Sight-fishing in this way can be exciting. Often an extra pair of eyes can be of help in spotting the fish so that you can accurately judge where to cast your bait.

2 **Throw ground bait** in the area most likely to produce fish. Mullet can sometimes be induced into feeding and taking the hook bait by these free offerings. Pieces of bread thrown into the water often work well because these will both sink and float. Bread is also a good hook bait.

3 **Keep a close eye** on the fish as they feed on the ground bait. You may need to add to this to keep them interested. Chest waders are ideal for estuary fishing because they provide protection as you enter the water to cast, land fish, and access different areas.

5 **Take a moment** to savor your success before releasing your catch. Fishing for mullet provides great sport on light tackle, and these fish can be wily adversaries.

4 **When a mullet bites,** be prepared for a powerful run, often toward snags (underwater obstructions). Be sure to try to turn fish away from areas where you might lose them. Keeping the rod high is one way to fight them, but sideways pressure can also work well to change their direction.

Shore-fishing for sea trout

Fishing for sea trout along the shores of northern Europe demands very different techniques from river-fishing for this species. Sea trout can be caught all year near these coasts, when they come inshore to hunt for small fish and shrimp.

Rod and rig set-up

Spinning rods, 9–10 ft (2.7–3 m) in length, work well for casting lures of ¾ to 1 oz (20–30 g), with small spinning or bait-casting reels to match. Braided lines are often preferred to mono for their direct feel. Spinning allows you to cover a lot of water efficiently, which can be crucial.

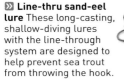

» Line-thru sand-eel lure These long-casting, shallow-diving lures with the line-through system are designed to help prevent sea trout from throwing the hook.

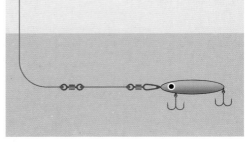

⌃ Lure-fishing rig
Use small spoons and spinners on a simple set-up. Many anglers like to use light lures in the shallows. But larger sea trout are often in deeper water, so a heavier lure will enable you to cast farther out.

Location and making a start

Success comes through learning where the fish are likely to be, and from working the coastline hard. First and last light are the best times to fish, but in summer, anglers often fish through the night. Look for long, shallow beaches, and shallow reefs or rocky ground—places where the fish can come in close to feed—and cover these first, before wading out. Seek shelter from onshore winds, which make casting trickier.

1 **Wade out slowly** to avoid spooking fish. Cover as much water as you can with your casts and vary the rate of your retrievals. If the sea trout ignore your lure, try letting it sink for a moment. This may induce a hit from a fish.

» Natural food Start fishing in areas where shrimp and various small baitfish are likely to be, such as near rocks and weed, as they are the reasons sea trout come inshore to feed. Many lures and flies successfully imitate shrimp and prawns.

2 **A big sea trout** is best landed in a net when shore-fishing. It is advisable to carry a small, portable landing net that can be clipped out of the way on your back until you need it. Sea trout caught in the ocean are usually brightly colored, with vivid markings. They begin to darken when they have spent time in a river.

3 **Wearing the right clothing** will enable you to enjoy your fishing. The colder months demand warm layers to let you fish for longer. Fly-fishing clothing is perfect; always wear polarized sunglasses, which help you spot fish and see more of the ground over which you are fishing. Glasses also protect your eyes.

Kayak fishing

Fishing from a kayak opens up new opportunities, from shallow inshore waters inaccessible on foot to targeting big fish offshore. Lure, bait, and fly anglers fish from kayaks in salt- and freshwater, and belly boats offer a good alternative when fishing on calm lakes.

Rod and rig set-up

Whether you fish with lures, flies, or bait, whatever fishing tackle you use when fishing from a kayak or belly boat is liable to get wet, and saltwater especially is very tough on fishing tackle. Shorter rods around 7–9 ft (2.1–2.7 m) long help with maneuverability on a kayak.

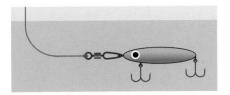

« Lure fishing rig A lure clip allows for easy lure changes to adapt to the fish you are targeting.

» Saltwater damage Wash your fishing tackle in freshwater after kayak fishing.

Modern fishing kayaks

The advances in designs and materials together with the increasing popularity of fishing from kayaks has given rise to so many different models. Basic kayaks can often be rented for fishing in very safe and shallow waters, but more and more anglers are buying and then customizing their kayaks for exploring more adventurous and remote waters. Traditionally, kayaks are propelled by a paddle, but increasingly kayaks are becoming available that can be moved around very efficiently via

pedal power, although it is essential to always carry a paddle and stow it away if you are not using it, just in case something goes wrong.

There are many safety issues to think about, and for the more adventurous kayak fishing, it is worth looking for some professional training. If you are going to move away from very shallow water where you can easily stand up, you need to be able to get back on your kayak if you capsize or fall off. Always check weather forecasts, know the times and size of the tides, and carry the correct safety equipment, such as a VHF radio, a compass, and a GPS unit.

1 **Kayaks allow for stealth,** which is of huge benefit if you are sight-fishing for specific species. When paddles are not in use, stow them securely so that they don't get lost or drop in the water and scare the fish.

2 **Keep your flies,** bait, or lures handy so that you can swap them around as required. If you are fishing in pairs, it's advisable for one angler to stay on "duty," paddling and steering while the other prepares their line.

3 **Cast your line** carefully and precisely. When targeting fish that live in and around the mangroves, accurate casting is required. Snook are one such species that often remains close to cover.

Belly-boat fishing

Also known as a float tube, a belly boat is a small, highly portable, inflatable fishing vessel. Used primarily for fly- and lure-fishing on lakes, belly boats are not recommended on moving water such as a river. The angler usually wears breathable, stocking-foot chest waders, and flippers or fins to help propel them around, and it is essential to wear a personal flotation device.

Pier fishing

Artificial structures often give easy and safe access to deeper water. Schools of small fish often gather around piers, breakwaters, and harbor walls, and bigger predators also congregate, attracted by this potential food source. Many people fish for their first time from a pier.

Rod and rig set-up

One of the most effective ways to fish from a pier is to set up a simple float-fishing rig. Use a longer spinning or casting rod to aid with casting the float out, and match it with a medium spinning reel. A float that carries a weight of 1–2 oz (30–60 g) is perfect for casting and fishing. Be careful when casting to avoid injury to others on the pier.

Weight

◄ Basic float rig A baited hook suspended under a float allows you to target fish that are not feeding on the bottom.

▶ Spinning reel A spinning reel offers tangle-free casting and is perfect for float-fishing.

Exploiting artificial structures

Piers often attract large numbers of fish taking advantage of the feeding opportunities offered by species that make their homes in the structure, such as crabs and crustaceans. Small fish often gather in the shelter of piers and harbor walls. Some piers offer exciting fishing for large species—for example, tarpon fishing from the piers of southern Florida. In parts of Australia, anglers target stingrays and sharks from the piers. Be sure to check that fishing is allowed from the pier you intend to go to.

1 **Choose your baits and equipment** to suit the waters and the likely targets. In northern European waters, float-fishing is effective for mackerel, garfish, pollack, or wrasse.

2 **Concentrate hard** on watching all movements of the float, and strike when it goes under the surface. The float is the bite indicator in float-fishing. When it suddenly goes under the surface or starts moving erratically, there is a fish eating the bait.

3 **When you have a bite,** strike and reel in. Set the bait about 6 ft (2 m) under the float to hook a mackerel. Garfish tend to swim at shallower depths, so set up the rig accordingly.

USING A DROP NET

Fishing from a pier may require the use of a drop net to land big fish if the distance down to the water is too great for a traditional landing net to be used. Having hooked your fish, lower the drop net into the water and steer the fish over the net. Then lift the net up with the fish in it. With practice this becomes an easy operation, especially if you have help available.

Long-range beach-fishing

In this form of fishing, an angler who is able to cast a long way out from a beach often has a distinct advantage. When fish are feeding far out or, perhaps, where there is a distant gully or sandbank that may hold fish, the angler who can reach them will catch more fish.

Rod and rig set-up

A long shore-fishing rod can cast farther than a shorter one, and can create extra leverage and compression when used by a good caster. Most long-range rods are at least 13 ft (3.9 m) long, and are rated to cast 4–6 oz (112–170 g). Modern materials make such rods light and responsive, but the most powerful are very stiff through the butt and midsections. Many sea anglers also use 15-ft (4.5-m) slow-action rods, which are easier to bend and cast. The longer and more forgiving the rod, the easier it is to put a proper bend into the rod, and gain maximum compression that sends the bait out farther.

>> **Clipped-down rig**
In a clipped-down, fixed paternoster rig, the hook is secured by the bait clip, and releases on impact with the water.

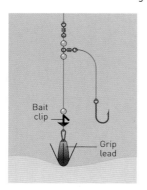

Bait
clip

Grip
lead

>> **Reel and line**
A modern 6000-size conventional reel is perfect for long-range beach-fishing. However, many anglers use big spinning reels, which are generally easier to use. Whichever reel you use should be loaded with 15-lb (6.75-kg) mono line, and a 60-lb (27-kg) shockleader for safety.

Location and preparation

Long-range beach-fishing has developed in order to reach fish on shallow, shelving beaches, and where deeper water, which often contains more fish, is farther out. Long-distance casting is a particularly useful skill to master if you need to clear rough ground to reach fish that live on the sandy and muddy bottoms farther out to sea. Many anglers now hone their technique in long-distance casting tournaments.

Always think about safety when distance casting, because the power buildup is immense, and this means that the lead and rig are moving at high speed, which is potentially dangerous to those nearby. Use a strong shockleader to take the strain during the cast; without it, the weaker mainline will snap.

1 **Fresh bait is key.** While being able to reach the fish is important, the freshness and quality of your bait is just as vital. When you are bottom-fishing, the more scent your bait releases into the water, the greater your chances of success. Check your baits at least every 20 minutes if you have had no bites.

2 **Stand on firm ground** away from other anglers to cast. Look into the sky during the power stroke, and release the line when the rod is at an angle of about 45 degrees to the ground; the lead should then head in that direction. Cast as far as you need to reach fish.

《 **Gripping the spool**
Clamp your thumb tightly onto the spool to hold it as you cast.

3 **Beware of striking too soon.** When you get a bite, be sure to allow the more hesitant fish species sufficient time to get the bait into their mouths. Be aware also of the need to strike quickly if the rod tip bends suddenly.

CASTING TIPS

The most important aspect of long-distance beachcasting is adding increased compression (or bend) to the rod during the entire length of the cast, in order to achieve greater casting distances. Look at where you want the bait, weight, or lure to go, and release in line with this point. Use a strong punch into the air with the top hand, and pull firmly into your chest with your bottom hand.

Beach-fishing for sharks

This is extreme shore-fishing—chasing very large fish from the beaches and rocks of remote locations, far from any kind of comfort. Sometimes the fish weigh more than the angler, such as the bronze whaler sharks caught on the desolate Skeleton Coast of Namibia.

Rod and rig set-up

Shark anglers use simple but robust gear, choosing long, powerful, shore-fishing rods that can hold big fish, and cope with casting large baits a long way out into the surf. A minimum rod length of 14 ft (4 m) is usual, but these rods are surprisingly light and easy to handle. Long rods are matched with strong conventional reels that hold at least 350 yd (320 m) of 30- to 40-lb (13.5–18-kg) main line. Big sharks run a long way when hooked and on occasion you may need all that line.

◉ **Bottom-fishing rig** A bottom-fishing rig works well for casting and fishing with big shark baits. Rigs need to be as tough and as simple as possible.

❯❯ **Large spinning reel** Spinning reels are far stronger than they used to be, and more and more anglers use them these days for chasing big fish from shore and boat.

Targeting sharks

Shark fishing is best done with a good guide. Sharks come inshore only when there is a plentiful food supply, and guides are able to "read" the water, looking for signs that show what kind of ground lies beneath the waves. Shark fishing relies on similar methods whether from the shore or a boat: scent-laden, bloody hook bait is used to appeal to the sharks' strong sense of smell. They can home in on these baits from a long distance. You will need to wear a fighting belt for this kind of fishing to secure the end of the rod while playing these potentially huge fish.

1 **Compress the rod** to harness the power that is necessary to cast big baits into the crashing waves. Safe casting with these big rods and reels takes practice and strength.

3 **When the shark tires,** let a wave bring it as close as possible to the beach. Then your guide will grab the shark just above the tail and begin to pull it out of the sea, using the surging water to help.

2 **Fight your shark** with the rod end secured in the fighting belt. When the shark slows, wind in line. When it runs again, let it run against the drag of the reel and brace yourself in a comfortable position.

4 **Unhook the shark,** clean it off with seawater, and take photographs of your catch; but keep it close to the water, and return it to the sea as soon as possible afterward—this is usually a job for two. When you have taken the shark back into the water, make sure it swims off strongly.

Surf-fishing for European sea bass

This classic style of shore-fishing originated on the Atlantic beaches of Ireland and southwest England, where tumbling surf and all kinds of underwater features hold everything the European sea bass angler looks for. There is something magical about fishing in the surf on a lonely beach.

Rod and rig set-up

There are many 11- to 12-ft (3.3–3.6-m) specialty bass rods on the market, but any rod that can cast baits or lures that weigh 2 to 4 oz (55–115 g) will work perfectly well. Match your rod with either a small conventional or a medium spinning reel. You will need a 15-lb (6.8-kg) main line, with a long, 40-lb (18-kg) shockleader.

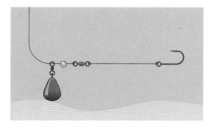

◀ **Bottom-fishing rig**
A standard bottom-fishing rig that fishes on the bottom is the usual set-up for this type of shore-fishing.

⌃ **Conventional reel** This small conventional reel, designed to hold 82 ft (25 m) of 15-lb (6.8-kg) line, is ideal for this type of fishing.

Reading the conditions

Many people look at a surf beach and see nothing but waves. However, the trained eye can see various patterns in the surf that show clearly the kind of terrain that lies beneath.

You will catch more European sea bass if you learn to "read" the water because they love to use unseen gullies and deeper holes to come in close to the shore to feed on sand eels, crabs, and shrimp. It takes practice, but in time you will see that a less "busy" area of surf among a mass of waves often signifies deeper water—either a gully, a drop-off, or a hole. An important element of your kit is a good pair of lightweight, breathable chest waders.

1 **Use a simple overhead style** of cast to put baits out where you believe the fish will be hunting, preferably in the gentle onshore surf—conditions that European sea bass like. Most European sea bass fishing is done at close range, so there is no need for distance casting and all the special expertise that goes with it.

2 **Hold the rod** so that you can sense any movements that may indicate a bite. Alternatively, hold the main line between your thumb and index finger.

3 **Use the forgiveness** of a light shore rod to cushion the powerful runs and shaking of the head of a hooked European sea bass. Strike only when the fish charges off and tightens up the line. Avoid striking on a slack- line bite—that is, when the European sea bass picks up the bait and runs toward you.

4 **Bring the fish slowly** toward you until you can grab it to remove the hook, before you release it.

HANDLING EUROPEAN SEA BASS

European sea bass have an extremely spiky dorsal fin, and razor-sharp edges to the gill covers, so handle them carefully. They have no real teeth, so grip their bottom lip firmly and lift them from the water gently, supporting them underneath so that the body does not bend uncomfortably.

Lure-fishing for European sea bass

European sea bass are highly predatory fish, adept at coming in close to the shoreline to hunt. Many shallow, rocky, weed-infested spots offer cover and food for hungry European sea bass, and these areas are perfect for the mobile angler who wants to fish with lures.

Rod and rig set-up

For lure-fishing for European sea bass, a 9- to 11-ft (2.7–3.3-m) spinning rod, rated to cast around 0.35 to 2oz (10–60g) will do the job, together with a medium-sized spinning reel. Load your reel with 10- to 15-lb (4.5–6.8-kg) mono or 15- to 30-lb (6.8–13.5-kg) braid. Chest waders are useful for reaching the best spots, but in summer many anglers wear no waterproofs (wet-wade). Carry your lures in a box that fits inside a small backpack.

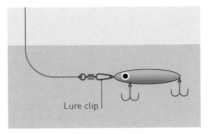

Lure clip

« Lure-fishing rig Join a short length of 20-lb (9-kg) fluorocarbon or clear mono leader to your main line, tie the end to a lure clip, and use that to chop and change your lures as required.

» Sand Eel Jerk Minnow A diving lure with a strong sand-eel and mackerel profile.

Choosing your location

European sea bass need cover to ambush their prey and will use rocks, seaweed, and gullies to trap hapless victims; try to cast lures in these locations. Take a look at a section of coastline at low tide and see what the outgoing sea has uncovered. You can then decide whether it is worth fishing the same ground when there is water over it. Note gullies and weed patches, and look for big rocks, around which the European sea bass will hunt. You need to go after European sea bass, instead of waiting for the fish to come to you. Be sure to keep a close eye on the tide and have a safe retreat through shallow water planned.

1 **European sea bass love movement,** so look for shallow water with plenty of movement, current or breaking waves, or rocky ground. Night fishing can also be highly effective.

Look for signs of current, because European sea bass will hunt their prey here

You can read the water to better understand where the fish might be

Make sure to fish through all the gullies; European sea bass love these areas

Fish close to the water when possible, but keep a close eye on conditions

2 **Play the fish** from the safest and easiest vantage point and work the hooked fish hard. When hooked, a European sea bass will head for the nearest snag. Apply plenty of pressure with the rod, and turn the fish away from danger.

3 **Return the European sea bass to the sea,** if possible. Take photographs and admire this efficient predator, but keep the fish close to water and return it quickly. Note the big predator eye and the spiked dorsal fin—not for nothing is this fish known as the wolf of the sea.

WHY USE A WEEDLESS HOOK?

Weedless hooks are also known as offset or worm hooks. They hugely reduce the risk of snagging your hook point when fishing rough or snaggy ground. European sea bass love this type of terrain.

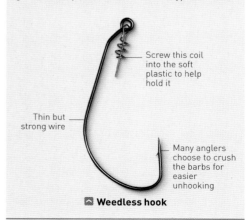

Screw this coil into the soft plastic to help hold it

Thin but strong wire

Many anglers choose to crush the barbs for easier unhooking

⌃ **Weedless hook**

Shore-fishing for striped bass

These magnificent fish inspire incredible levels of devotion. As the "stripers" migrate up and down the northeast coast of the US, "striper junkies" (as these anglers are often known) will follow, from bays to inlets, estuaries to beaches, rocky shores to canals, and saltwater into freshwater.

Rod and rig set-up

There is no one way to target striped bass from the shore; indeed, anglers will fish with lures, baits, and flies. If lure-fishing, in general you are either looking for a lure rod around 7–8 ft (2.1–2.4 m) long, which can handle with lures up to about 2 oz (60 g), or you might need to fish bigger lures at range, which calls for a longer, more powerful lure rod.

Reel stem

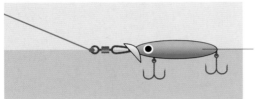

Slim profile and rear-weighted for long-distance casting

》 Spinning reel
The heavier the lure, the easier it is to cast, especially with a larger spinning reel. These reels allow for effective line management and also provide sufficient retrieval speed to work the many different types of lures.

Big chunky handle for added grip

⌃ **Surface lure** Pencil poppers are one of the most popular types of surface lure for striped bass fishing. Takes can be very aggressive.

Targeting striped bass from shore

Striped bass migrate on the hunt for food, and at various times of the season they might be feeding on baitfish such as mackerel, bunker (menhaden), sand eels, and herring. Sometimes striped bass will be so focused on a particular baitfish that they will refuse almost anything that doesn't at least conform to the size and profile of that particular food source. You will need to carry a selection of lures with different profiles, colors, and swimming actions.

1 **Look for fish-holding features,** such as boulder fields and rocky promontories. Anglers will often wear chest waders and wade out to fish locations like these. Carry your lures with you in either a rucksack or a specialist lure bag.

2 **Putting lures out** a long way is not always needed, but the ability to do so can often help. Lure rods for striped bass fishing are so varied, but surf-based fishing in particular tends to call for bigger lures, which in turn require longer and more powerful rods.

SURFACE LURES

Explosive topwater takes are incredibly exciting, and striped bass will often hit surface lures. Pencil poppers come in many shapes and sizes, and in places such as the Cape Cod Canal they can be a deadly lure for big striped bass. You will need a relatively long, powerful rod. To get the surface lure working properly on the retrieve, place the rod between your legs, and almost "shake" the rod tip, which then imparts action on the lure.

3 **Large striped bass** can be a real handful. Once you have landed your fish, handle it carefully and remove the hooks. Many anglers release all their fish, but if you want to take one to eat, then make sure to be very aware of local fishing regulations.

Night-fishing for striped bass

Many of the biggest striped bass caught from the shore are landed at first light, last light, and when it gets dark, as this is often when big fish will move close inshore to feed. Striped bass will hit lures as readily at night as they will during the day, but make sure you keep light off the water and keep noise to a minimum, especially when fishing calm conditions. Anglers will often be very secretive about their best fishing spots.

« **Fishing guides** If you are new to a particular kind of fishing or location, hiring a good local fishing guide can pay dividends.

Rock-edge fishing for pollack

The hard-fighting pollack is known for its ability to crash-dive once hooked. One of the classic species of fish for rock-based anglers to target, fishing for pollack can take anglers to some truly beautiful locations.

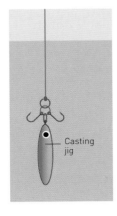

Rod and rig set-up

Pollack respond very well to lure-fishing tactics. A powerful lure rod rated around 0.70–2 oz (20–60 g) and 8–10 in (20–25 cm) length will deal with most rock-fishing situations. In general you will need to get your lure down deep to where the pollack are located.

◀ **Casting jig**
Great lures for getting down deep and covering lots of water.

Casting jig

▶ **Different colors**
On some days pollack can show a marked preference for specific lure colors. Carry a selection.

Pure rock-fishing

This fish is one of the quintessential rock-edge fishing species, often found in wild and out-of-the-way locations. You don't actually have to venture far from the beaten track, but in general you will find better pollack-fishing away from areas that are heavily fished. Pollack inhabit very rocky and reefy waters, which they use as cover to ambush their prey. Look for current, structure (rocks, reefs, weed, gullies), and deeper water that drops away from rock edges, and you are likely to find pollack. Although pollack do feed well during the day and will often do so hardest on a flooding tide, at around last light they will often come up closer to the surface.

1 **Choose your ground,** and be aware that pollack may literally be feeding in the waters under the rocks beneath your feet, so you will need to fish close to the edge of the rocks. Fish in calm conditions only and keep a watch out for swells. Wear good, grippy footwear.

2 **Hit the bottom** with your lure. You need to feel it literally "tap" the bottom as you let it drop through the water column. Now start your retrieval. Tackle losses are inevitable.

3 **Prepare to crash-dive,** as a pollack's first instinct is to crash-dive for the bottom or the nearest snag, so you cannot mistake it when a pollack hits your lure or fly or bait. Put as much pressure on a hooked fish as you can.

SAFE FISHING

Pollack-fishing can take place in some potentially dangerous locations. Wearing a lightweight, auto-inflate life jacket is very important and will hugely help your chances of survival if the worst happens and you are washed into the sea. Also carry a means of communication that you know will work in the areas in which you are fishing.

Lure-fishing for wrasse

It was only relatively recently that a few forward-thinking anglers in the Channel Islands worked out that wrasse were a species that could be targeted on lures. Traditionally a fish for bait anglers only, wrasse are now very much a target of saltwater anglers who fish with lure gear.

Rod and rig set-up

Wrasse are hard-fighting fish that usually dive for cover once hooked, so lure rods need to be around 8ft (2.4m) long and fairly powerful for setting hooks and dragging fish away from snags. The Texas rig is very effective when presenting soft plastic lures on the bottom for wrasse. Use cone weights of around ½–¾oz (10–20g), with strong size 1/0 to 3/0 weedless hooks.

》 Wrasse-fishing rig
The Texas rig, adopted from freshwater bass-fishing in the US, is perfect for saltwater wrasse-fishing with lures.

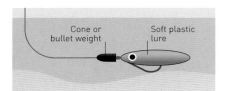

Cone or bullet weight   Soft plastic lure

》 Spinning reel
Spinning reels matched to relatively short, powerful lure rods are trouble-free and perfect for wrasse-fishing.

Targeting wrasse

Wrasse will feed hardest on a flooding tide, and they frequent rocky ground, so this is where you need to fish. Look for shallow reefs and boulder fields, and move around to cover as much ground as possible. This is where lure-fishing is so effective. Think on your feet and remember that wrasse might be feeding literally right beneath your rod tip.

1 Keep your lures moving
Casting into rocky ground inevitably means losing lures, but use a Texas rig, bury your hookpoint away in the back of the soft plastic, and keep the lure twitching along the bottom. Wrasse bites can be gentle plucks on your rod tip, or savage smashes into your lure.

2 Change lure colors Sometimes wrasse will hit almost any color soft plastic; on other days they will be very fussy. In general, dark greens, browns, and blacks are good colors to carry. Experiment with colors of lure, but be aware that this fish's preferences can change during the season. Nobody really knows why.

WRASSE DO TAKE LURES

Wrasse seem to be either very inquisitive or aggressive fish when it comes to how hard they hit lures. If bites are a little hesitant, you can often literally tease fish onto your lure by keeping it in place and shaking your rod tip up and down to subtly move it. Often this seems to annoy the wrasse into engulfing your lure.

3 Up and away It is essential to time your strike, to pull hard, and to pull the wrasse up and away from any snags as you strike. Wrasse will pull hard to get into cover, and once back in the rocks are virtually impossible to get out.

Inshore boat-fishing for striped bass

Among the most popular and important saltwater species in the US, striped bass, or "stripers," are migratory fish. The best places to fish for them have prime times of year when the most or biggest fish can be caught, from boats or inshore, using baits, lures, or flies.

Rod and rig set-up

A short, powerful spinning or casting rod of 8 ft (2.4 m) is perfect for boat-fishing for stripers, when using lures or bait (live and dead). Combine it with a spinning or conventional reel. Modern braid main lines are a good choice because they provide such direct contact with the fish, and are much stronger than monolines of similar width. However, it is important to adjust the drag (or clutch) on your reel to compensate for their lack of stretch. A #9 saltwater fly-fishing set-up works well. Carry floating and sinking lines.

◀ **Basic float rig** For fishing in a current and near underwater structures, use a basic float rig with a 50-lb (23-kg) mono leader and a sharp 6/0 hook.

Strong saltwater hook

▲ **Soft plastic lure** Striped bass respond well to lure-fishing techniques. Soft lures on heavy jig heads help you to fish deep water and strong currents.

Boat-fishing for striped bass

Like many saltwater fish, stripers use cover to hunt and feed around, and many boat-anglers use the wind and currents to push their baits and lures close to likely fish-holding areas. A favored method in many areas is to steer or anchor the boat precisely so that your float-fished cut bait (cut-up fish) works its way back toward an underwater structure, such as shallow, rocky ground, or perhaps a bridge or pier. It is also exciting to ease boats close to the structure and cast into the best-looking spots. Take up a stable and comfortable casting position and cover as much water as possible.

To maneuver close to a structure, you must be very capable of handling a boat in this kind of situation, or have an extremely knowledgeable skipper. Never take a boat anywhere near a rocky shore if you lack experience. Watch out at all times for other water traffic and keep an eye on the state of the sea and weather. Remember that tides rise and fall, sometimes quite significantly.

1 **Start to introduce** chunks of baitfish (mackerel works well) into the tide, once the boat is anchored, so that they drift toward the fish-holding areas. As with freshwater ground-baiting, little and often is the key; you want the fish to be interested, but not full. Place a chunk on your hook, set the float, and use the tide or current to drift the bait back toward the structure.

2 **React quickly.** Hold the rod at all times for bait and lure fishing and then react to any firm bites by striking to help set the hook. Keep a good bend in the rod to tire the fish out and protect the hookhold.

3 **When you hook a striper,** play it out from the structure as hard as you can—it will try to find sanctuary. On a boat, the easiest way to land a fish is by using a net, especially when the water is choppy. Landing nets with large openings make it comparatively straightforward to steer the fish in and over the net so that your companion can scoop it up.

4 **Striped bass** are one of those species that can be targeted by bait, lure, and fly anglers. You can fish for them in a wide variety of inshore waters as they migrate up and down the east coast of the US each year. Stripers are a true sport fish.

Inshore saltwater fishing

Small boats allow anglers to fish in waters that might be inaccessible to larger boats. Those that have a shallow draft can be used in shallow water and confined spaces. For ultra-shallow waters in tropical seas, there are special flats boats.

Rod and rig setup

Most anglers who fish from boats carry a variety of rods and reels. They must be stowed carefully to avoid damage as you move around the boat. It is useful to have a short, powerful spinning or casting rod that is suitable for spinning, jigging, float-fishing, and bottom-fishing.

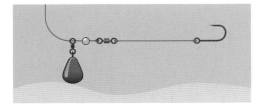

▶ **Bottom-fishing rig** A typical bottom-fishing rig used for this type of fishing. Use a wire trace for fish with sharp teeth.

▲ **Round bait-casting reel** When filled with braid, a round bait-casting reel is a good all-around boat reel. Surprisingly large fish can be landed on this type of bait-casting reel.

Warm-climate small-boat fishing

In warm waters there are plenty of species that feed either close to or right at the surface. Many areas close to shore hold good stocks of fish, and a small boat may be the only way of accessing them. Channels, flats, and mangrove areas, for instance, may be accessible only in a boat, and yield species such as snook, tarpon, snappers, and bonefish.

As you cruise around in the boat, keep an eye open for signs of fish activity. For example, a school of jacks voraciously feeding on bait on the surface or flocks of birds diving may indicate that there are predatory fish swimming below. The faster you can get close to such an area, the greater your chances of success. It is worth always having a lure-fishing rod set up with a surface popper (see p.58) to cast into an area of this type of fish activity.

Safety considerations

Wherever you choose to fish, take the right safety equipment: life jackets for everybody, plus a VHF radio and distress flares. Do not rely on cell phones for your safety. If you are thinking of buying a boat, for your own safety, be sure to attend an appropriate course.

1 **Shallow water** can often offer remarkably good fishing, and the chance to sight-fish for many species is a large part of the appeal. Many of the specialist inshore boats are designed to access these shallow, calm waters.

2 **Keep a tight line.** So many different species, and so many different ways to catch them. Inshore saltwater anglers will employ bait, lure, and fly techniques to tempt a huge variety of species of fish. Rods are generally fairly short, which makes for easier and more precise use when fishing from a boat.

3 **There's plenty of scope to fish** how you like when you are saltwater fishing inshore, both for species that you might take home to eat and species you might want to target purely for the sporting challenge. Sheepshead, for example (*see* photo), are prized for their eating, whereas tarpon are not eaten, but are one of the world's premier sport fish.

LURE-FISHING FOR GIANT TREVALLY

Generally accepted as one of the hardest-fighting saltwater fish on Earth, the giant trevally, or "GT" as they are mostly known by anglers, offers a truly brutal experience to lure, fly, and bait anglers. Casting big surface lures over tropical reefs is an incredibly exciting way to fish, and GTs love to literally smash lures and then make very strong runs for structure. You will break rods, reels, lines, and even bodies, but getting a big giant trevally on lure-fishing tackle is one of the ultimate fishing experiences.

Boat-fishing for tarpon

Tarpon are among the most impressive and hard-fighting fish in the world, famous for their awesome speed, power, and acrobatic jumps, as well as their ability to throw hooks. They grow very large and represent a great challenge on any kind of rig.

Rod and rig set-up

Short, powerful rods are used for boat-fishing; for tarpon they are often heavy-rated spinning or casting rods that have sufficient strength to cope with this extreme sport. Many anglers prefer monolines of around 30-lb (13.5-kg) breaking strain—the inherent stretch of this type of line can help cushion the impact of the tarpon's runs and jumps. But increasingly, heavy braid main lines are used, which offer a greater strength-to-diameter ratio than mono. Anglers using such tackle are playing the tarpon as hard as possible, but nevertheless this fish will often still get away.

◀ **Tarpon rig** Use a float, a sharp 6/0 or 7/0 hook, and a short length of 100-lb (45-kg) biting (or "rubbing") leader.

⌃ **Conventional reel** Strong, modern conventional or spinning reels work equally well for this type of fishing. An effective drag system that will help you tire this powerful fish is also essential.

Choosing your location

The Florida Keys are perfect for fishing tarpon—during their migration they are found here feeding on a mass of baitfish. They feed more readily in low light—dawn or dusk, or at night—and many anglers and guides are well practiced at hunting them during complete darkness. At other times, the numerous road bridges cast shadow in the water, offering the tarpon the cover or darker light they prefer. The deeper the water under the bridge, the greater your chances during daylight hours.

Position the boat at anchor so that the tide will take your float-fished (or free-lined) baits back to where the tarpon are holding up.

There is no mistaking a tarpon bite—the float disappears and/or your line suddenly tightens up and pulls violently away. For this reason, it is vital that everybody on board knows exactly what to do the moment a fish is hooked—this is high-adrenaline fishing.

1 **Fish in the shadows** and deeper water beneath a bridge where tarpon are feeding during the daytime. They will be staying within the shadow lines. You will often see their big shapes on your fishfinder. Try to set your hook with repeated short strikes and then hold on. The fish will usually jump the moment it is hooked, and this is when it may manage to throw the hook. If the hook holds, be prepared for an awesome fight.

2 **Pursue the fish.** Your skipper will raise the anchor and head in the same direction as the fish. Get line back on the reel fast to fight on a short line—this gives more control when the fish charges off. "Bow to the fish" as the tarpon jumps out of the water, by lowering the rod tip to create slack line, which protects against the violent head-shaking of the fish.

3 **Landing a tarpon** is best done by grabbing the hard bottom lip while wearing gloves, and then unhooking. Tarpon are very carefully looked after and are rarely taken out of the water; most guides lean over, grab the fish, remove the hook, wait for a few photographs to be taken, and then release the fish.

HOOKING AND UNHOOKING TIPS

Tarpon are notorious for shedding hooks. Their hard, bony mouths are tricky to set a hook into, and their head-shaking tactics throw hooks too. With J-hooks, strike repeatedly when the fish hits your bait; with circle hooks, let the fish tighten up against the reel. If you strike a circle hook, you will pull it straight out of the fish's mouth. Circle hooks are relatively easy to unhook and present no risk of being swallowed, which could cause damage to the fish. Tarpon also readily take flies and lures; indeed there is a strong argument for them being the ultimate sporting fish.

Slow trolling for salmon

Chinook and coho are among the salmon species that school in the Pacific Ocean to feed prior to returning to rivers to spawn. This is when many anglers use trolling methods for them at sea. Whether close to shore or miles from land, the methods used are similar.

Rod and rig set-up

A downrigger uses a wire line and heavy weight to hold lures down deep. This means you do not have a weight on your rod, which gives a different feel when you fight the fish. Use soft-tipped rods because they bend over easily when the line is clipped to the downrigger. Braided mainlines are advised.

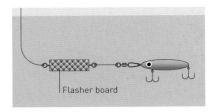

Salmon rig set-up A lure is usually fished behind a reflective "flasher board." This is a plastic board that spins enticingly when it is trolled at the correct speed. The board's movement attracts the salmon, which then see your lure just beyond.

Flasher board

Conventional reel Conventional reels are popular, as are "mooching" reels. The latter do not have a drag system or gears. The handle revolves when a fish takes the line.

How a downrigger works

A downrigger is an electronic or mechanical winching device that keeps lures at a set depth (usually fairly deep) when trolling. It does this by means of a thin, strong wire line with a heavy weight at the end. Just above the weight is a special line clip to which your rig is attached; rig and weight are then lowered via the downrigger. Your mainline is held in place by the clip until a fish hits your lure. The heavy weight and thin wire cut through the water as they are slowly trolled behind the boat.

Downrigger set-up The mainline from the rod is threaded though the line clip on the weighted downrigger wire, to secure the rig at the required depth. As soon as a fish takes the lure, the clip releases the line, and the rod tip springs forward.

Downrigger in action Most boats use at least two downriggers, many of which are electronically controlled. Linked into the boat's power system, they will do all the winding in of the heavy weight for you. Downriggers have a long arm that sticks out from the side of the boat, which helps prevent the lures from tangling. Use the fish-finder and the downrigger's depth counter to fish the correct depths without snagging.

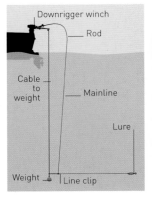

Downrigger winch

Rod

Cable to weight

Mainline

Lure

Weight

Line clip

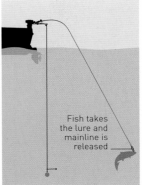

Fish takes the lure and mainline is released

DOWNRIGGER TECHNIQUES

Clip your line into the line clip on the downrigger and put your reel in free-spool mode (remember to control it). Let the downrigger drop the weight down, controlling your reel as your lure descends. Stop the weight at your chosen depth, click your reel into gear, and wind your line down tight to the clip. Set your drag for when a fish hits, and then place your rod into its holder.

Trolling in action

Trolling for salmon is generally done at a slow, constant speed, often with a small engine. Once the lures are set on the downriggers, steer the boat through fish-holding areas. Chinook and coho can put up a dogged fight, especially the large chinook, which is often caught when trolling near the bottom. Stock levels of these fish are monitored and the numbers that anglers can keep are tightly controlled. This protects salmon stocks, ensuring that plenty of fish can get back into the rivers to spawn.

1 **When a fish bites,** your rod tip suddenly springs back because the clip has freed your line. Grab the rod and wind down hard on the reel right until you can feel the kicking fish. Salmon can fight powerfully and aggressively in the open sea. The soft-tipped rod helps protect your hook-hold by absorbing the fish's lunges.

2 **Land your fish** with the help of a landing net, and remove the hook with care. Coho salmon are superb fish and one of the most prized of Pacific salmon species. Respect the rules regarding the number of fish you can keep, and return as many as possible to the water.

Lure-fishing for tuna

Tuna species are some of the hardest-fighting fish in the world. In certain locations you can cast lures at big, fast-moving bluefin tuna, but smaller, more manageable bluefin tuna—such as those in the Mediterranean—offer good sport without the need for really powerful gear and long, exhausting fights.

Rod and rig set-up

Hard-fighting fish such as tuna will test all the different components in your set-up. Rods need to be fairly short, 6¾–8¾ft (2–2.6m), to gain maximum leverage against these fish, but they also need to be flexible enough to cast lures again and again. Knots such as the modern and incredibly strong FG knot are required to secure the fluorocarbon leader to the braid.

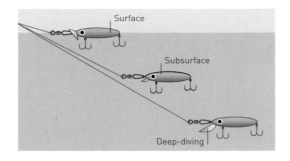

» Lure options
Choose the type of lure and swimming depth depending on what the tuna are feeding on.

Toughened lure body

» Savage Gear 3D Mack Stick
Many different types of hard and soft lures catch tuna, but any lure and its components need to be incredibly strong and well made.

Preparation and planning

Tuna are some of the fastest, strongest fish in the sea and will quickly show up any flaws in an angler's tackle and technique, so plan for the size of tuna you might expect, and tackle up accordingly. Tie leaders to main lines before you head out, and really tighten and test all knots. Take spare rods and reels to allow for breakages or the need to change lures quickly.

Make sure you're prepared physically, too. Casting lures at bluefish tuna with stand-up tackle is very tough on the angler, so be realistic about the size of fish you choose to chase and where you choose to chase them.

1 **Look for feeding birds** A species such as bluefin tuna is constantly on the move as they hunt for food, so keep a sharp lookout for schools of tuna bursting on the surface on bait. Sometimes, where you might expect to find tuna, the best sign of activity will be birds trying to feed on bait that has been driven to the surface by feeding tuna.

2 **Be stealthy** It is incredibly exciting to see bluefin tuna smashing into bait, but do not make the mistake of thinking you can just charge in with your boat. For all their aggressive feeding habits, tuna can in fact be a very wary fish, and it is very common to see signs of feeding fish, only for them to disappear and move somewhere else as you approach in your boat.

3 **Try to predict where the fish will be** Tuna are so fast that somehow you need to try to predict where they are going to be, not where they were when you cast, and then put in a very accurate cast to get your lure in front of the fish.

4 **Hold on** It is almost impossible to describe how hard bluefin tuna fight. Certain areas are known for holding specific sizes of tuna, which in turn attracts different kinds of anglers and how they prefer to fish. Sometimes, however strong your tackle, they are simply too big to tackle on stand-up lure-fishing rods and reels. This is when trolling tackle on fighting chairs is used.

BLUEFIN TUNA

The largest of the tuna species, bluefin tuna migrate through all the oceans of the world on their endless hunt for prey. Highly prized as an eating fish, stocks of bluefin tuna have been heavily overfished by commercial fleets. A recovery plan has shown good signs of efficacy.

Wreck-fishing

On a featureless seabed, a wreck acts as a haven for fish. Small fish shelter from the tide and use the structure as a refuge, which attracts larger predators that come to feed on them. Some species live in and around wrecks all the time; others may simply be passing through.

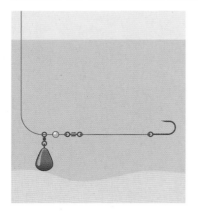

Rod and rig set-up

You will need a powerful rod to support the heavy weights needed to take lures and baits to the depths required. Wreck-fishing is likely to require a 20–50-lb (9–23-kg) boat rod, with a conventional reel to match. Braided main lines are usually the best choice. On a large tide (spring tide), you can allow your boat to drift over a wreck. On a smaller tide (neap tide), anchoring over the wreck is an option.

◅ **Bottom-fishing rig** An effective way to fish with big baits near wrecks on the sea bottom is to use a simple bottom-fishing rig.

⌃ **Large conventional reel** Choose a reel that will hold enough line to get your baits right to the bottom in deep water.

Fishing for conger eels

Powerful conger eels thrive in and around wrecks and are targeted by many sea anglers. Congers feed tight to the bottom, and a key to fishing for them is to use fresh, scent-laden baits. When they start to home in on the baits, action can be hectic; once hooked, an eel will try to run for cover.

You will need to "pump and wind" (lift the rod and wind it in as you lower it) repeatedly. Sometimes conger eels feed far from the wreck, and an experienced skipper may choose to anchor a fair distance away.

1 **Take the boat close** to the structure. A good skipper, using the latest electronic aids, can take a boat to the best fishing with great accuracy. They are often familiar with the waters in the area and know how to anchor and how to drift over wrecks and reefs properly.

2 **Drop the bait down,** hold your rod, and wait for a bite. Being able to feel exactly what is going on with your bait is vital for fish that may bite only gently. Do not be overeager to strike when a conger bites; the biggest eels often bite the gentlest. To be sure the conger takes the bait properly, wait a few moments to allow a bite to develop before winding into the fish.

3 **Work closely with the skipper** when landing a conger eel. A conger eel will spin furiously on the hook as you try to land it, so take care.

4 **Beware of the powerful tail** of a conger eel as you bring it on board. These fish often thrash around dangerously and can cause real harm. Most conger eels caught by anglers are successfully returned to the water. Many are unhooked at the side of the boat without being brought on board, but it is possible to lift surprisingly big conger eels on board by grabbing the strong trace. To avoid injury, always wear gloves when doing so.

USING TECHNICAL AIDS

Successful modern wreck-fishing revolves around the effective use of modern electronic navigational aids. In fact, most boat-fishing requires some knowledge of how to use them. A GPS (Global Positioning System) unit displays the boat's exact location, speed, and direction, and is invaluable when finding relatively small features, such as wrecks.

Boat-fishing for sharks

Sharks are the most efficient predators in the sea, and fishing for them is hugely exciting. Incredible creatures that deserve our respect and admiration, they are sadly greatly endangered, so anglers must fish responsibly and release all catch unharmed.

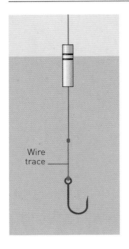

Wire trace

Rod and rig set-up

When targeting large sharks, use powerful rods and reels. Boat rods are fairly short, to give maximum leverage, and for ease of use in restricted spaces. You will need a minimum rod rating of 30 lb (13.5 kg). Load your reel with plenty of line for long runs. Strong wire traces are essential, and circle hooks ensure that the fish is hooked no deeper than the side of the mouth. Remember not to strike when using circle hooks—let the shark run against the reel-drag to set the hook. Consider wearing a butt pad for protection during the fight.

◀ **Floating rig** Suspend bait under a basic float. Set baits at various depths to find out where the sharks are feeding.

▲ **Large conventional reel** Big-game style conventional reels offer the power you need to cope with the demands of shark fishing.

Attracting the quarry

When shark fishing, the trick is to put enticing smells and scents into the water to attract the sharks to you. Essentially you set up the boat as a source of food. The idea is that the sharks pick up the scent trail drifting away with the tide and are lured to the boat, where you have chum sacks (see right) tied overboard, and baits suspended around the boat under floats. Often the first sign of success is a fin working its way up the slick, or one of the reels exploding into life as a shark charges off with a bait in its mouth. Either will provoke controlled mayhem in the boat crew as everybody instantly snaps into full fishing mode.

1 **Prepare your tackle well.** Quiet periods are often broken by a shark run and a well-prepared boat helps everything to go as planned. Keep the decks clear for sudden activity—the skipper might have to give chase, or the angler may get pulled all around the boat.

CHUMMING

Chum, or "rubby dubby," is usually made from chopped fish, blood, fish oil, and perhaps bran. This is placed in mesh sacks over the side of the boat so the small food particles and oil are carried downtide. There are various chum "recipes," but all appeal to the hunting instinct of the shark or other prey.

2 **Work as a team** to get a shark to the side of the boat for unhooking. Wear gloves when you grab the leader, and never under any circumstances wrap it around your hand for grip. If a shark runs again when you have line around your hand, your hand could be seriously injured.

3 **Keep safety in mind** at all times when landing a shark. Here, one person is grabbing the shark's tail and another holds the leader to control its twisting head. Do not be tempted to try to take the hook out by hand.

4 **Remove the hook** without necessarily bringing the shark on board—lean over the side and use a pair of pliers. If the hook is deep, cut the wire as close to the hook as possible; it will soon rust out and cause no harm to the fish.

Vertical jigging

Many anglers consider vertical jigging to be one of the most effective ways to use lures (or "jigs"). This technique is used for saltwater species, such as dogtooth tuna, yellowtail kingfish, and big giant trevally, as well as freshwater fish, such as smallmouth bass and walleye.

Rod and rig set-up

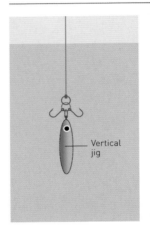

Jigging rods must be light and strong, to cope with continually working the sometimes-heavy jigs in deep water, and then lifting big, powerful fish. These rods are about 7–8 ft (2–2.4 m) in length and rated to the lines or the weights of the jigs. Jigging requires the use of braided main lines, which reduce stretch and drag in the water, and allow you to produce the required movement in the lure. Line with a high breaking strain can be used for strong fish, but always use a mono "rubbing" leader that resists abrasion and sharp teeth.

Vertical jig

◄ **Vertical jig rig** Rig assist (or stinger) hooks above the jig using Kevlar cord and heavy-duty split rings.

⌃ **Spinning reel** Strong saltwater spinning reels are perfect for vertical jigging, but some anglers prefer conventional reels. Choose good quality—this type of fishing is hard on the equipment.

Modern techniques

Jigging is an old fishing technique that has been improved by modern methods and materials, as well as new technology. Light but powerful rods have helped anglers to land huge fish that would have previously required far heavier tackle. Electronic fish finders are used to locate the fish and allow you to place the jig near them. Special braided lines that change color along their length help you judge the exact depth of your jig.

Once the jig is in place, you need to make it come to life and appeal to the fish. There are many slightly different ways of working the jig, but the basic technique is to lift up the rod to lift the jig, and then lower the rod to allow it to flutter back down. Whether you reel in at the same time depends on where you are fishing and the species you are targeting. Vertical jigging is an active way of fishing—the longer your jig dances in fish-holding areas, the greater your chance of success. Vertical jigs are ideal for fast-moving predatory fish, but can be used to catch a variety of other species in warm and cold waters.

1 **Be prepared** for some physical fishing. When chasing some of the hard-fighting and fast-moving tropical species of fish, vertical jigging can become a very physical way to fish. It is hard to imagine how hard some of these fish can hit your jigs, and then how hard they can fight in deep water. It is also incredibly tough on your fishing tackle, with broken rods, reels, and lines not uncommon.

2 **Stand comfortably** and drop the jig to the desired depth. Now lift (jerk) the rod as you turn the reel-handle upward, and drop the rod as you turn the reel-handle downward. You can also jerk the rod up without reeling. Some warm-water fish respond very well to aggressive movements of the jig.

◀ **Maintain contact** Braid main lines enable you to keep a very direct contact with the lure. Modern spinning reels designed for saltwater use are very robust and will handle big fish and tough fishing.

3 **Set the drag** on your reel to match the strength of the braid. This will enable you to catch very big fish using vertical jigging techniques. Use the power of the rod and braid to lift hard into the fish, and then pump and wind repeatedly to tire the fish and get line back on the reel. Make sure you remain stable and comfortable on the deck of the boat.

4 **Use a butt pad** when playing the fish, in order to protect your groin and lower stomach area from the butt of the rod. A butt pad also provides a central pivot point that enables you to apply pressure more effectively to the fish. Deepwater reefs often produce a wide range of large, colorful species of fish that are attracted to vertical jigs.

Big-game fishing

Searching the deep oceans for some of the largest fish on the planet is a serious sport that calls for special boats, crews, and skippers. The best fishing is expensive and time-consuming, but for many anglers, trolling for hard-fighting tuna and marlin is as exciting as fishing gets.

Rod and rig set-up

Special large lever-drag conventional reels—and rods to match—are required. Reels must hold hundreds of yards of line and the rods must withstand a lot of pressure from large, fast-moving fish. Even a small marlin of around 200 lb (90 kg) can take over 600 ft (180 m) of line in a few seconds. The boats used are usually specifically designed for big-game fishing, and offer a variety of comforts while you troll for what can be very long periods of time.

>> **Strong rig** Troll lures and baits just under or on the surface. Mono biting leaders of 300 lb (136 kg) or more are common.

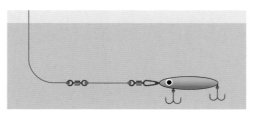

>> **Marlin lure** The head of a typical marlin lure allows it to skim along the water's surface at up to 10 knots. The hooks sit behind the lure's head.

Trolling multiple lures

There are various popular patterns used for trolling a team of lures when big-game fishing. The lines are set up by the crew so that the lures do not tangle, but you should fish close enough together to "close all the holes"—big gaps in the pattern that might allow an interested fish to come in and find no lure to hit.

To spread the lures outside the boat's wake, the lines are clipped to outriggers.

The "stinger" lure is the term used to describe the one that is farthest from the boat, often also the smallest.

The rods are placed into holders and the skipper trolls the lures through the areas where fish are thought to be patrolling. The angler sits in a "fighting chair" rigged up for playing the big fish from. It is often a waiting game.

>> **Trolling** When trolling blue water for large game fish, periods of inactivity are interspersed by high-energy moments when a fish hits.

▧ **Trolling set-up** The arrangement of rods is designed to fish the lures at specific speeds for the target species. Lures are trolled at a constant speed through known fish-holding areas. When a fish hits one of the lures, the other rods are quickly wound in.

Outrigger

Rod

Line

Fishing for marlin

Most marlin fishing is done by trolling undersea islands, humps, and walls, or current lines and color changes, often miles offshore beyond the continental shelf. Like many other species, the marlin has periods when it is more active, often linked to the lunar cycle; these are optimum fishing times.

1 **When you have a bite** from a smaller fish, it is possible to stand up to fight, using a butt pad (to protect your groin from the rod's butt) and often a shoulder harness as well. The reel's drag is usually set at about 25 percent of the mainline's breaking strain, which can put huge pressure on a fish, while protecting the line.

2 **Many big fish have to be tackled** from a fighting chair that takes some of the strain by enabling you to sit down and clip in the rod. The skipper and crew help set the hooks by gunning the engines when you get a hit, and will steer the boat so you can follow the running fish. If you can get the fish close enough to the boat for someone to grab the leader with a gloved hand, this counts as a catch. The person who does this must know exactly what to do.

3 **The marlin may be tagged** before release. A crew member will then hold the marlin's bill with a gloved hand as the boat moves, to allow oxygenated water to run through its gills. The fish is released when it has regained strength.

FINDING MARLIN

Most of the big marlin destinations have a resident fleet of high-tech big-game boats with experienced skippers and crews on hand. Such skippers have their favorite areas to fish, but generally, marlin are found through a combination of a thorough understanding of their behavior, and the use of modern fish-spotting electronics. Marlin track schools of baitfish, and prefer to remain in deep water, often some way offshore. Once in the area, trolling lures is an effective way of covering a lot of ground. Skippers know how to position the boat carefully so that it does not spook the fish.

Fly-fishing

The gentle art of fly-fishing is completely absorbing. From the most fundamental and traditional ways of presenting flies to fish, in both saltwater and freshwater, to more modern approaches to the discipline of fly-fishing, these strategies will help you catch all manner of fish species in a wonderful variety of waters. Casting artificial flies in rivers, lakes, and seas can be an intoxicating mix of the old and the new.

Reservoir and lake fly-fishing

Fly-fishing quietly from open boats is a wonderful way to fish, and in time the skills become second nature. When you take a boat out on a large lake or reservoir—having stowed your equipment—your main consideration is where the fish might be feeding.

Rod and rig set-up

A 10-ft (3-m) #5 to #7 fly-fishing rod and matched reel will cover most fly-fishing situations on open water, such as reservoirs and lakes, including dry-fly fishing with floating lines, and nymph-fishing with intermediate or sinking lines. Most fly-anglers on boats use a large, top-opening boat-style tackle bag to hold their fly boxes, spare reels, lines, flies, leaders, and other tackle. It is always advisable to wear a life jacket, and in some places it is mandatory.

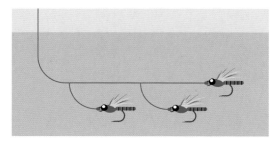

≪ The rig It can be very effective to use a team of flies (usually two or three) when fishing on a reservoir or lake. The point fly, which is the one farthest from the fly line, might be a heavy fly that helps the others sink a bit deeper.

≫ Bright line You will find it easier to see a colored fly line. Attach a long, clear leader to avoid spooking the fish.

Using the boat

Many lakes and reservoirs have fleets of small, open boats available to rent for fly-fishing. Often, conservation regulations permit only electric motors with 12V batteries, but speed is not important, and a quiet boat will spook fewer fish. Many anglers like to bring foldable seats for comfort during a long day on the water. Keep tackle bags close by you, to minimize movement on board.

When you are fishing in pairs, the least experienced angler should sit with a clear casting arc to their strongest side. If right-handed, they should sit farthest forward, facing out from the left-hand side of the boat; if left-handed, they should face the other way.

Tackle bag

Oars and spare rods

Folding seat

Battery

Electric motor

Landing net

≫ Packing the boat Stow rods carefully where they cannot be stepped on, and store tackle neatly in bags or boxes. Leave as much clear space as possible for casting, playing, and landing fish.

Spare files

Finding the fish

Present dry flies and nymphs just below the surface where there are gentle ripples on top of the water, but fish may also be present in flat-calm stretches of water flanked by gentle ripples. In a small boat, always cast one at a time, and remain sitting down. The person casting must be sure to cast their line safely away from their fishing companion in the boat.

1 **Having cast a long line** to cover a large section of water with your fly, fish right back to the boat. Lift the fly gently from the water in case a fish is following it in.

2 **Maneuver the boat** to explore different fish-holding spots. In hot, still weather, look for fish around artificially oxygenated areas with bubbles on the surface. Features such as dam walls, overhanging trees, and other structures may also attract fish. Sit down to play the fish.

3 **Use a landing net** to bring your catch on board; keep the rod high, and draw the fish over the waiting net opening rather than chasing the fish with the net.

Fly-fishing on small rivers

Fly-fishing for trout and grayling in small rivers is one of the most delicate forms of angling. Tumbling water tends to have a hypnotic effect on the angler, and nobody tires of seeing these beautiful fish. Fishing for them requires light tactics and a deft touch.

Rod and rig set-up

A light, 8-ft (2.4-m) #4 or #5 fly rod is usually suitable for fly-fishing in a river of this type. The rod should be matched with a small fly reel loaded with a floating line. Catching trout and grayling with dry flies as they rise to the surface to feed on insects is the classic way of taking them, but be prepared to fish with weighted nymphs (see Freshwater wet flies, p.62) if dry flies are not working. Tapered leaders no heavier than 4-lb (1.8-kg) breaking strain are adequate for most conditions.

» **Dry-fly rig** A simple dry-fly rig works well for trout and grayling that are feeding on the surface. However, you can also use wet-fly tactics. Be sure to check the local regulations for what methods are allowed on the waters you are fishing.

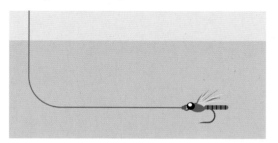

⌃ **Small-river fly reel** A small, lightweight fly reel is perfectly suited to fishing small rivers. This reel holds enough line for most situations.

Targeting trout and grayling

Look for these fish around landscape features and structures, whether overhanging branches, moving white water, sunken branches, or undercut banks. Fishing close to fast-moving water means that the fish are less likely to see you. Classic upstream dry-fly fishing, as described here, is perfect for delicate presentation to freely rising fish. However, as an alternative to a simple dry-fly rig, you could try a dry fly with a weighted nymph below—a useful way to fish simultaneously on the surface and along or near to the bottom. While accurate and delicate casting is an essential river-fishing technique, the ability to control how the river affects your fly and line is also vital, a technique termed "mending the line" (see below). Ideally, a dry fly should act naturally in the water; when you cast upstream, allow your fly to gently drift downstream in the current.

1 **After casting** and as your line starts to straighten after landing on the water, point your rod tip down the line and then delicately flip your arm and wrist upstream. This is called "mending the line" and is a way of allowing your fly to drift farther by adding some slack into the fly line, either during the cast, or when your fly line hits the water.

2 **Be prepared to change fly** if your initial choice is not working. Carry a selection of flies in their boxes in your fly-vest or jacket pocket, so that you can change flies while in the river. The less you move around, the less the fish will be spooked. Always be careful of your footing when wading in a river.

3 **Having landed your fish,** return it to the water. Hold it close to the surface of the water and gently slip it back in. Wild brown trout are pretty fish and, even if they might not be the largest fish you will catch, to take them from a small river is a true privilege.

CHECKING FOR LARVAE AND GRUBS

It can be extremely useful to scour around the river bottom, checking the types of indigenous grubs and larvae on which the fish in the particular waters you are fishing are feeding. This enables you to match your pattern of fly to the natural prey you find, which may increase your chance of a catch. Many landing nets have a finer net attached that can be spread out across the opening of the net and used to sift the river bottom.

Wet fly-fishing on lakes

Novice fly-anglers are well advised to start fly-fishing with wet flies on small bodies of still water; larger lakes and reservoirs can be daunting for a newcomer to the sport. Well-stocked commercial fisheries tend to be easiest to fish. Rainbow trout are a common target.

Rod and rig set-up

A #7 fly rod and reel suit this type of wet fly-fishing perfectly. You should either carry two reels or use one with an interchangeable cartridge, because you will need to carry a floating and an intermediate or sinking line, for a variety of situations. Your range of wet flies should include a variety of patterns (see pp.62–63). Big lure patterns may attract trout, but carry some dry flies as well.

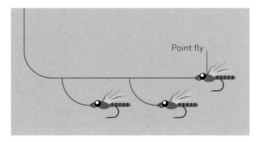

Team of flies Fishing a team of flies allows you to set them up in different ways. Try a weighted wet fly as the point fly, to help sink the others deeper.

Damsel nymph medium (olive) Excellent for use if trout are rejecting bigger, brighter imitations, the damsel nymph medium should be used with intermediate or floating fly lines, with varied retrieves.

Stillwater fishing

When considering where to cast, look for fish-holding areas such as natural bays, small streams coming into the lake, and vegetation at the water's edge. Watch for birds feasting on hatching insects; fish might also be feeding in these areas as the larvae head to the surface. Look for fish taking flies off the surface, or water movement as fish cruise around. Don't forget to talk to local anglers and the people who run the fisheries because nothing beats local advice on fly patterns, fish movements, and water conditions.

1 **Use a smooth overhead cast** to put your flies out on the water. A team of flies is prone to tangling, so cast gently. Start with floating line, suitable for both wet and dry flies; in high sun, or cold weather, change to intermediate or fast-sinking line to take wet flies down deeper.

2 **Cast and retrieve continually** to give flies maximum time in the water. Making a figure-eight movement as you retrieve creates extra fly movement. Finally, consider tying on a single, garish lure pattern, then cast and retrieve quickly on floating and intermediate lines.

3 **Keep your line tight** once a fish is hooked. Keep a good bend in the rod, and use it to steer the fish over the waiting net, until it can be scooped up. Do not chase the fish with the net. If on your own, extend the net with one hand, and bring the fish over the net with the other.

4 **Hold the fish** in the water and let it regain its strength before releasing it, if appropriate. Some fisheries are "put and take" only, where the fish you catch must be quickly and efficiently dispatched, to then take home and eat. The fishery records the numbers of fish taken, and frequently restocks.

Czech nymphing

Czech nymphing is an extremely effective method of fly-fishing in which a team of weighted flies is fished close to the bottom of the river. No long casting is required, but the delicate presentation is a skill that takes time to master.

Rod and rig set-up

Equip yourself with a 10-ft (3-m) #5 to #7 fly rod, which gives a high degree of control when working a team of flies. Use a fly reel to match, and load it with a floating line. Make a leader no more than 6 ft (1.8 m) in length. A strike indicator can help keep the flies at the right depth, and also acts as a visual bite detector.

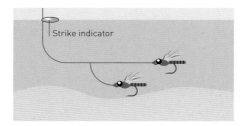

Strike indicator

◄◄ **Team of flies** The point fly is the lightest of the team of flies, designed to rise slightly in the water; tie on one or two heavier-weighted nymphs as droppers. These bounce on or close to the bottom.

⌃ **Small fly reel** Small fly reels work best for Czech nymphing since there is no need to hold lots of backing.

Czech-nymphing techniques

Study the river and work out where the fish will be. They may be feeding among rocks and boulders, or over gravel banks, so wade out close to where you want to fish. It is essential for you to enter the water so that you can flick the flies out the short distance required to maintain control of the short fly line as the flies drift downstream.

When Czech nymphing, fish with a short line to maintain direct contact with your flies. Strip a short length of line off your reel and make a simple sideways or overhead cast upstream to cover your chosen area on the drift down. Weighted flies sink quickly, so be alert the moment your line hits the water. The current will take your sinking flies downstream and through the places where you think the fish will be. The movement of the water will make the flies flutter and work, but you need to keep the rod high and allow the fly line to just touch the surface.

Bites vary, but be prepared to strike or lift into a fish at any time. While your flies may snag on rocks and give false bites, it is vital to concentrate hard and strike anything that looks like a bite.

1 **Pick the right flies** to imitate foods that species such as yellowfish, trout, or grayling may feed on underwater. Czech Nymph and Copper John flies work well. Look at the undersides of stones and small boulders to find out what is in the river, and what the fish are likely to be feeding on.

2 Fish with a short line to keep your flies close to the rod tip. Maintain contact as the flies drift downstream, then lift up and cast or flick again, covering as large an area of water as you can. Move around slowly and steadily.

3 Be prepared to strike or lift into a fish at any time. The strike indicator may suddenly disappear under the water, your line may visibly tighten, or the flies may stop suddenly. When you have landed a fish, unhook it, and release it carefully. Yellowfish from the rocky terrain in the Vaal and Orange river systems in South Africa respond well to Czech nymphing.

GRAVEL GUARDS

Some rivers are warm enough to permit wet wading (wading without chest waders). However, it is always advisable to wear felt-soled boots to protect your feet and give extra grip. It is also recommended that you wrap neoprene gravel guards around the bottoms of your calves and the tops of the boots to prevent stones and gravel from getting into your boots.

Sight-fishing for wild brown trout

Locating wild brown trout in crystal-clear rivers, and then casting small flies at them, is one of the purest forms of fly-fishing. Big wild brown trout are found in many parts of the world. They are often wary and tricky to catch, but the rewards of success are worth the effort.

Rod and rig set-up

A 9-ft (2.7-m) fly rod rated #5 or #6, and a nonreflective fly reel, are perfect. Choose dull-colored, nonreflective, floating lines, matched to the rod rating. Clear, tapered leaders are essential, and may be up to 16 ft (5 m) long to avoid spooking the fish. Tailor rigs to local conditions. A good pair of polarized sunglasses is vital, and a wide-brimmed hat or a dull-colored baseball cap is also handy.

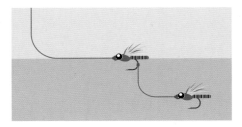

◀ New Zealand dropper
Try using a New Zealand dropper rig. In this rig the dropper fly (often a nymph) is tied to the bend of the dry fly's hook. As well as fishing effectively, the dry fly acts as a strike-indicator for the wet fly.

⌃ Humpy dry fly The hair on the "hump" of this classic dry fly gives added buoyancy for fishing moving and often slightly turbulent water. The most commonly used sizes of Humpy flies are 10 to 18.

Location and preparation

Sight-fishing calls for a stealthy approach because the fish will have a perfect line of sight to all approaching anglers. Wear dull-colored clothing and ensure that none of your fishing gear is reflective.

The largest numbers of fish will be in fairly shallow water, but it can take practice to spot them. Make sure you are wearing polarized sunglasses and concentrate hard on seeing "through" the water—often, in such clear water, there will be fish you simply do not see at first. A sound casting technique, involving as few false casts as possible, will make it less likely that the fish will see your lines moving around; try to avoid using too many false casts.

In very clear water, wading is not advised because of the risk of spooking the fish, so position yourself as low down and as far back as you can, and step lightly on the river bank.

1 **Once you have spotted** trout, prepare to cover the area as efficiently as possible. Strip the required line from your reel, make a couple of false casts, and then quietly and smoothly drop the fly above the area, so that the current pulls it down over the fish. Mend the line (*see* p.172), if necessary, when it lands on the water— the aim is to have the fly drift naturally.

2 **Big, wild brown trout** can be extremely wary, and it often requires real skill even to put a fly over them, let alone successfully land one. If a fish does take your dry fly off the surface, make yourself hesitate for a second before striking—let the fish really take the fly properly. This is hard because seeing a fish come up is exciting. Wild trout are powerful and usually go on a run toward the nearest snag. Fight the fish hard, without breaking the leader, and maneuver yourself to put pressure on the fish.

3 **Bring the trout** over your waiting net, either alone, by tiring out the fish, or with the help of your guide. It is a challenge to do this with a rod in one hand and net in the other, but immensely satisfying when accomplished successfully.

Fly-fishing for Atlantic salmon

Anglers have fly-fished for Atlantic salmon for hundreds of years in some of the world's most beautiful river scenery. Some large rivers are fished with double-handed fly rods and with graceful Spey casting, whereas smaller rivers are better suited to smaller, single-handed rods.

Rod and rig set-up

Choose a standard #8 single-handed fly rod and matched reel, or a #8 or #9 double-hander. You will need a rod that is light to handle, depending on where you fish. Floating lines are normally used, along with tapered leaders. Some rivers ban the use of weighted flies, so at times you will need to use a line with a weighted tip (sink-tip). You may be required to use barbless hooks.

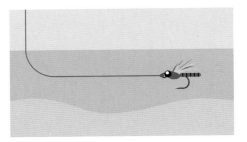

◀ **Single-fly rig** Use a single weighted fly for salmon fishing. A heavily weighted tube fly is often used, to sink the fly as fast as possible, but often the sheer speed of the current means that the fly never sinks very deep.

◈ **Salmon-fishing fly reel** A salmon reel that you intend to use for double-handed Spey casting has to be fairly large to hold the length and thickness of line needed. Reels for single-handed fly-fishing are smaller.

Location and preparation

Salmon stop feeding when they enter a river to head for their spawning grounds. Nobody knows whether they attack anglers' flies because of a feeding instinct, annoyance at the sight of a fly drifting past them again and again, competition among the school, or for some other reason. However, there is nothing complicated about fly-fishing for salmon; you just need to know where the fish will swim, and have the skill to cast and retrieve your fly. It is worth securing the services of a good guide who knows the river well, because salmon are predictable in where they like to be. The fish will not stay in the fastest parts of the river, but will look for natural pools, or eddies.

Having chosen your spot, you need to put out your fly repeatedly, and let it fish with the river flow. Generally, flies are cast out across the stream, or slightly downstream, and allowed to swing naturally with the current, before being retrieved and cast again.

1 **Choose your fly carefully.** Many salmon anglers and guides have a favorite fly that tends to work well. Some use the same fly virtually all the time, and catch plenty of fish. Thinking anglers will change the fly after repeated casting, for the salmon will have seen, and possibly refused, the fly on many occasions. The theory is that a change of fly may produce a take.

2 **Cover the water** by casting your line either directly
across the stretch of river, or slightly downstream. Then
mend (adjust) the line, and allow the current to swing your fly
across the water you want to fish. Let the fly hang for a while;
when it has swung in close to the bank, strip back, and then
cast again. The longer your fly spends in the water, the greater
your chance of catching a salmon.

3 **Strike if the line suddenly tightens.** It is essential to
keep a tight line in order to maintain the hook-hold when
fighting the fish. Be sure to follow instructions from your guide
on how to land the salmon.

4 **Take care of this magnificent fish** when unhooking
it. Keep it in the water, turning the fish slightly on its
side to help calm it down. A barbless hook is usually very
easy to remove. Many salmon rivers operate a catch-and-
release-only policy.

⌃ **A fish to admire** Atlantic salmon are special fish, and the
capture of a large specimen will be remembered for a long
time. A darker coloration is an indication that the fish has
been in the river for a while. When they first come in from
the sea, they are a bright chrome-silver color, and often
have sea lice on their bodies.

Fly-fishing for steelhead

Migratory rainbow trout are known the world over as steelhead. These magnificent fish are renowned fighters, and offer one of the greatest fly-fishing challenges. Fishing often takes place surrounded by some of the wildest and most majestic scenery imaginable.

Rod and rig set-up

Long, double-handed rods and Spey-casting techniques are used on the big steelhead rivers. To cast heavy lines and flies, you need a long rod that will pick the line off the water and take it across the river. Try a 13- to 14-ft (3.9–4.2-m) #9 double-handed rod, with a large fly reel holding a floating Spey line and plenty of backing.

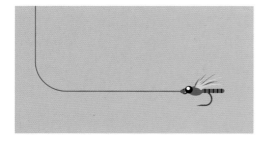

Wet-fly rig A tapered leader is looped to the end of the thick floating Spey line. The big fly will sink down into the water to a depth determined by the speed of the current.

Steelhead fly Most steelhead flies are large and brightly colored. This Purple String Leach is designed to appeal to the predatory instinct in the fish, and also to show up well in murky water. Big flies are hard to cast, so protect your eyes with sunglasses.

Going steelhead fishing

Most of the famous steelhead rivers are in British Columbia, Canada, and along the west coast of the US. There are various runs of fish during the year, but most traveling anglers choose to target steelhead in either spring or fall; locals also fish in the depths of winter. Fly-fishing for steelhead is similar to fly-fishing for salmon or big sea trout. You cast the fly out across the river, let the thick fly line swing the fly around in the current, then draw it in toward the bank. The big difference is that at least half the steelhead caught are taken "on the dangle"—this is when the fly swings in near the bank and the angler lets it hang there for a few seconds to allow the current to move the fly. Steelhead are looking for the least amount of current to battle as they head upriver, and this tends to be close to the river bank. Look for a consistent flow to the water with no great depth, and wade out to no more than calf or mid-thigh depth. Take warm, layered clothing with you to deal with the possibility of cold conditions, plus good-quality breathable chest waders and wading jacket.

1 **Fish the dangle.** Your natural reaction would be to cast again as the fly swings around in the current and in toward the river bank. Instead, allow the fly to hang in the current straight down your rod tip for at least ten seconds before casting out again.

2 **Play a fast-running steelhead hard.** Let the fish run when it wants to, but keep a bend in the rod at all times, and work on retrieving line when the fish tires and stops. Tuck a double-handed rod into your stomach for extra support.

3 **Land the steelhead** with a net. Be aware of keeping a tight line to the fish at all times, and work with your guide to bring the fish over the waiting net. A fly-angler will always release a steelhead; indeed, many rivers operate a barbless-hook-only, catch-and-release policy.

SAFE WADING

Wading is an essential part of fishing, so learn to wade safely. A wading belt pulls tight around your waders to slow the flow of water into the legs and feet if you fall. Wade slowly—watch how the river flows, then decide where to place your feet. Perceptions of depth can be misleading, so use a wading stick, or your rod to measure the depth and help keep you stable as you wade out. Never wade beyond the point where you feel safe.

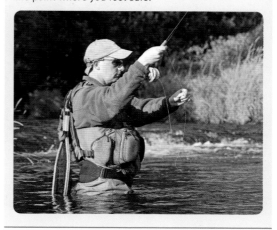

River-fishing for tiger fish

One of the most ferocious freshwater fish, the voracious tiger fish inhabits the Zambezi River of central Africa. It presents a challenge for adventurous fly-anglers. Some of the best fishing for this fish is in the Caprivi Strip, when the flood waters begin to trickle off the plains.

Rod and rig set-up

Choose a 9-ft (2.7-m) #9 fly rod, matched with a reel of comparable size. A multisection, saltwater fly-fishing rod will work well, and is easy to travel with. Your reel should have a good drag system, as tiger fish fight hard when hooked. Most fly-fishing for tiger fish is done with modern, fast-sinking lines that help take the flies down to the feeding fish. Carry a spare rod and reel when traveling overseas, to cover any mishaps.

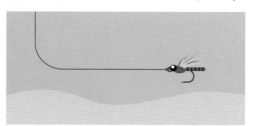

➤ **Tiger fish rig** Use a single fly on a razor-sharp, strong size 1/0 hook. Patterns include Gray or Black Clouser Minnows, Blue Deceivers, or a fly that resembles a baby tiger fish. Include a short section of wire trace in front of the fly.

➤ **Medium fly reel** You will need a durable reel, as used for salmon fishing, with a smooth drag system that will help you play this hard-fighting fish.

Targeting tiger fish

The threat posed by large, wild animals makes it safer to fish the warm Zambezi waters from a boat. Anchor the boat close to swirling currents and eddies, where flood water runs off the plains into the river. Cast the fly directly downstream into the powerful current, wait for the fast-sinking fly line to sink down well, then start retrieving the fly at a slow, constant pace. If you find lots of small fish moving around, then tiger fish are not far away. Often they crash into baitfish close to the surface early in the morning, so be rigged up and ready to fish the moment you arrive at your spot.

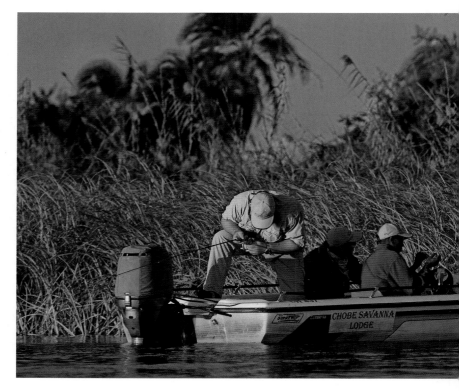

1 **Warn other anglers** before casting heavy fly lines and fast-moving flies, which present a potentially dangerous combination. It is wise for others to duck down while you cast.

Setting the hook

The huge teeth of this fish give it a hard, bony mouth, in which it is difficult to set the hook. The bite from a tiger fish is savage, and will come with little or no warning; because you are fishing without being able to see your quarry, and are retrieving the fly slowly, you cannot fully prepare yourself for the moment of impact. When you feel a hit, work hard to set the hook home; repeatedly strip-strike as hard as possible. To strip-strike, do not use the rod to set the hook; rather,

keep the rod pointing at the fish and use your stripping hand to keep pulling the line back and forth as hard as possible.

A hooked tiger fish will often jump clean out of the water; if this happens, immediately point your rod downward toward the fish. To disorient the fish, change direction on it; if the fish is running one way, turn the rod and line in the opposite direction. Forcing it to change direction can make the difference between landing and not landing this fast-running, hard-fighting fish.

2 **Work hard to change** the direction of the rod and line to the fish, to help disorient it. Keep your balance by planting your feet wide apart on a stable platform within the boat.

3 **Handle the fish with care,** both for the fish's safety and to protect your fingers, while the special moment is captured in a photograph. Then gently slip this magnificent predator back into the water.

UNHOOKING A TIGER FISH

Take safety precautions when handling fish that have big, sharp teeth. Use a gripping tool (the Boga-Grip is the most widely used) to clasp the fish's bottom jaw (this does it no harm at all), and use pliers to remove the fly. Avoid placing your fingers near the teeth.

Fly-fishing for carp

Fishing for carp on fly-fishing tackle is perhaps not the purest form of fly-fishing, but it attracts modern anglers who are looking for a new challenge, and is fantastic fun. Carp often feed on or just below the surface, which makes them perfect for targeting on fly-fishing tackle.

Rod and rig set-up

Use #7 to #9 fly rods and matched reels with a visible floating line and a fluorocarbon leader. Try to find out how big the carp you are fishing are likely to be, so you can plan your tackle needs. Use more powerful tackle if big carp are a possibility. Carp fly-fishing is often done in snaggy areas where it is important to be able to put pressure on running fish.

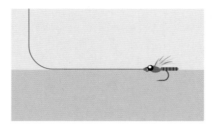

⌃ **Floating-line rig** You are mainly targeting carp that are feeding off the surface, so floating lines are essential. If the fly sinks after a while, add some floatant (normally a gel) to keep it on the surface.

⌃ **Bonio carp fly** Use flies that resemble bread or dog biscuits. This small fly looks like a dog biscuit and will float on the surface among the real biscuits that have been introduced. The aim is to get the carp to eat it confidently.

Location and time

Don't target waters where there is huge pressure on only a few big carp. It is far better to fish where there are carp populations of all sizes that are willing to come up to the surface to feed. First and last light are the best times to find carp surface-feeding. Cloud cover and still conditions are also more likely to bring success than very bright sunlight on the water, which often drives fish to the bottom.

1 **Use the roll cast,** which does not entail a back-cast, to put out flies when casting room is restricted. Many small carp waters are surrounded by extensive vegetation, which makes for harder casting. The roll cast enables the fly-angler to put flies out a fair distance.

Using flies and baits

Carp are extremely adept at feeding off the surface; their mouths are perfectly designed to suck in particles of food. With this in mind, it is worthwhile spending some time throwing bits of bread and dog biscuits into the water and watching their feeding habits. This technique is as useful to the fly-angler as it is to the bait- and lure-carp angler.

Fish that feed off the surface are often very wary, so approach stealthily—do not break natural horizons, wear relatively dull clothing (many carp anglers dress in camouflage colors), and keep noise to a minimum.

Once the carp you want to fish for are feeding happily and coming up for food on a regular basis, you can cast your fly in among the offerings, and wait for a bite.

Striking and playing

The secret is not to strike the moment you see a carp closing in on your bait, but rather to steel yourself to wait until it has very visibly engulfed your fly. Now strike and start playing the fish. Be very alert; carp are powerful fish that know their surroundings well— be prepared for a hard fight.

2 **Playing a carp** takes skill. When hooked, larger fish will be determined to reach snags, so it is vital to keep the rod bent into the fish. If the rod is hardly bent, the fish is not under enough pressure. Have a landing net and a carp bed close by.

3 **The safest and most humane way** to land carp is with a soft-meshed landing net on a long handle. Be sure to bring the carp over the landing net using the rod, rather than chasing the fish with the net. Many carp are lost by going after the fish and bumping the hook out or breaking the line.

Fly-fishing for pike

The pike is a hugely popular freshwater species, often caught with bait and lures, but increasing numbers of anglers from the fly-fishing world are realizing that this magnificent predator is also extremely eager to take flies. Pike offer a world-class fly-fishing challenge.

Rod and rig set-up

Pike flies are heavy and the quarry can grow large, so use a #9 fly rod and reel. Saltwater fly rods of 9 ft (2.7 m) in length are perfect because they often have a fast action, which helps lines and flies cut through the wind. Take reels or spools loaded with floating and intermediate lines for versatility. Be sure to carry an unhooking tool.

☒ Bunny bug pike fly Big and bold, pike flies are not subtle. A Bunny Bug on a 2/0 or 3/0 hook is typical. Try different designs until you find one that works on the waters you are fishing.

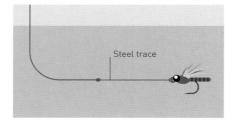

Steel trace

◀ Wire trace Use a thin, flexible wire trace that is easy to tie, such as the coated variety. Flies are usually fished below the surface, but in warmer water pike will often take poppers and crease flies on the surface.

Choosing your location

Not all fly-fishing waters contain pike, and those that do may not allow anglers to fish for them. However, with their increased popularity, many fisheries are encouraging anglers to try their luck if pike are present. Large pike are solitary and like to lurk in cover and then pounce on their prey, so when you get to the lake, ask local anglers for tips and look for fish-holding features. If there are trout, which pike feed on, think about where they might be. The best places to start are near structures and cover—weed beds, sunken trees, or inlets—but don't forget, pike also feed in open water.

1 **Position the boat** near the kind of cover that a pike would hide in. Work out how the wind will affect the boat and set it up accordingly. This will allow you to cover the water successfully.

Casting, striking, and playing

It is essential to cover as much water as possible with your fly; the pike could be anywhere. Their keen senses will alert them to your fly in the water, so use powerful and efficient casting to keep it working for as long as possible. The basic overhead cast is sufficient, but more line speed will be built up to move a big fly through the air if you use a double-haul to the cast. Big flies are subject to wind resistance, so the faster you can move the fly in the cast, the farther it will go out and the more softly it will land on the water. You may see pike come at your fly and then suddenly turn away. If this happens, repeat the cast and retrieve a couple of times to see if the fish is interested—more often than not, it will be. When a pike takes the fly, it is almost like hitting a brick wall—everything suddenly stops and then a split-second later the fish usually charges off. There is often no time or need to strike, as a hungry pike will engulf the fly with ease. These fish are known for doing a lot of head-shaking during the fight, so keep a tight line to the fish at all times. Do not go out on the water without a buoyancy aid; many countries enforce a strict policy that fly-anglers on boats must wear one at all times.

2 **Palming the reel** in conjuction with using the drag system on your reel is a simple way to apply more drag when fighting a fish. Use your hand to apply pressure to the spool, but take your hand away quickly if the fish suddenly starts to run. The technique is effective, but it takes some practice.

3 **Use a large soft-mesh net** for landing pike. These fish require delicate handling because they are often exhausted by the fight. Remove the hook with long-nose pliers at the side of the boat, or on board on a carp mat. Hold the pike in the water and wait for it to revive before letting it go.

Loch-style fly-fishing

Fishing large, open waters from a boat calls for a combination of boat-handling skills and the ability to find fish. Open, windswept waters, such as the Scottish lochs, can be stunning places to fish. A common technique, often referred to as loch-fishing, is to fish a team of flies.

Rod and rig set-up

There is seldom a need for long casting when fly-fishing from a boat, so a standard 10-ft (3-m) #6 or #7 fly rod and matched reel are suitable. Although the fish may be small, a slightly overpowered rod helps when casting heavy lines in strong wind. Floating lines are commonly used, but carry a reel or spare spool loaded with an intermediate line. Match the lines to the rod.

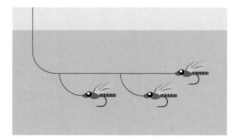

◄ **Team of flies** Fish a team of three wet flies on a light, 4–6-lb (2–2.75-kg) leader. Start with sizes 14 and 12, and change flies regularly if you are not catching. Weighted flies help get the team down more quickly, and deeper.

⬢ **Hare's-ear nymph** This is a pattern tied to imitate various nymphs. It is tied either unweighted or weighted, and rabbit fur (not hare's) is the usual body material. A size 12 is a good all-around size for loch-fishing.

Loch-fishing techniques

Wear a life jacket or buoyancy aid at all times. Set the boat to drift broadside to the wind, with the anglers casting downwind. A drogue is often used to help slow the drift, especially in a strong wind, but if you are fishing with a guide, or gillie, then they may use oars to keep the boat moving at the right angle and speed. Wild brown trout will come close to the boat, so do not cast too far. More importantly, match the retrieval of your team of flies to the weather conditions. Less wind calls for a slower retrieval, often a figure-eight; a stronger breeze calls for a faster retrieval, to keep you in constant contact with the flies. If two of you are fishing, the better caster should fish close to the engine, unless one of you is left-handed.

1 **Organize your gear neatly,** and stow it out of the way. Fly lines need to be stripped in and recast continually, and will snag on items left around.

2 **Cast within your capabilities;** long leaders carrying a team of flies are prone to tangle if you time a cast badly by trying too hard. Work with your boat partner, and alternate your casts. Keep a close eye on the activity of fish on the surface and adjust flies accordingly.

3 **Keep in contact** with your team of flies at all times. Watch your line on the surface for signs of a fish hitting a fly. Often you will feel the fish first, but the windier the conditions, the more you must watch the line.

4 **Land the fish** with a net as normal, steering the fish over the waiting net and lifting it up. A wild brown trout from unspoiled waters is a creature of real beauty. Some may be small, but it is possible to catch really big specimens.

Fly-fishing for bonefish

Many inshore waters of the world's tropical regions consist of large areas of very shallow water where the bottom is generally hard sand, coral, mud, and turtle grass. These "flats" are home to bonefish, a species that is hugely adept at feeding in such "skinny" water.

Rod and rig set-up

Fishing very shallow water calls for floating fly lines, plenty of backing to deal with fast-running fish, and a long, tapered leader. A #8 or #9 fly-fishing rod and matching reel will serve you perfectly on the flats, but above all, make sure the drag system on your reel can cope with the explosive run of a hooked bonefish. Few fish run as fast when hooked, making this fish one of the ultimate saltwater prizes for fly-anglers.

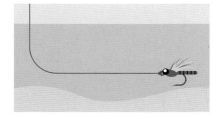

⏏ **Single-fly rig** Bonefish are fished for with single, weighted flies that are gently retrieved along the bottom, where the bonefish feed when they are on the flats.

⏏ **Clouser Minnow** Available in several colors, of which this is one of the most common, the Clouser Minnow is highly effective for catching bonefish. The weighted eyes invert the fly as it is twitched along the bottom. Carry various colors in your fly box.

Targeting bonefish

Without doubt some of the most exciting and visual fishing there is, fly-fishing on saltwater flats is all about being able to see the fish that you are casting at. Fishing in very shallow water calls for an array of different skills that will put any angler to the test. An essential part of your gear is a pair of good polarized sunglasses, which will help you to see through the water by cutting the glare.

Bonefish, a common species in shallow tropical waters, are easily spooked, which calls for a very measured approach. Stalk them slowly and quietly, watching out for moving schools of fish and movement on the surface of the water. Bonefish feed hard on the bottom and when they put their heads down to do this, their tails often become visible as they break the surface of the water. Known as "tailing," this is an unmistakable sign of the presence of bonefish.

Step gently and slowly to enable you to get within casting range of the fish. Generally, you will aim to cast in front of the fish, but be careful not to alarm them by allowing your line to land over them. Bonefish are celebrated for being a very "honest" fish. This refers to the fact that if you make the right cast in the right place, more often than not the fish will take your fly.

1 **Fish with an experienced guide,** to help you spot the bonefish. The more you fish the flats, the better you will become at seeing fish, but a good guide will always spot more fish than you, and will advise on exactly where to cast and how to fish the fly.

2 **Cast fast, accurate lines** to avoid spooking the fish. A tight loop shows a good fly-casting style. In these locations, there is often a breeze, so the more proficient you are at casting, the more likely you are to succeed in placing flies where the bonefish can see them.

3 **When a bonefish takes the fly,** set the hook as fast as you can. Lift the rod high in order to keep the line away from the coral. Bonefish will run very fast when hooked, and may do so repeatedly.

4 **To land the fish,** most fly-anglers take their catch when it begins to tire. Even so, it may still charge off again, so be ready to grab the fish, calm it down, remove the hook, then gently release it unharmed.

Fly-fishing for milkfish

It is only within the last 10 to 15 years that forward-thinking anglers have worked out how to target large, flats-based milkfish on the fly. Noted for their immense power and speed, these warm-water dwellers are extremely wary, and anglers require a high level of skill to catch them.

Rod and rig set-up

You need to use a more robust version of the tackle used for catching bonefish (see p.192). The same kind of leader and floating line will work well, but consider using a powerful 9-ft (2.7-m) fly rod—#9 or even #10—with a matched fly reel that has a smooth drag system. Make sure that you have plenty of backing line because these fish are capable of long runs.

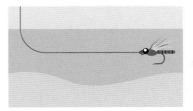

⬆ **Milkfish fly rig** Use a floating fly line and long fluorocarbon leader. The milkfish fly must float just under the surface, like algae. Allow it to drift with the current, known as dead-drifting the fly.

⬆ **Arno's milky dream** Milkfish feed on algae and plankton, and this fly, which imitates algae, is the only one that has been successful in catching them.

Casting and retrieving

Seeing the milkfish on the flats is often the easiest part of this kind of fishing. The pursuit of this elusive quarry takes plenty of patience and involves some luck. The wind and current need to be working together effectively to allow the very light fly to drift down to the milkfish in such a way as to convince them that it is the same as the food that they are eating. Milkfish are extremely suspicious and will often repeatedly ignore the fly. If it does not sit just below the surface, be prepared to add or remove material to alter its buoyancy.

1 **Cast ahead and uptide** of a school of milkfish and allow the fly to "dead drift" down to them. Retrieve the fly once it has passed below the school, and repeat the cast.

2 **Keep up the pressure** on the hooked fish until you can land it. As a milkfish begins to tire, it may swim in circles around you for some time.

Striking, playing, and landing

When a milkfish decides to take the fly, set the hook home by "strip-striking" (sharply pulling line with the rod pointed at the fish) as quickly as possible, and then hold on. These fish are incredibly fast and will often jump repeatedly when hooked. Although you can play and land a milkfish purely by wading, as described below, some anglers have a boat waiting nearby. Once the fish is hooked, the angler gets into the boat as fast as possible to chase it, in an attempt to avoid having all the line taken off their reel (getting "spooled"). Whichever way you play these fish, it is essential to fight them hard by getting line back onto the reel as quickly as you can, regularly changing direction on the fish via the rod, and always watching out for sharks. Milkfish are among the hardest fish of the flats to hook, let alone land, but are worth the effort. Your determination will be well rewarded.

FLY-FISHING INNOVATOR

Fly-fishing for milkfish has been revolutionized by the development of an algae-imitating fly by Arno Mattee (below), a noted South African fly-fishing guide. Over many years working in the Seychelles, he studied the feeding habits of the milkfish and designed a fly that it would take, now named Arno's Milky Dream.

3 **Land the milkfish** with the help of a companion. Be prepared for even a tired fish to run again at this stage. To land the fish, grab it by the tail and hold it securely for unhooking and release.

Fly-fishing for giant trevally

In some tropical areas, giant trevally can be fished for on the flats. When these powerful and aggressive fish move into shallow water to hunt and feed, they become perfect targets for thrill-seeking fly-anglers. This is one of the most extreme forms of fly-fishing.

Rod and rig set-up

The giant trevally is a brute of a fish, so select your tackle accordingly. Take nothing less than a powerful, four-piece #12 fly rod (see pp.36–37), and carry a spare in case of breakages. You will need a fly reel to match, loaded with plenty of backing line and a #12 saltwater floating line (see p.48). Check and recheck all knots regularly because giant trevally pull amazingly hard.

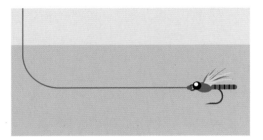

◀ **Wet-fly rig** Use a single, large fly (size 6/0 or 8/0)—for example, a saltwater fly called a Flashy Profile—and a mono leader of around 120-lb (54-kg) breaking strain. Avoid tapered leaders.

▲ **Saltwater fly reel** Take a large saltwater fly reel of the best quality you can afford and, as with rods, be sure to carry a spare.

Before you start fishing

Fly-fishing for giant trevally is as much about preparing mentally as physically and technically. Prepare yourself to do battle with one of the most aggressive predators in the sea. Whereas most fly-fishing is about gently casting to fish, this type of fishing is about attracting the attention of the fish by the force with which the fly hits the water, and then fighting your quarry as hard as you physically can. Carry plenty of drinking water with you to prevent dehydration; places like the remote Seychelles atolls can be very hot and draining. However, there are few fishing experiences as exciting as this kind of sight-fishing.

1 **Cast a big fly near** a fish within your comfortable range, and strip (pull in) the fly as fast as you can. When you wear polarized sunglasses, their black shapes are easy to spot.

2 **Fight giant trevally hard.**
You need to play these fish as hard as they play you. You can apply huge pressure on a running fish by keeping the rod low and fighting the fish "on the reel"—keeping the angle to the fish less acute, and making the fish work directly against the drag of the reel, instead of only against the bend of the rod. This combination works well on these really strong fish. Tuck the rod butt into your body, and make the fish work for every bit of line it takes from your reel.

3 **Wear a glove** to hold the sharp "wrist" of the giant trevally's tail safely. Not many catches beat that of this magnificent tropical predator. All giant trevally are unhooked and released after the fight, so make sure to revive them and give them all the respect they deserve.

Fly-fishing from a flats boat

Many of the world's saltwater flats systems are successfully fly-fished from skiffs or flats boats, and catches can be spectacular. Shallow-draft, fast boats make it possible to fish a lot of water, and to move to a different spot quickly if the fish are not biting.

Rod and rig set-up

Permit, snook, and bonefish can be fished for with #8 fly-fishing rods, or #9 for larger permit. Tarpon demand a #12 rod if big fish are expected; they are uncontrollable on anything less, for all but the most experienced anglers. Floating lines are required to fish the flats, and use a single fly for permit, snook, and tarpon fishing.

Chartreuse-and-White Clouser Minnow One of the world's most consistently successful flies for saltwater fly-fishing, the Clouser Minnow imitates various baitfish. The chartreuse-and-white version works well for tarpon and snook. Clouser Minnows can also work for permit, but generally these fish prefer crab patterns.

Flats-fishing set-up Use a single fly. For permit, try a weighted crab pattern and cast just in front of the fish, then twitch back toward you. Tarpon will take large flies just under the surface.

PERMIT FISHING

Permit are among the most sought-after flats species, and to take a permit on the fly is a serious challenge. They can be choosy when presented with a fly and simply refuse all fly patterns; or they may spook immediately. However, when one finally goes tail up and takes a fly, the lucky angler is about to engage in one of the most spectacular fights it is possible to have on a fly rod.

On the flats

Many of the world's best flats-fishing destinations offer fishing from skiffs, with competent and knowledgeable guides who will go out of their way to help you. While the aim is to take you to the fishing grounds fast, the special advantage of a flats boat is the poling platform at the back of the boat—once you are on the flats and near the fish, the guide will cut the engine, raise it, and take up position on the platform. Guides on these boats generally use a long, carbon-fiber pole to move you around quietly. Standing high up, and therefore able to spot fish more easily, they brief you with a series of simple instructions. Keep your spare line coiled neatly on the casting platform, and be ready to cast an accurate line at all times (remembering your guide is standing behind you). It is often possible to creep up close to fish, and the closer you can get, the easier the cast, especially when there is a wind blowing. In time, you will learn to see the fish really well and cast accordingly.

1 **Stow your gear safely** for the journey to the flats because the boats go extremely fast over shallow water. Often your guide will take the boat through a maze of mangroves and channels—on extensive flats systems, the fish can be spread out in different areas.

2 **Cast as close as you can** to the spot your guide advises. The faster you can place a fly in front of the fish, the better your chance of connecting; the fish are constantly moving and you may get only one chance. Double-hauling (see pp.86–87) is a useful skill in this situation.

Fly-fishing for European sea bass

European sea bass are among the few species of the seas of northern Europe that can be successfully caught on the fly. They will take flies, lures, and baits with equal relish. European sea bass have always been a much sought-after target and are attractive to anglers from all disciplines.

Rod and rig set-up

The perfect outfit for European sea bass fly-fishing is a #8 saltwater fly-fishing rod (see pp.36–37). This will have a degree of built-in protection against corrosion for sea fishing, but if you already possess a #8 rod and reel that you use for reservoir-fishing, this will work just as well. Remember to wash them thoroughly with fresh water afterward. A floating fly line is generally the best all-around choice for catching European sea bass, for when they are moving in shallow water, they will feed close to or on the surface.

>> **Wet-fly rig** Single, sinking (wet) flies are most useful when saltwater fly-fishing. European sea bass also go for poppers and crease flies (see pp.64–65). A long, tapered leader is ideal.

⌃ **Bass fly** Most bass flies imitate small prey, such as sand eels. Specialty bass flies are tied with saltwater hooks.

Mobile and adaptable

Although it is not in the least bit complicated, fly-fishing for European sea bass is very different from fishing in a reservoir. The more you move around and the more water you cover, the greater your chances of success. Travel as light as you can and walk to find the fish. European sea bass are not difficult to catch, but the trick is to find them—this is where a fly-angler can benefit from a sea-angler's knowledge. It is often useful to fish with a lure-angler, as you can help each other work out where the fish are and at what range they seem to be feeding. When you start to fish, keep an open mind and think carefully about the prevailing conditions—wind direction, times and direction of the tides, and light levels. Look for the same kind of terrain you would try when lure-fishing for European sea bass (see pp.140–141). A fly-angler can often catch large numbers of small, schooling bass (known as "schoolies"), but the challenge is to find large fish. First and last light are considered the best times to chase them.

1 **Cast in the right place** by putting yourself where you judge the fish will be, but always play safe and know the tide times. Wear chest waders to enable you to access more ground, and use a line-tray to catch the loose line as you strip back, to prevent it from tangling on the rocks. Knowing how to double-haul (see pp.86–87) can be helpful when casting fly lines in strong winds.

2 **Play the bass out** and bring it to hand while you are in the water, then unhook and release it. Watch out for its spiky dorsal fin and the razor-sharp gill plates. When they want to take the fly, European sea bass simply hit it—there are no false bites or hesitant takes. This makes them great to fish, although you may have to work the terrain hard. Many of the bass you catch will probably be on the small side, but even so they are a hugely satisfying quarry.

SAFETY ON THE ROCKS

Angling from rocks is unpredictable, but with a little care it can be reasonably safe. Study weather forecasts and understand their implications. Ensure that you tell someone where you are going and tell them the time you expect to be back, and stick to it. Carry a cell phone in a waterproof case. Use felt-soled waders for grip on rocks, and remember that seaweed is always slippery.

3 **Return as many fish** as you can and check local size limits as well; only bass of a certain size can be kept, and there are often strict bag limits too. Watching this bass swim strongly away after you have caught and released it is a pleasure. Few other sea fish in northern European waters attract so much dedication and passion.

Ultra-deep-water fly-fishing

In recent years, fly lines have developed to allow big, weighted flies to be put down far below the surface to catch fish that frequent these deeper waters. This type of fishing has certainly opened up new realms to the adventurous fly-angler.

Rod and rig set-up

Look for a #14 or even a #15 fly rod for targeting the heaviest fish, but often a good #12 will do. Choose a reel that is sufficiently big and powerful to stand up to the demands of this form of fishing. There are various fly lines on the market that are designed to sink very fast. Be sure to think about where you are fishing, and how deep you are trying to sink your fly, before buying one. Good fly lines are not cheap, so they are worth taking care of. It is good practice always to strip the lines off your reel after a trip and rinse them down with fresh water. Choose a big, weighted fly to match your quarry.

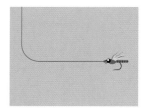

◀◀ Deep-sinking fly rig
The single, weighted fly sits at the end of a powerful but shortish leader; long leaders are likely to tangle on the way down. Use a wire biting-leader if the target species has very large teeth.

▶▶ Large reel Angling for big fish at a depth of 65 ft (20 m) or more puts huge strain on a fly reel, so use the best-quality saltwater model you can afford and match its size to the rod. It must have a sealed drag system that works efficiently during the playing of fish.

Using deep-sinking lines

Deep-sinking lines have been developed to put flies down to depths that were previously unreachable with fly-fishing methods. You can use this technique to target species such as marlin and sailfish, usually after they have been teased to the side of the boat with bait. Casting ultra-fast-sinking fly lines and big, weighted flies is not about any kind of finesse; indeed, there is often no formal cast when heaving out the gear. Remember that the faster a boat moves with wind and tide, the harder it is to get thick fly lines down deep, because the drag on them in the water is great compared with braid or even mono lines. When it is successful, this form of fishing can be spectacular.

1 **You need to work** to make a large, weighted fly come alive for your prey. The best technique is to position yourself against the gunwale of the boat and get comfortable, and then put the fly through its paces. Be prepared to respond to a bite at any time.

2 **Fly rods can bend** at alarming angles. This is to be expected when a big fish takes your fly many yards below you, and is exactly how a rod is designed to work against fish. The more bend you put in the rod, the more pressure is being exerted on the fish to come up. Even then, you will lose your share of decent fish that simply will not budge.

3 **Deep-water fly-fishing** often reveals very different species of fish from those you would expect. This green jobfish is a member of the snapper family that lives around rocks and reefs from the Indian Ocean to the eastern Pacific.

Fish
Species

Just what is that fish you have caught, or what species is it that you can see swimming in front of you? What are they feeding on and where else might you find them? This section contains authoritative descriptions of a selection of the world's premier sporting quarries.

It is staggering how many different kinds of fish you can catch on rod and line. Some are so obscure that they could only be called "sport" fish by very few anglers. Most of the fish in this section are very popular sport-fishing species wherever they are found. While a few might be less targeted than others due to their locations, rest assured that you could spend ten lifetimes trying to catch all the fish species in this book.

Take time to study the feeding and breeding habits of fish, for the more you begin to learn about how fish behave, the better you can work out how to catch them. Fish can be so gloriously predictable, yet at times unexpectedly different, that you could be excused a flicker of fishing rage when you can't catch them. We know huge amounts about Pacific salmon, for example, such as when they run the rivers, when they spawn,

⌃ **Unique features** Many fish have features that make them instantly identifiable, such as the mouth of this thick-lipped gray mullet.

and when they school at sea prior to entering the rivers. Nevertheless, there are yearly differences and fluctuations because nature itself is amazingly unpredictable. Learn all you can about the species that you are targeting, but at the same time, remember that you are on the same learning curve as every other angler. While an enormous amount is known about many fish, it can be reassuring to know that there is still plenty to discover about many of the rare or less-studied species.

Take note of how widespread some fish species are, and how many can be fished for using a wide variety of techniques. Learning to identify what you catch is also an essential part of fishing. The ability to recognize key species is crucial to ensure that you do not break local laws by fishing for, catching, or perhaps taking to eat a fish that is restricted. Being able to identify fish can also add to your enjoyment; it is exciting when you catch something completely unexpected. While you can target certain species with some precision, you never really know what might take your bait, lure, or fly.

⌃ **Natural glory** To see a fish such as this trout moving naturally through water is one of the great sights in fishing. Learning about fish only adds to your enjoyment.

Freshwater fish

There is a wealth of different freshwater fish species to catch, in a variety of locations all over the world, from tumbling streams and broad rivers to quiet ponds and vast lakes. The fish that swim in freshwater are fantastically varied, and their different colors, sizes, habitats, and feeding habits fascinate anglers. Some freshwater anglers become so absorbed that they devote a lifetime to the pursuit of just a handful of species.

Brown trout and Sea trout
Salmo trutta

WEIGHT Up to 110 lb (50 kg).

TYPES OF WATER Streams, rivers, lakes, and reservoirs; coastal waters (sea trout).

DISTRIBUTION Temperate regions worldwide.

FISHING METHODS Primarily fly-fishing, but can also be caught with bait and lures.

The brown trout (*Salmo trutta*, morpha: *fario*), and its seagoing form, the sea trout (*Salmo trutta*, morpha: *trutta*), is one of the most important game-fishing species and is found throughout the world. The species is native to Europe and western Asia, but over hundreds of years it has been gradually introduced into many other temperate regions. The brown trout has a brownish body with distinct red and black spots, but there are many variations according to habitat and genetic makeup. This species can be found in a variety of waters, from the smallest streams to large lakes and reservoirs.

It feeds principally on insects, larvae, and small fish. At times, as most trout anglers discover, this species can be extremely choosy about what it will eat.

Sea trout
The sea trout is a silvery-blue-colored, migratory form of brown trout that spends its early life in freshwater, but enters the sea between the ages of one and five years. It eventually returns to the rivers to spawn. The preference of this form of the species is for cold, fast-flowing water. The rivers of southern Argentina are well known for their abundant populations of large sea trout. During its river-dwelling phase, the sea trout gradually darkens, but never reverts completely to the coloration of a brown trout. Unlike the Atlantic salmon, the sea trout does not need floodwater to move up the spawning rivers. However, a flooding river does tend to attract this species in large numbers. The sea trout often moves most confidently at night, and the best fishing for this species tends to be at the end of the day. Some anglers prefer to fish for sea trout after dark.

⬙ Fly-fishing in Chile
The crystal-clear rivers and streams of Chile provide an ideal environment for brown trout. Fly-fishing in these waters requires patience and skill.

Black and red spots

⌃ Brown trout

Silver-blue coloration

Spots above and below lateral line

Squared-off tail

⌃ Sea trout

CANNIBAL BROWN TROUT

Large, predatory brown trout are known as ferox, or cannibal, trout. Once thought to be a different species, it is now known that these are simply brown trout that have changed to a diet based mainly on fish—sometimes including small members of its own species. The ferox trout has a hooked jaw and lives longer than most brown trout.

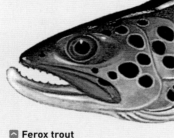

⌃ Ferox trout

Rainbow trout and Steelhead

Oncorhynchus mykiss

WEIGHT Up to 55 lb (25 kg).

TYPES OF WATER Rivers, lakes; coastal waters (steelhead).

DISTRIBUTION Temperate waters worldwide.

FISHING METHODS Fly-fishing, less commonly bait- and lure-fishing.

The rainbow trout and its seagoing form (both *Oncorhynchus mykiss*) are among the principal game-fishing quarries, and have been introduced in temperate waters worldwide. The species includes many subspecies, including the Kamloops, Kern River, and Shasta rainbow trout. Great numbers are successfully bred in lakes and reservoirs, but there are various wild strains that spend their lives in rivers and, if allowed, will run to the sea and ultimately return to the rivers to spawn. Rainbow trout that have migrated to sea are known as steelhead. Any stock of rainbow trout can migrate like this if given the chance.

Physical characteristics

Rainbow trout vary hugely in appearance but they are distinguished by a pink stripe along the lateral line. They are speckled black along their sides, back, upper fins, and tail. In North America, rainbow trout can reach up to 55 lb (25 kg), but in Europe, they more commonly reach a maximum weight of around 24 lb (11 kg).

They feed mainly on insects and their larvae and may also take crustaceans, fish eggs, and small fish. Wild rainbow trout are known for being hard fighters when hooked.

Steelhead fishing

Steelhead are famous among fly-anglers for their intense silvery coloration and their impressive and powerful fighting abilities. The longer a sea-run steelhead spends in the river, the more its appearance tends to revert to that of a "standard" rainbow trout.

Without doubt, the most famous steelhead fishing in the world occurs in British Columbia on the west coast of Canada, where the fall runs of bright chrome fish are legendary. Steelhead smolts

CUTTHROAT TROUT

This relative of the rainbow trout is native to western North America. It can be identified primarily by the telltale red "cutthroat" mark that is found under the chin and the pronounced black spots over much of the body. The overall body color of this species varies from mainly dark green to green-blue on the back.

🔺 **Cutthroat trout**

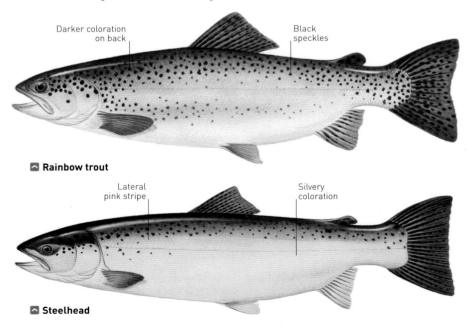

Darker coloration on back

Black speckles

🔺 **Rainbow trout**

Lateral pink stripe

Silvery coloration

🔺 **Steelhead**

(two- or three-year-old fish) inhabit the Pacific waters along the west coast of North America, feeding on schools of small fish from Alaska down to Mexico. Increasingly, steelhead are also found in the waters around New Zealand. The larger fish are the most successful at returning to the rivers to spawn. Fly-fishing is the most popular way to target steelhead, mainly when they are returning from the sea to spawn.

Steelhead river The rivers of northern California are known for their steelhead. For the fly-angler, these stunning locations can provide an unrivaled experience.

STEELHEAD AND RIVER HEALTH

Observation of steelhead populations is a useful way to measure the health of a river system. In order to thrive, steelhead need cold, clear water, so fluctuations in their numbers often point toward problems with the waters of a river, such as increased pollution. This is important not only from a wildlife conservation perspective, but also for the prosperity of an area. An abundance of steelhead brings more anglers to an area, and more money into the local economy.

Lake trout
Salvelinus namaycush

WEIGHT Up to 72 lb (33 kg).

TYPES OF WATER Lakes, streams.

DISTRIBUTION North America; introduced to South America, Asia, and Europe.

FISHING METHODS Lure- and fly-fishing.

Lake trout can reach up to 5 ft (1.5 m) in length, with a distinctly forked tail, and do not have the dark spots of most other trout species. They are usually found in lakes and streams, and are fast-swimming, aggressive predators, feeding on all kinds of organisms from plankton to small mammals. Adult lake trout are known to eat smaller lake trout. They spawn when they reach the age of five to six years. The females release their eggs over the rocky bottoms of lakes. This enables the eggs to lie in crevices on the bottom. Fly-fishing and spinning are the favorite fishing methods, but many anglers prefer to troll lures behind boats.

Greenish coloration

Forked tail

Pale spots

Dolly varden
Salvelinus malma

WEIGHT Up to 41 lb (18.5 kg).

TYPES OF WATER Lakes, and rivers; migrating to sea.

DISTRIBUTION North America; Arctic Ocean; northeastern and northwestern Pacific Ocean.

FISHING METHODS Lure-, bait-, and fly-fishing.

Dolly varden are part of the char family. They grow to about 4¼ ft (1.3 m) in length, and their light spots distinguish them from trout and salmon. Mature male dolly varden develop a distinctive bright red coloration along the lower body, and their fins take on a red-black tinge with white edges; over time they develop an extended lower jaw. Mature females are similar in color but less bright. Sea-going dolly varden are more silvery, with plenty of

MIGRATORY BEHAVIOR IN ALASKA

Dolly varden from northern Alaska tend to overwinter in rivers, whereas south-Alaskan dolly varden spend the winter in lakes. It is believed that they search for lakes on a random basis, by swimming up various rivers until they find one with a lake at the top. Both male and female dolly varden must return for spawning to the river in which they were spawned themselves.

red-orange spots on their flanks, and a greenish brown dorsal fin. Dolly varden spawn in streams during fall; the eggs are deposited in channels dug out by the females with their tails. The young migrate to sea at three or four years old, during May and June. Migrating fish then overwinter in freshwater, with distinct river and lake populations.

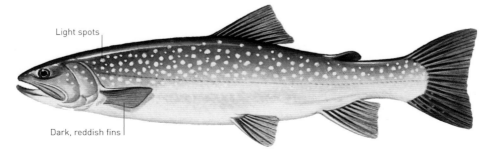

Light spots

Dark, reddish fins

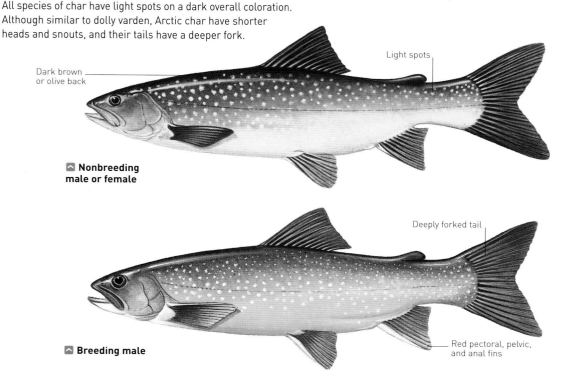

◀ Clean-water species Arctic char need uncontaminated, well-oxygenated water to survive. This means that the best fishing is in the unspoiled waters of the north.

Arctic char

Salvelinus alpinus

WEIGHT Up to 33 lb (15 kg).

TYPES OF WATER Clean, cold lakes and large rivers; some migrating to sea.

DISTRIBUTION North America; Arctic Ocean; Scandinavia; Iceland; Greenland; northern North Atlantic Ocean; occasionally northern UK.

FISHING METHODS Lure-, bait-, and fly-fishing.

All species of char have light spots on a dark overall coloration. Although similar to dolly varden, Arctic char have shorter heads and snouts, and their tails have a deeper fork.

These fish can reach a maximum length of about 3¼ ft (1 m). Their backs are dark brown or olive, with lighter sides fading to a light-colored belly. Colors vary considerably at spawning time, especially in male Arctic char—the whole body may become gold or orange in color, and the lower fins often develop white edges. This species is believed to spawn in alternate years from August to October.

Arctic char are a popular angling quarry in the lakes of Kodiak Island in Alaska. They also congregate in the big lakes throughout Bristol Bay in Alaska from May to July, to feed on the salmon smolts that migrate toward the sea at this time.

Dark brown or olive back

Light spots

⌃ Nonbreeding male or female

Deeply forked tail

⌃ Breeding male

Red pectoral, pelvic, and anal fins

Atlantic salmon
Salmo salar

WEIGHT Up to 104 lb (47 kg).	

TYPES OF WATER Cold, fast-flowing rivers.

DISTRIBUTION North Atlantic, Baltic, and Arctic Ocean; introduced to Australasia and Argentina.

FISHING METHODS Fly-fishing.

The Atlantic salmon is a hugely important game fish and a highly prized catch, especially among fly-anglers. These fish can grow to large sizes and are extremely powerful swimmers, built for endurance and speed.

Before Atlantic salmon spawn, they spend several years feeding in the cold ocean waters, but once the urge to spawn comes, they return to the rivers in which they were born. A proportion of adult Atlantic salmon die after spawning, but some survive and these return to the sea. Young salmon (smolts) migrate to the sea after about two years.

Atlantic salmon stocks are under increasing commercial pressure and the salmon-farming industry is expanding to satisfy the immense demand for this fish. However, there are places where sport-fishing for Atlantic salmon can still be truly excellent, such as the Kola Peninsula in northern Russia, parts of eastern Canada, and some of the great Norwegian salmon-river systems. The species has also been introduced into Australia, New Zealand, and Argentina.

Various fishing methods are used, but fly-fishing is the most popular. Atlantic salmon do not feed during the return journey to their spawning rivers, so the angler must tempt them to take the fly.

Leaping salmon
Atlantic salmon returning to their native rivers to spawn must swim against the flow of the river. They often leap spectacularly up rocky falls or other obstructions to reach the spawning grounds.

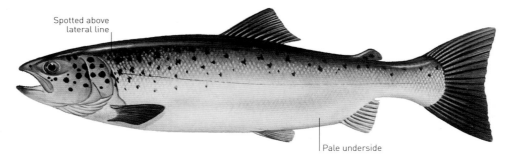

Spotted above lateral line

Pale underside

Chinook salmon

Oncorhynchus tshawytscha

WEIGHT Up to 134 lb (61 kg).

TYPES OF WATER Rivers, lakes, and oceans.

DISTRIBUTION Arctic Ocean and north Pacific Ocean and the rivers that flow into them.

FISHING METHODS Trolling (offshore and estuaries); lure- and fly-fishing (rivers).

These highly prized game fish are also known as king salmon. Chinook are the largest Pacific salmon, and they are immensely hard-fighting, powerful fish. Like all salmon, they begin their lives in freshwater. Chinook salmon fry can migrate to sea when they are only three months old, but generally they remain in the spawning rivers for one to three years before migrating to the oceans, where they feed and mature. These salmon can migrate huge distances at sea; then they return to the rivers they were born in, spawn once, and die. Adult Chinook in the oceans are dark green to blue-black on the head and back, and silvery underneath. As they migrate inland, the breeding colors appear, with tinges of brownish reds and purples.

Offshore trolling

Chinook salmon are among several Pacific salmon species that are successfully caught when feeding in the ocean, prior to returning to rivers for spawning. Anglers take them by trolling just offshore and in the estuaries, as the fish return. They can be caught in large numbers when big schools are found. Like virtually all salmon, Chinook do not feed when they enter river systems, so the river angler must induce the salmon to take lures or flies when they would not do so naturally.

⏏ **Migrating salmon school** At times, the cold waters of the Alaska rivers are filled with dense, migrating schools of Chinook salmon. These large numbers of fish, intent on reaching their spawning ground, are easy prey for large mammals, such as bears.

TYPES OF CHINOOK

There are two types of Chinook salmon: the "stream type," found mostly in the headwaters of larger river systems, and the "ocean type," found mostly in coastal streams and rivers. Stream-type Chinook spend a long time in freshwater, whereas those of the ocean type often remain in freshwater for only a year before migrating to the ocean. During their ocean-living phase, ocean-type Chinook salmon usually remain in coastal waters.

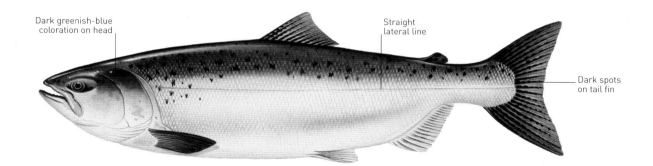

Dark greenish-blue coloration on head

Straight lateral line

Dark spots on tail fin

Coho salmon
Oncorhynchus kisutch

WEIGHT Up to 33 lb (15 kg).

TYPES OF WATER Rivers, lakes, oceans.

DISTRIBUTION North Pacific Ocean and the rivers that flow into it.

FISHING METHODS Trolling with lures (offshore); spinning and fly-fishing (rivers).

The coho salmon is an extremely important game species to anglers. At sea, coho salmon are a dark metallic blue-green with small black spots on the upper sides, and silver paling to white underneath. When running inland for the spawning season, the fish turn bright green on the head and back, red on the sides, and dark underneath.

Young coho salmon will usually spend one to two years in their spawning rivers and then migrate at night either to the sea or to lakes. Here they feed on plankton, crustaceans, small fish, and jellyfish. Some never leave the freshwater lakes and, while they may be sexually mature, they never spawn. Like all Pacific salmon, coho return to the river in which they were born to breed and then die after spawning. In rivers, coho salmon do not tend to mix with the more aggressive salmon species like the chum and the Chinook (opposite).

A prized quarry

Coho salmon are renowned for being very hard-fighting fish and, while not as large as the Chinook salmon, they are nevertheless a highly prized quarry. Inland, they are caught by spinning and fly-fishing. Fly anglers, especially, look for slower-moving waters in which to fish for this species. At sea, anglers catch coho salmon mainly by trolling, using downriggers and lures.

Dark spots on upper part of tail fin

Pale gum line of lower jaw

☑ **Coho salmon fishing**
Anglers fish from boats in the waters of Giltoyees River, Douglas Channel, British Columbia, as the coho salmon run in from the Pacific.

Largemouth bass
Micropterus salmoides

WEIGHT Up to 22¼ lb (10 kg).

TYPES OF WATER Lakes, ponds, rivers, and creeks.

DISTRIBUTION North America from Canada to northern Mexico.

FISHING METHODS Bait-, lure-, and fly-fishing.

A member of the black bass family, which are active and sometimes cannibalistic predators, the largemouth bass has an upper jaw that extends to behind its eye—hence the name. This species feeds predominantly on smaller fish, frogs, and crayfish, but does not feed during spawning. As the water warms up, so does its metabolism: the preferred temperatures for feeding are from 50–80° F (10–27° C); it feeds most heavily from 68–80° F (20–27° C). Like all species of black bass, the largemouth bass

⏫ **Largemouth bass** Largemouth bass prefer tranquil, clear waters where they can search for prey among the small fish and other creatures that hide in reeds or among bankside vegetation.

thrives in clear water with either overgrown banks or extensive reed beds. The biggest largemouth bass are found in the rivers of Florida. A whole industry has grown up in the US around these immensely popular fish, with professional tournament circuits and huge prize money to be won.

Other black bass species

The smallmouth bass (*Micropterus dolomieui*), distinguished by a jaw that does not extend beyond the eye, is a renowned hard-fighting fish. The spotted bass (*Micropterus punctulatus*) is named after the dark spots along the flank and belly areas, and a dark spot on the gill cover. Its mouth does not extend beyond the eye. It is found mainly in the Mississippi and Ohio River basins.

Spiny first dorsal fin

Soft-rayed second dorsal fin

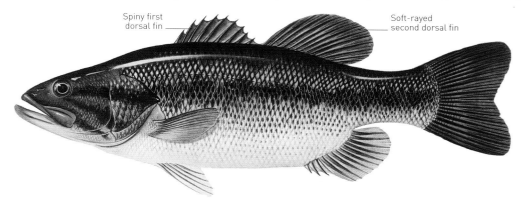

Black crappie

Pomoxis nigromaculatus

WEIGHT Up to 6 lb (2.75 kg).

TYPES OF WATER Ponds, rivers, and lakes.

DISTRIBUTION North America.

FISHING METHODS Very light tackle, bait-, lure-, and fly-fishing.

The black crappie and its close relative the white crappie (*Pomoxis annularis*) are very popular fish in parts of the US, both for sport and for eating. The black crappie tends to be bigger than the white crappie, but neither reach large sizes. These species are relatives of the black bass family and are generally found in the same kinds of waters, such as ponds, rivers, and lakes. The black crappie thrives better in slightly clearer water than the white. Crappies tend to school around weed beds and over mud or sand, and feed on small insect larvae and crustaceans. Larger individuals will also eat small fish.

A favorite time to fish for crappies is when the water starts to warm up in spring. These fish spawn when the water reaches around 52°F (11°C), but just before spawning, when the temperature of the water is 48–51°F (9–10°C), they move into shallow water and feed voraciously. They are often found in coves, around rocks, and among sunken trees. Fishing with small jigs is a popular strategy.

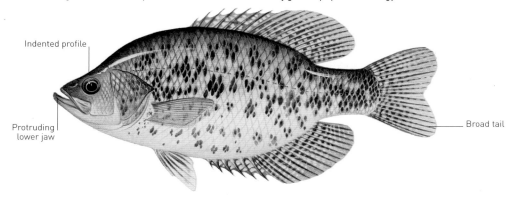

Indented profile

Protruding lower jaw

Broad tail

Tench

Tinca tinca

WEIGHT Up to 16½ lb (7.5 kg).

TYPES OF WATER Slow-moving or still water in ponds, lakes, or rivers.

DISTRIBUTION Europe and Asia.

FISHING METHODS Predominantly bait-fishing, usually float-fishing or bottom-fishing.

Tench are a popular fishing quarry throughout Europe, and are known as dogged fighters when hooked. They live in relatively warm ponds and lakes, but can inhabit the slow-moving or still lower sections of some rivers. They are famous for feeding hardest around dawn, on the edge of dense vegetation such as reed beds. During winter, tench are known to remain in the mud and not feed.

Tench breed in shallow water, and the larvae remain attached to plants for a few days after hatching. They are slow-growing fish and their small scales are covered in a dense layer of protective slime. Male tench have a longer pelvic fin than the female. Dawn is traditionally considered by anglers to be the best time of day for tench fishing.

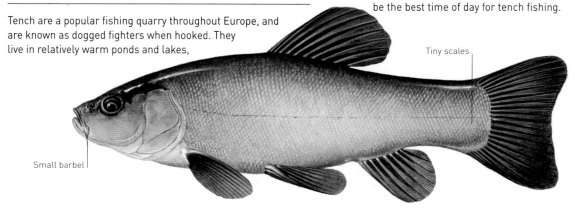

Tiny scales

Small barbel

◀ **Barbels on barbels**
The distinctive barbels (or barbules) of this species enable the fish to feed on bottom-dwelling invertebrates, which they can grab from the surface of the river bed or dig up from the bottom.

Barbel

Barbus barbus

WEIGHT Up to 26½ lb (12 kg).

TYPES OF WATER Medium- to fast-running rivers.

DISTRIBUTION Europe (not Ireland and Scotland) and Asia.

FISHING METHODS Float-fishing and bottom-fishing, especially with a swimfeeder; also fly-fishing.

The barbel is viewed by many freshwater anglers as perhaps the classic river fish to target. An immensely powerful and hard-fighting fish, the barbel has classic, sleek lines that enable it to feed tight to the bottom, using its fleshy lips to scoop up crustaceans, mollusks, and insect larvae. Barbel can often be sight-fished for, due to their preference for fast-running, clean water. There are various subspecies of barbel that are extensively fished for in parts of Europe, and they can at times be targeted with dry flies. The four barbels (or barbules) on their downturned mouth, from which these fish get their name, give them extra taste and touch abilities.

Barbel spawn from May to June, tending to migrate farther upstream to shed small yellow eggs, usually over a sandy bottom in shallow water. These eggs hatch in about two weeks. Young barbel have a greenish color, and can look similar to gudgeon, although gudgeon have two barbels on the mouth compared to the barbel's four.

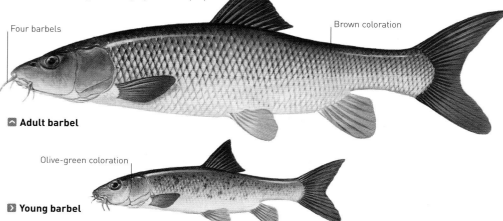

Four barbels

Brown coloration

◢ **Adult barbel**

Olive-green coloration

▶ **Young barbel**

Common carp
Cyprinus carpio

WEIGHT Up to 81 lb (37 kg).

TYPES OF WATER Large bodies of slow-moving or still water, such as natural and artificial lakes; prefers an environment with a soft or muddy bottom.

DISTRIBUTION Europe and Asia; introduced in North America and Australasia.

FISHING METHODS Bait-fishing (float-fishing, freelining, or bottom-fishing); also fly-fishing with imitation flies.

The common (or king) carp is an immensely popular fishing quarry throughout Europe, and is growing more popular in other areas of the world. Part of the attraction of this species as a target for anglers is the fact that individuals can grow to a very large size. In warm, food-rich waters, carp grow fast and can easily put on about 2 lb (1 kg) in weight every year.

The common carp is a deep-bodied fish. It has no scales on the head, but its body is covered with them. The varied diet of this species includes

⌃ **Caught and released** Large carp in protected waters are usually returned carefully to the water after being caught, to give other anglers the chance of good sport. They may live to be caught and released many times.

plants, insects, worms, and crustaceans, which it sucks in with a vacuumlike action. The common carp can spawn only when the water temperature rises to about 64° F (18° C). In Europe this is usually from late May to June. These long-lived fish can reach an age of more than 40 years old.

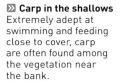

» **Carp in the shallows** Extremely adept at swimming and feeding close to cover, carp are often found among the vegetation near the bank.

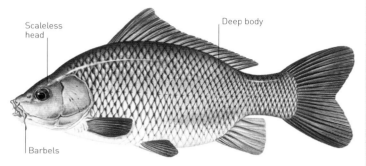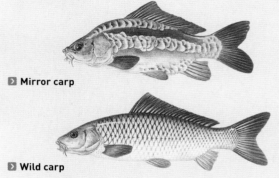

The common carp has evolved after hundreds of years of selective breeding. There are three varieties of common carp that are fished for, the standard common carp, the mirror carp (see panel, right), and the leather carp. The crucian carp (*Carassius carassius*), a separate species, is a popular target among some freshwater anglers. Highly tolerant of variable conditions, it lives in ponds and lakes and burrows into the mud during dry periods or in winter.

Scaleless head

Deep body

Barbels

CARP VARIETIES

The common carp is descended from the wild carp that were introduced from Asia to Europe for food purposes during the Middle Ages. Found in only a few waters today, wild carp have a more elongated body and usually weigh under 15 lb (7 kg). The mirror carp, a variety of the modern common carp, is completely covered with large, irregularly shaped scales. There are a number of types of mirror carp; the linear type (below) has a distinct line of scales along its lateral line.

▶ **Mirror carp**

▶ **Wild carp**

Roach
Rutilus rutilus

WEIGHT Up to 4 lb (1.8 kg).

TYPES OF WATER Stlll and slow-moving waters.

DISTRIBUTION Europe and Asia.

FISHING METHODS Bait-fishing, mainly bottom-fishing and float-fishing.

The roach is one of the most popular freshwater fishing quarries in Europe. This species has an upturned mouth, much like the rudd (opposite), that enables it to take food from the surface of the water. The roach inhabits mainly slow-moving rivers, canals, and well-vegetated still waters. Known for its ability to thrive in muddy or poor-quality water, the roach can also thrive in brackish inshore conditions, migrating up rivers from the sea in order to breed. It feeds primarily on insects, crustaceans, mollusks, and plants—adult roach seem to prefer the latter.

The roach dislikes bright light and is most easily caught in cloudy conditions. It spawns among vegetation, from late spring through to summer. This species often interbreeds with the common bream (below) and rudd (opposite). The roach multiplies fast and, where introduced, may become a pest. This shy fish can be caught using a variety of bait-fishing methods.

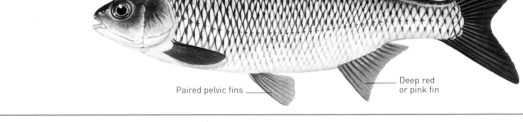

Red iris

Paired pelvic fins

Deep red or pink fin

Common bream
Abramis brama

WEIGHT Up to 13¼ lb (6 kg).

TYPES OF WATER Still and slow-moving waters.

DISTRIBUTION From Europe to central Asia.

FISHING METHODS Bait-fishing, either float-fishing or bottom-fishing.

The most widely fished freshwater bream species is the common bream (also known as the bronze bream). It is found in still and slow-running waters, principally lakes, rivers, and ponds, often swimming in large schools. Many places in Europe are famous for huge catches of schooling bream. Bream tend to feed on insects and small crustaceans, but larger ones are known to feed on smaller fish. Not a particularly hard-fighting species, common bream are nevertheless much sought after by many anglers. The roach-bream hybrid is common in some places where schools of roach and bream spawn in the same areas. The distinctive common bream of Ireland's Shannon River system tend to have striped markings and are often larger than common bream found elsewhere.

Scaleless head

Deep narrow body

Long anal fin

European chub
Squalius cephalus

WEIGHT Up to 17¾ lb (8 kg).

TYPES OF WATER Rivers and lakes.

DISTRIBUTION Europe and Asia.

FISHING METHODS Bait-fishing, mainly bottom-fishing and float-fishing; can be caught on flies.

A solid body and strong, rounded fins characterize this popular freshwater fishing target. It is found in rivers, and sometimes in lakes. The European chub prefers medium- to fast-flowing clean water; it is also known to enter brackish water in the eastern Baltic. While young European chub form schools, adults are solitary fish. Spawning is from April to June in sheltered waters.

Adults of this species are powerful and opportunistic feeders, whose natural diet includes frogs, worms, smaller fish, crustaceans, insects, and seeds and berries that fall into the water from overhanging trees. They take a wide variety of baits; bread is particularly effective.

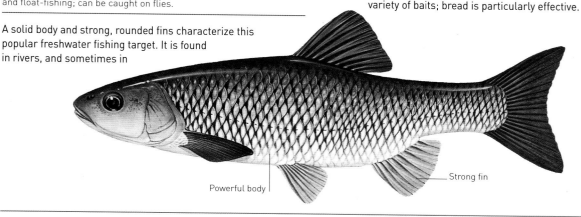

Powerful body

Strong fin

Rudd
Scardinius erythrophthalmus

WEIGHT Up to 4½ lb (2 kg).

TYPES OF WATER Still and slow-moving waters.

DISTRIBUTION Europe and Asia.

FISHING METHODS Bait-fishing, mainly bottom-fishing and float-fishing.

At first glance, the rudd looks very much like a roach (opposite), but there are two main differences: a rudd's dorsal fin is set farther back than that of a roach and, while a roach has red irises, a rudd's are yellow to orange. This species is found mainly in relatively still waters, such as canals, ponds, and marshlands. It prefers thickly overgrown areas near the banks. The rudd is happy to feed closer to the surface than the roach, but the diets of both species are similar—mainly small crustaceans, aquatic plants, and insect larvae. Rudd spawn from late spring to early summer (May and June).

A favorite quarry of many freshwater anglers, the rudd has been introduced widely in Europe and Asia. It responds well to small, natural baits, such as bread and maggots, and can be successfully fished "on the drop," a technique in which there is little or no weight under a float, allowing the bait to sink naturally down through the water.

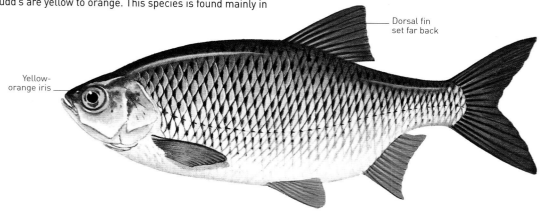

Dorsal fin set far back

Yellow-orange iris

Grayling

Thymallus thymallus

WEIGHT Up to 15 lb (6.7 kg).

TYPES OF WATER Rivers, streams, occasionally lakes.

DISTRIBUTION Northern North America and northern Europe.

FISHING METHODS Bait-, lure-, and fly-fishing.

The grayling is not a particularly large fish, growing to a maximum of about 2 ft (60 cm) in length, but it has a highly distinctive, large dorsal fin. It is gregarious, forming schools, and prefers to live in well-oxygenated, running water. It is commonly found in rivers, and in North America it can be found in lakes. It is particularly susceptible to pollution and thrives best in clean water, usually in the upper parts of a river with a gravel or sandy bottom. It feeds predominantly on a varied diet of insects, nymphs, worms, and crustaceans.

They spawn in spring and early summer in gravel-bottomed, shallow parts of the river. Grayling of the North American lakes come into the streams for spawning. The use of small lures or spinners, or baits, are among the most common methods used to target fish of this species. Fly-fishing techniques can also be effective.

DWARFING

In waters where large numbers of grayling congregate, the amount of food available to each fish is limited, and small, deep-bodied individuals, with a weight no more than half the maximum recorded, are common. The large dorsal fin still gives the fish extra leverage against the angler, making the grayling a popular catch.

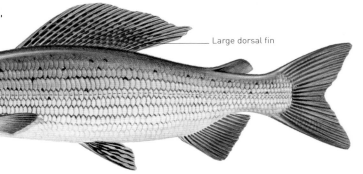

Large dorsal fin

《 Distinctive dorsal fin
The oversized dorsal fin becomes more highly colored in the breeding season and is used by the male grayling to wrap over the female during spawning.

« **A camouflaged hunter** The barred and spotted markings of the northern pike give good camouflage for this voracious predator, hiding among weed beds. Its sharp teeth are able to deal with quite large prey.

Northern pike

Esox lucius

WEIGHT Up to 77 lb (35 kg).

TYPES OF WATER Quiet lakes, ponds, and rivers; occasionally brackish waters.

DISTRIBUTION North America; Europe; and central Asia.

FISHING METHODS Bait-, lure-, and fly-fishing.

The northern pike is an extremely adept, streamlined predator. Its body is designed principally for intense bursts of high speed, while a long, flat snout, plenty of extremely sharp teeth, and complex jaws enable it to take relatively large prey fish and even small aquatic animals. This fish prefers a solitary existence, and it is a skillful and aggressive feeder, often using weeds for cover. It can also be cannibalistic, attacking smaller fish of its own species. It inhabits clear lakes, ponds, and rivers, and is considered a territorial fish. On some coastlines, the northern pike enters brackish water to feed on sea fish.

It is generally accepted that some of the largest pike are to be found in the larger lochs of Scotland and Ireland. Most of the specimens caught are much smaller than the maximum recorded weight: 10–20 lb (4.5–9 kg) is more common for line-caught pike. Northern pike are usually targeted with baits and lures. Some massive pike have also been caught on fly-fishing tackle. Their sharp teeth require the use of wire traces. A close relative, the huge muskellunge or "muskie" (*Esox masquinongy*) of North America is a popular quarry that can grow larger than the northern pike.

Protruding lower jaw

Wels catfish
Silurus glanis

WEIGHT Up to 675 lb (306 kg).

TYPES OF WATER Deep water in weedy lakes, slow-moving rivers, brackish waters.

DISTRIBUTION Europe and Asia.

FISHING METHODS Bait-fishing.

Although the giant wels catfish is native only to eastern and central Europe, it has been introduced into a far wider area, including much of western Europe and Asia. It is among the largest freshwater fish in the world and is considered an exciting sporting challenge. The Ebro River in Spain is one of the most famous places to fish for this big catfish. The wels catfish has a body with no scales, a broad, blunt head, and six distinctive barbels around the mouth. It is a voracious predator that will feed extensively on local fish populations, small mammals, and even waterfowl, and is most active at night.

A specialized form of fishing that is sometimes used is for a helper to take lines with baits too large to be cast, from the bank out into the river by boat. The baits are then anchored with light lines. Powerful rods, reels, and lines are needed to subdue these huge fish. Various other catfish species are fished for throughout the world, especially in the US, where favored species include the blue catfish (*Ictalurus furcatus*) and the channel catfish (*Ictalurus punctatus*).

Broad head

Scaleless body

>> **Voracious appetite**
A male wels catfish looks ferocious, with long barbels and a wide mouth—and indeed he is, feeding on mammals and waterfowl as well as smaller fish.

Zander

Sander lucioperca

WEIGHT Up to 44 lb (20 kg).

TYPES OF WATER Deep lakes, canals, and rivers.

DISTRIBUTION Eastern, central, and northern Europe; western Asia.

FISHING METHODS Bait-, lure-, and fly-fishing.

Also known as the pike perch, the zander is native to the Danube River and other northern and central European waters, but it has been extensively introduced elsewhere for sport-fishing purposes. It is a voracious predator of small fish and is blamed for drastically reducing stocks of local freshwater species in some areas. The zander prefers the deep waters of lakes, canals, and rivers and remains around deep trenches during the winter months. In spring it moves upstream for spawning. After spawning, it remains in pools for about two weeks before spreading out again.

The zander has reflective material behind its eyeballs that enables it to hunt effectively in low-light conditions, and it is often most active at night. A smaller relative, the walleye (*Sander vitreus*), is the largest of the North American perch species, and a popular angling quarry.

Spineless gill cover

Large teeth

Slender body

European perch

Perca fluviatilis

WEIGHT Up to 10½ lb (4.75 kg).

TYPES OF WATER Warm, slow-moving rivers, lakes, and ponds.

DISTRIBUTION Europe and Asia.

FISHING METHODS Bait-, lure-, and fly-fishing.

The European perch inhabits rivers, lakes, and ponds, but avoids fast-flowing and excessively cold waters. It is also found in brackish waters in some regions. It is distinctively marked with five to nine transverse black bands on the body, yellow-brown pectoral fins, and red pelvic and anal fins. The European perch is a predatory species that takes a wide variety of invertebrates and small fish. It spawns in spring. The eggs are not eaten by other fish, helping their chances of survival.

Young perch tend to hunt in schools and can often be observed chasing prey close to the edges of rivers and lakes. Older fish tend to feed most in the morning and the evening, especially in the few hours before complete darkness.

Anglers who wish to target this fish need a thorough understanding of its habits, but most importantly, the water must have a good supply of its favored prey. Those seeking to catch large specimens often choose to fish around obstacles in or near the water, such as overhanging branches and sunken trees.

Greenish-yellow coloration

Yellow-brown pectoral fins

Transverse black bands

Nile perch
Lates niloticus

WEIGHT Up to 440 lb (200 kg).

TYPES OF WATER Lakes and large rivers;
occasionally brackish waters.

DISTRIBUTION Northern, central, and eastern Africa.

FISHING METHODS Mainly lure- and bait-fishing; also fly-fishing.

Nile perch inhabit lakes and various river systems in Africa, including the Nile, and are a popular fishing quarry. They can grow very large, up to 6 ft (2 m) in length, and are adept at living in waters of all depths. They are voracious predators, feeding predominantly on smaller fish, while the juveniles also feed on crustaceans, and on various insects.

They are fished for on many lakes, including Lake Nasser in Egypt and Lake Victoria in central Africa (source of the White Nile), and in Uganda around Murchison Falls. They can be caught using a variety of techniques. Lures and baits account for most Nile perch, but many anglers believe that it is possible to take large Nile perch on fly-fishing tackle, using big flies and powerful tackle. Lake Nasser is one of the locations where this might be possible, especially when Nile perch enter shallow water to prey on tilapia that have moved into the shallows to spawn.

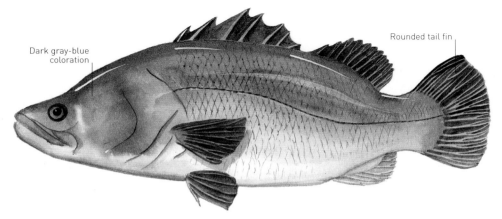

Dark gray-blue coloration

Rounded tail fin

» **Turbulent perch waters** Nile perch grow to a massive size in the fast-moving waters around Murchison Falls. Fishing these waters calls for steady feet and strong tackle.

« Armor-plated fish
Golden mahseer thrive in conditions, including rapids, in which lesser fish simply cannot survive. The angler needs to be prepared for a huge challenge from a strong fighter.

Golden mahseer

Tor putitora

WEIGHT Up to 119 lb (54 kg).

TYPES OF WATER Lakes and fast-flowing rivers.

DISTRIBUTION Asia, particularly the Indian subcontinent.

FISHING METHODS Bait-, lure-, and fly-fishing.

The immensely powerful golden mahseer is a distinctively large-scaled member of the carp family. Golden mahseer in northern India tend to have a slender body shape, while the southern Indian representatives of the species have deeper bodies, and can grow very large—up to 9 ft (2.75 m) in length.

Golden mahseer prefer fast-flowing rivers with rocky bottoms. They are omnivorous, feeding on fish, insect larvae, zooplankton, and plants. Adults ascend the streams to breed over gravel and stones, returning to lower reaches of the rivers, or to lakes and river-fed ponds, after breeding.

They are a classic freshwater fishing species; it takes an adventurous angler to brave the heat of southern India, and to fish big river systems such as the Kaveri (Cauvery). Here, the golden mahseer feed in the fastest rapids and rocky areas, and many fish will hit baits and lures with such power that they are lost during the fight. Fishing with baits and lures usually works well, but if the conditions are right, golden mahseer can also be caught with big flies on very powerful fishing tackle.

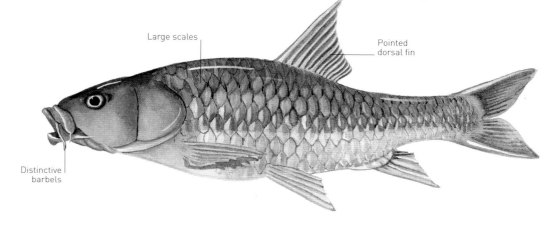

Large scales

Pointed dorsal fin

Distinctive barbels

Tiger fish
Hydrocynus vittatus

WEIGHT Up to 62lb (28kg).

TYPES OF WATER Warm rivers and lakes.

DISTRIBUTION Africa.

FISHING METHODS Bait-, lure-, and fly-fishing.

Tiger fish are ferocious freshwater predators that swim in certain warm river systems in southern and central Africa, and are especially well known in the Zambezi. A popular species among anglers because of their voracious appetites and hard-fighting abilities, tiger fish are also targeted commercially in many areas by local subsistence fishermen.

Growing up to a yard (meter) long, tiger fish are instantly recognizable by their protruding front teeth. They prefer to live in warm, well-oxygenated waters, principally the bigger rivers and lakes inhabited by large numbers of

GOLIATH TIGER FISH

Huge goliath tiger fish (*Hydrocynus goliath*) live predominantly in the Congo River system. They grow to more than 100 lb (45 kg) and are renowned as tough fighters. Angling for these fish demands big hooks and substantial wire traces. However, due to political conflict in the Democratic Republic of Congo, in recent years it has been virtually impossible for traveling anglers to target these massive predatory fish.

smaller prey species (tiger fish target most smaller species of fish). They tend to collect in schools of similar-sized fish, with only the larger specimens remaining solitary. Spinning and bait-fishing are the usual ways of fishing for tiger fish, but recently fly-fishing has also become popular, especially on the Zambezi. Tiger fish have hard, bony mouths, and it can be difficult to hook them securely. They will often jump when hooked.

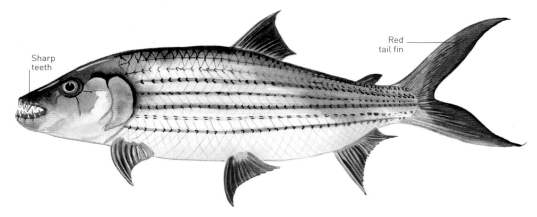

Sharp teeth

Red tail fin

» Distinctive profile
Few fish are as instantly recognizable as the tiger fish, with its sharp, protruding teeth and large, predatory eyes.

Smallmouth yellowfish
Labeobarbus aeneus

WEIGHT Up to 17lb (7.75kg).

TYPES OF WATER Fast-flowing rivers.

DISTRIBUTION Africa, specifically the Vaal and Orange River systems of South Africa.

FISHING METHODS Bait- and fly-fishing.

Smallmouth yellowfish are greenish above, and golden-yellow underneath and around the mouth and tail fin. They grow to about 1¾ ft (50 cm) in length. They prefer the fast-flowing, clear sections, with rocky or sandy bottoms, and tend to swim in shoals of up to 30 fish.

Smallmouth yellowfish feed aggressively and move constantly, often working among boulders in fast sections of rapids, and are adept at rooting out insect larvae. They will eat almost anything from plankton up to the size of a small fish. They usually begin to feed at the base of a system of rapids, gradually working their way upstream. Smallmouth yellowfish breed in spring and summer, moving upstream to find suitable gravel breeding beds.

LARGEMOUTH YELLOWFISH

Largemouth yellowfish (*Labeobarbus kimberleyensis*) are found only in South Africa. They are a large-scaled freshwater fish and are more silvery than the predominantly golden yellow-colored smallmouth. True predators, they fight extremely hard. Although close relatives of the barbel, yellowfish in fact are far closer in feeding habits to trout and grayling, and should be fished for accordingly.

While Czech nymphing (*see* pp.174–175) techniques are usually the most effective, at times these fish will take dry flies.

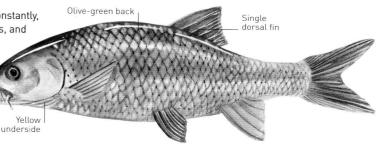
Olive-green back
Single dorsal fin
Yellow underside

Golden dorado
Salminus brasiliensis

WEIGHT Up to 75lb (34kg).

TYPES OF WATER Rivers and river basins, relatively warm waters.

DISTRIBUTION Central South America.

FISHING METHODS Bait-, lure-, and fly-fishing.

Known simply as "dorado" in South America—dorado means "golden" in Spanish—these fish are known as golden dorado to anglers around the rest of the world. Prized by anglers all over

Central South America, over the last 20 years or so these magnificent fish have become one of the premier freshwater targets for fly anglers. Golden dorado prefer warmer rivers and river basins, and will migrate many miles upstream to spawn during spring and summer. They will also follow shoals of baitfish.

In some respects golden dorado are the ultimate freshwater game fish—a powerful predator that grows to a large size, with the females growing larger than males. Golden dorado hit lures, flies, and bait with incredible aggression; they fight very hard and will jump repeatedly in an effort to shed the hook; and they are a truly beautiful fish. It is essential to use short wire traces because their teeth are so sharp. Like many species of fish the golden dorado is in decline in some areas.

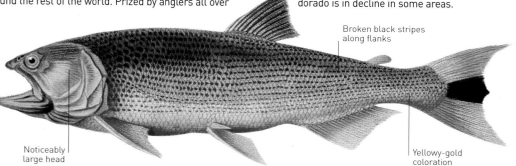
Broken black stripes along flanks
Noticeably large head
Yellowy-gold coloration

Saltwater fish

Almost every part of every ocean contains fish, and it is the sheer scale of possibilities that makes learning about the fish that swim in the sea so fascinating. All that you learn must be continually refined and adapted, as you begin to understand the fish you chase and their varied habits. Some of the largest and most aggressive sporting fish are targeted in the world's seas and oceans, which include many wonderfully exciting environments.

Atlantic cod

Gadus morhua

WEIGHT Up to 212 lb (96 kg).

TYPES OF WATER Temperate and cold waters, from shoreline to continental shelf.

DISTRIBUTION North Atlantic Ocean.

FISHING METHODS Bait- and lure-fishing.

Subject to intense commercial pressure for centuries, the Atlantic cod stocks of Britain, Greenland, and Newfoundland are close to total collapse; only rigorously enforced conservation methods will ensure the survival of this species. However, in countries such as Norway and Iceland it is still possible to enjoy fishing for large cod, both from boats and the shore.

Cod can grow up to 6½ ft (2 m) long. Their coloration can vary from brown to green or gray on the back, paling to white or silver underneath.

Wide-ranging and omnivorous

Atlantic cod inhabit a wide range of habitats, including estuaries, inshore waters, wrecks, reefs, and deepwater fjords, right out to the edge of the continental shelf. They are most likely to come close inshore during rough seas. Atlantic cod are voracious feeders, eating everything from weed and invertebrates to small fish, even including the young of their own species. They school in large numbers, close to the bottom. They are caught mainly on baits and lures (jigs, pirks, or shads) fished from the bottom to mid-waters, but they can also be caught using big flies close to the seabed.

Schooling Atlantic cod Atlantic cod are a favorite fish for sport and for the table. Although they can grow to very large sizes, they often come close inshore, where they can be targeted by anglers from the beach or rocks, or from boats.

White lateral line

Single barbel

Square-ended tail

Ling
Molva molva

WEIGHT Up to 99 lb (45 kg).

TYPES OF WATER Deep, inshore, temperate waters, on rocky bottoms.

DISTRIBUTION North Atlantic Ocean; Mediterranean.

FISHING METHODS Bait- and lure-fishing.

A member of the cod family, the ling can grow to an impressive size. This species is reddish brown on the back and pale underneath, and its sides have a marbled pattern. The ling has a long chin barbel and a black spot is sometimes discernible on the rear of the first dorsal fin. The second dorsal fin and the anal fin are relatively long. Its diet includes fish, crustaceans,

FISHING FOR LING

Generally fished for close to the seabed, ling respond well to fish baits fished tight to the bottom, but are also successfully targeted by anglers using baited and unbaited lures (pirks and large jigs). The biggest specimens of ling that are caught on rod and line tend to be found in deep water around the Norwegian coastline during late winter and early spring.

and other bottom-dwelling invertebrates. The ling will often take baits intended for conger eels, and also lures intended for pollack and coalfish. It is often found in large numbers around deepwater wrecks and reefs, but is also occasionally targeted from the shore when the water is deep.

Chin barbel

Stout tail fin

Coalfish
Pollachius virens

WEIGHT Up to 70 lb (32 kg).

TYPES OF WATER Temperate and cold waters, deep, over rocks, and inshore.

DISTRIBUTION North Atlantic Ocean and Arctic Ocean.

FISHING METHODS Lure- and fly-fishing.

Coalfish are known as pollack in some parts of the world and coalfish or saithe in others. To distinguish a coalfish from its relative the pollack (*Pollachius pollachius*), look for a bottom jaw

that does not protrude, a more silvery overall color, and a prominent white lateral line that does not have a distinct curve. Coalfish form large schools that feed primarily on smaller fish and crustaceans.

The largest coalfish are found over reefs and wrecks, but in areas of extremely deep water and fast tides, big coalfish will come inshore. A more powerful fighting fish than the pollack, coalfish will repeatedly crash-dive for the bottom when hooked. Lures tend to be the most effective means of catching coalfish, but because they often come higher in the water to feed than pollack, for example, big flies fished at the correct depths can also be successfully used to catch this species.

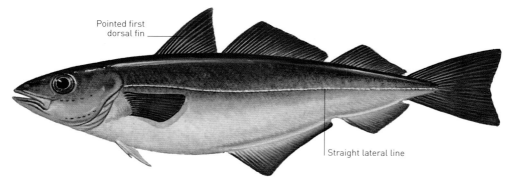

Pointed first dorsal fin

Straight lateral line

Pollack
Pollachius pollachius

WEIGHT Up to 39½ lb (18 kg).

TYPES OF WATER Coastal waters.

DISTRIBUTION Northeastern Atlantic Ocean.

FISHING METHODS Bait-, lure-, and fly-fishing, from shore or boats.

Pollack are gaining increased value as a commercial fish as cod stocks suffer from a dramatic decline. They are recognized primarily by a protruding lower jaw, a dark top half of the body (often greenish-brown), and a prominent lateral line with a distinct curve to it.

Pollack can be found from the shoreline through to deep water, though they tend to inhabit areas of rough or broken ground; specimens found on sandy bottoms are usually smaller. Traditionally, the largest pollack have been caught when fishing over deepwater wrecks, especially off the southwest of England, but many northern European coastlines hold good populations of these fish. They feed mainly on smaller fish and occasionally on crustaceans. Other species that are sometimes encountered in similar waters include the haddock (*Melanogrammus aeglefinus*), in deep water, and the whiting (*Merlangius merlangus*), part of the cod family that may be caught from the shore in the winter months but prefers deeper waters at other times of year.

Fishing for pollack
An accessible fish for the shore angler, pollack are known for their powerful crash-dive upon being hooked. Lure-fishing works well for pollack, but they will take baits off the bottom at times. Fly-fishing may also be effective when the water is not too deep.

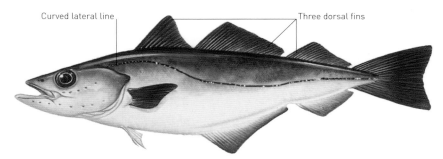

Curved lateral line

Three dorsal fins

☑ **Fishing for pollack**
A rocky coastline is the ideal place for adventurous sea anglers to find large, strong pollack.

European sea bass

Dicentrarchus labrax

WEIGHT Up to 26½ lb (12 kg).

TYPES OF WATER Coastal waters, estuaries.

DISTRIBUTION Northeastern and eastern Atlantic Ocean.

FISHING METHODS Bait-, lure-, and fly-fishing, from shore or boats.

European sea bass, known simply as bass to anglers throughout Europe, are important sport fish, where they are fished for from boats close to shore, and from the shore. They are under extreme commercial fishing pressure because of their eating qualities.

Instantly recognizable, with a spiked dorsal fin, gray-blue back, silver sides, and white belly,

European sea bass tend to form large schools when young (small sea bass are known as school bass or "schoolies"). They inhabit coastal waters to a depth of about 328 ft (100 m) and move up into estuaries, creeks, and on rare occasions river systems in summer. European sea bass can feed in shallow water over rocks, weed, mud, and sand, and are therefore much sought after by shore-anglers. They migrate farther offshore in colder weather and their range seems to be spreading farther north, perhaps as a result of warming oceans. They spawn in the spring or early summer.

Aggressive predators, European sea bass feed mainly on shrimps and mollusks, but also on other fish. A variety of baits and lures are used. They can also be caught on flies.

⌃ Schooling bass
Young European sea bass form large schools in shallow coastal waters and estuaries, often feeding in very shallow water.

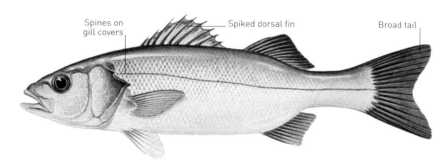

Spines on gill covers   Spiked dorsal fin   Broad tail

Conger eel
Conger conger

WEIGHT Up to 242 lb (110 kg).

TYPES OF WATER Shallow or deep coastal waters, over broken ground, reefs, and wrecks.

DISTRIBUTION Northeastern and east-central Atlantic Ocean; Mediterranean.

FISHING METHODS Bottom-fished baits.

Conger eels grow up to 10 ft (3 m) in length, and have a slender appearance. They are scaleless, dark gray, and pale underneath, with a continuous, vertical fin. They inhabit an extreme range of depths, from the shallowest water close to the shore to waters more than 1,640 ft (500 m) deep. Conger eels feed on the bottom on fish and crustaceans.

Large conger eels are most often caught in deep water, mostly over reefs, wrecks, and broken ground, but can also be targeted from the shore. These large specimens are best fished for at night but can be caught during the day in very deep water. Some of the largest conger eels have been caught from deepwater wrecks off the south coast of England, where charter boats specialize in fishing for them. The largest congers are likely to be female.

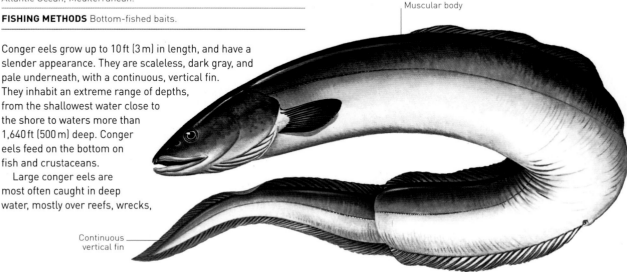

Muscular body

Continuous vertical fin

Ballan wrasse
Labrus bergylta

WEIGHT Up to 10 lb (4.5 kg).

TYPES OF WATER Shallow coastal waters.

DISTRIBUTION Northeastern and east-central Atlantic Ocean.

FISHING METHODS Bait- or lure-fishing, on the bottom or with deep floats.

The ballan wrasse is a solidly built fish up to 2 ft (60 cm) in length, with a deep body and large head. A small mouth protrudes with thick, fleshy lips and large, strong, rounded teeth. A large dorsal fin extends down the back; coloration varies between shades of olive, brown, dark green, and red, usually with white spots all over. This species is usually found in rocky locations in water less than 66 ft (20 m) in depth, so is popular among shore anglers. It feeds mainly on mollusks and crustaceans, crushing them with powerful front teeth.

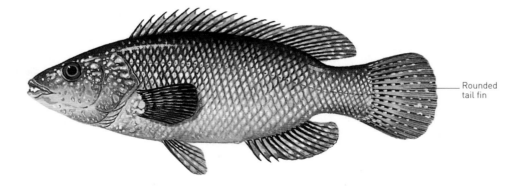

Rounded tail fin

Redfish
Sciaenops ocellatus

WEIGHT Up to 100 lb (45 kg).

TYPES OF WATER Coastal waters and estuaries.

DISTRIBUTION West-central Atlantic Ocean.

FISHING METHODS Bait-, lure-, and fly-fishing from boats or the shore.

The redfish, also called red drum, channel bass, spottail bass, or "croaker" (see below), is one of the most important sport-fishing species in the southern US. Redfish may grow to about 5 ft (1.5 m) in length, although most adults are much smaller. They have an overall red coloration, with one or more dark spots at the base of the tail.

Redfish are found predominantly in coastal waters and estuaries, mostly over sand and muddy bottoms. They prefer to feed in the surf zone, mainly on mollusks, crustaceans, and small fish. When redfish move into shallow and clear water on saltwater flats, it may be possible to sight-fish for them, and here they give excellent sport. In shallow water it is important to approach quietly because redfish spook easily.

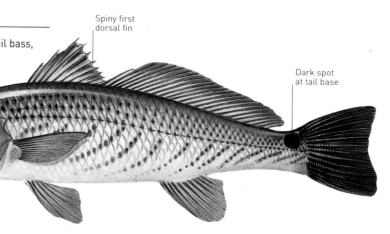

Spiny first dorsal fin

Dark spot at tail base

Black drum
Pogonias cromis

WEIGHT Up to 110 lb (50 kg).

TYPES OF WATER Coastal waters and estuaries.

DISTRIBUTION Western Atlantic Ocean, from Nova Scotia to Argentina, including the Caribbean.

FISHING METHODS Bait-fishing from shore, piers, or boats.

The black drum is a broad, chunky-looking fish with a tall back, and plenty of distinctive barbels under the lower jaw, used for smelling and feeling out prey. The adult black drum has a white underside, but the overall coloration varies from light gray through to almost bronze. The four or five dark vertical bars on the flank disappear with age.

Both black drum and redfish (see above) are often called "croakers" because of their ability to make croaking (or drumming) sounds via an air bladder. Black drum are best at doing this, and anglers can sometimes hear passing schools because of these sounds. Texas is a favored place to fish for large black drum, especially during February and March, when they gather for spawning.

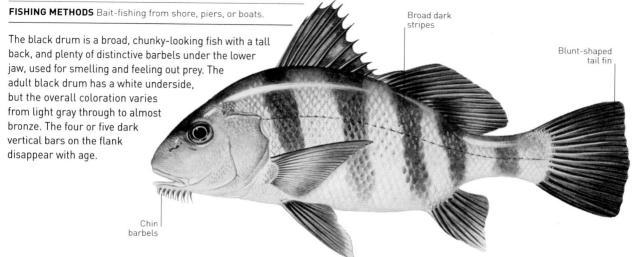

Broad dark stripes

Blunt-shaped tail fin

Chin barbels

Blue marlin
Makaira nigricans

WEIGHT Up to 1,810 lb (820 kg).

TYPES OF WATER Warm, deep waters.

DISTRIBUTION Atlantic Ocean; Indian Ocean; and Pacific Ocean.

FISHING METHODS Trolling with lures and baits.

The striking blue marlin may grow to 16 ft (5 m) in length. As with the black marlin, a cross section of the stout bill is round in profile, and it has two dorsal fins; importantly, the height of the large, first dorsal fin of the blue marlin measures less than the depth of the body. The impressive, bladelike, pectoral fins can be depressed down the sides of the body. Blue marlin are a rich, blue-black color on the upper body, blending into silver underneath, with about fifteen rows of lighter blue stripes on the flanks.

Found in the Pacific, Indian, and Atlantic oceans, the blue marlin tends to prefer deep water. It is a solitary fish that feeds mainly on smaller fish—principally tuna species—and also squid and crustaceans, using its powerful bill

⏏ Deep-water camouflage The largest numbers of blue marlin are said to be found where the water color is blue, possibly because it provides the best camouflage. Anglers prefer to fish for them when the water is clear.

to slash at its intended prey. Fishing for blue marlin is generally by trolling with lures and baits from big-game boats. When hooked, blue marlin jump repeatedly, and give long, powerful runs that may last for many hours. No angler will ever forget a fight with a blue marlin; its strength, endurance, and spectacular jumps leave an indelible impression.

MARLIN SWORDS

Marlin use their bill (or sword) primarily as a tool for hunting and capturing prey. The bill is a sharp spike covered with lots of small serrations and it is used to slash at prey fish in the water. Marlin have also been reported using their bill to both spear and stun their victims. When a marlin is caught, it is vital, from the point of view of safety, that the person grabbing the bill when the marlin is next to the boat does so with gloved hands.

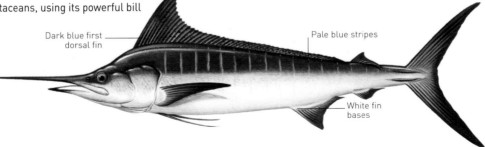

Dark blue first dorsal fin

Pale blue stripes

White fin bases

White marlin
Tetrapturus albidus

WEIGHT Up to 180 lb (82 kg).

TYPES OF WATER Warm waters.

DISTRIBUTION Atlantic Ocean; Caribbean; Mediterranean.

FISHING METHODS Trolling with lures and baits; and fly-fishing.

White marlin are much smaller than other marlin species, up to 10 ft (3 m) in length. Their body color varies from dark blue to dark brown on top, fading down to a silvery white underbelly. There are distinct spots on the large dorsal fin, and the tips of the first dorsal, pectoral, and anal fins are rounded. Sometimes the flanks have rows of rather indistinct, whitish stripes. White marlin are found offshore in the Atlantic Ocean, the Gulf of Mexico, the Caribbean Sea, and parts of the Mediterranean. They are a migratory species, moving into higher latitudes as the waters warm with the seasons. They feed on smaller open-water fish, and squid.

Trolling from big-game boats is the normal method of fishing, but white marlin are fantastic quarry for light-tackle anglers, and can be fished for effectively with lures, baitfish, and flies when the fish are teased close to the boat. They tend to stay close to schools of baitfish, and structural areas such as reefs and canyons offer the best chances of catching a white marlin.

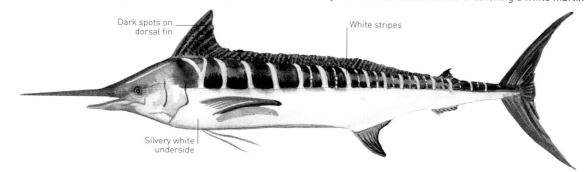

Dark spots on dorsal fin

White stripes

Silvery white underside

Bull huss
Scyliorhinus stellaris

WEIGHT Up to 26 lb (12 kg).

TYPES OF WATER Temperate coastal waters.

DISTRIBUTION Northeastern Atlantic Ocean.

FISHING METHODS Bottom-fished baits.

Also known as the nursehound, the bull huss grows to about 5½ ft (1.7 m) in length. The overall color varies greatly, but the upper body is often light brown in coloration, and is covered with dark spots, and sometimes a few white spots as well. The bull huss has two dorsal fins, set well back; the distinctive nasal flaps form two lobes. Small bull huss can often be mistaken for dogfish, but the nasal flaps on a dogfish form only one lobe. This is the best way to distinguish the species. Bull huss feed on smaller fish, mollusks, and crustaceans. They mate in the fall and the females carry eggs that develop internally for about eight months. Young bull huss are almost perfect replicas of adult fish.

Bull huss are fished for mainly in UK and Irish waters, where they are found over rocky and broken ground, often in very shallow water, and their coloration blends into the background. They are not known for their hard-fighting abilities, but bull huss are a popular shore-fishing quarry, and large specimens can also be caught from boats.

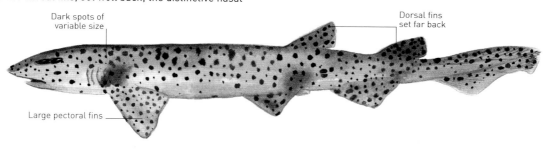

Dark spots of variable size

Dorsal fins set far back

Large pectoral fins

Atlantic halibut
Hippoglossus hippoglossus

WEIGHT Up to 705 lb (320 kg).

TYPES OF WATER Deep, cold water.

DISTRIBUTION Northern Atlantic Ocean.

FISHING METHODS Bait- and lure-fishing, from boats.

One of the largest sea fish, Atlantic halibut have large mouths and slightly forked tails; their upper bodies are greenish-brown to dark brown, and the undersides are white to gray. The eyes are on the upper side of the right-hand side of the body. A lateral line curves over the large pectoral fin. Halibut feed on other fish and large crustaceans. In some areas they have become rare due to overfishing.

Sport-fishing for halibut
Atlantic halibut are fished for by anglers primarily from boats over deep water. They are fished for with baits and big lures, either at anchor or drifting, or by using downriggers and slow-trolling. It is also possible, in rare circumstances, to catch them from the shore. Halibut fight hard, and need to be handled with care when landing to avoid injury to both angler and fish.

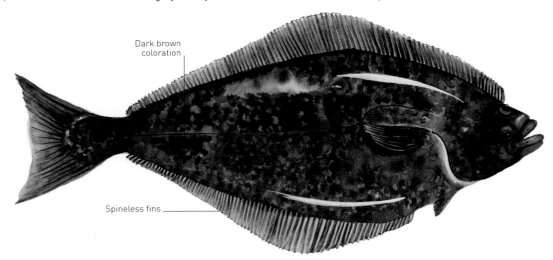

Dark brown coloration

Spineless fins

Winter flounder
Pseudopleuronectes americanus

WEIGHT Up to 8¼ lb (3.8 kg).

TYPES OF WATER Soft to moderately hard bottoms in coastal waters.

DISTRIBUTION Western Atlantic Ocean from Labrador, Canada, to Georgia, US.

FISHING METHODS Bait fishing.

The winter flounder is a popular game fish for anglers fishing the coastal waters of the eastern shores of North America. It occurs in waters from tidal shallows to a maximum depth of 400 ft (120 m). This fish is usually mainly brown in coloration, often with dark spots. A similar species, the European flounder (*Platichthys flesus*), is found in coastal and brackish waters from western Europe to the Black Sea, and is often present in estuaries. Also a popular target for anglers, it is generally smaller than the winter flounder, reaching a maximum weight of 7 lb (3.25 kg).

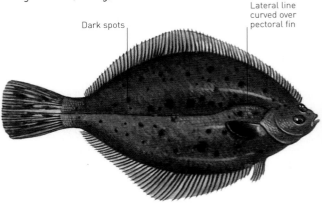

Dark spots

Lateral line curved over pectoral fin

European plaice
Pleuronectes platessa

WEIGHT Up to 15½ lb (7 kg).

TYPES OF WATER Shallow water.

DISTRIBUTION Northeast Atlantic Ocean; Mediterranean.

FISHING METHOD Bait-fishing.

Plaice have been heavily overfished, but still provide good catches in certain areas. They are right-sided flatfish (with their eyes on their upper right-hand side). The coloration of the upper parts is brown with bright orange spots; the underside is white.

Plaice live over mixed bottoms, from clean sand to mussel beds, and will remain stationary for long periods. They are active in shallow water at night, but may spend the day buried in the sand. Their preferred depth range is from 30–164 ft (10–50 m), where they feed mainly on worms and thin-shelled mollusks. Anglers normally target plaice by bottom-fishing with baits.

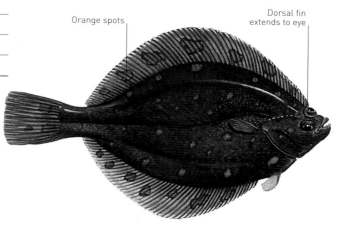

Orange spots

Dorsal fin extends to eye

Turbot
Psetta maxima

WEIGHT Up to 55 lb (25 kg).

TYPES OF WATER Shallow coastal and brackish water.

DISTRIBUTION Northeast Atlantic Ocean to Arctic Circle; Mediterranean.

FISHING METHOD Bait-fishing.

The turbot is an almost circular species of flatfish, and is highly prized for eating. Its upper parts and underside are scaleless. Coloration is usually sandy brown, with brown or black speckles all over the body and fins; but turbot can change color to match their background, hence their reputation for camouflage. The underside is white.

Turbot live on sandy, rocky, or mixed sea beds, and are relatively common in brackish water. They feed on other bottom-living fish, crustaceans, and bivalves (shellfish such as clams and mussels). While turbot can sometimes be caught from the shore, most are taken by fishing from boats in relatively shallow water—for example, over sandbanks. They are targeted on the bottom using a variety of baits, such as fish or squid.

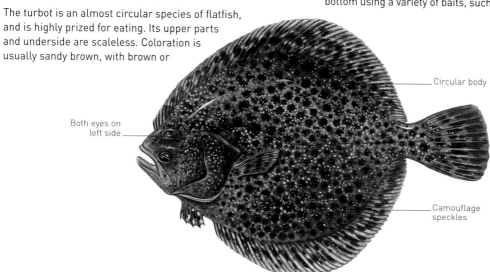

Both eyes on left side

Circular body

Camouflage speckles

Striped bass

Morone saxatilis

WEIGHT Up to 125½ lb (57 kg).

TYPES OF WATER Coastal waters; freshwater and brackish rivers.

DISTRIBUTION Western Atlantic Ocean.

FISHING METHODS Bait-, lure-, and fly-fishing.

The striped bass is an important saltwater sport-fishing species in North America. It is colored greenish-gray above, becoming paler beneath, with six to nine dark horizontal stripes. Adult striped bass feed on fish and crustaceans, and they stop feeding before spawning. These large fish migrate into freshwater to spawn during the spring, and there are various fresh and brackish water populations from Louisiana to

⌃ Schooling striped bass Striped bass are mainly saltwater fish, but some populations are landlocked in North American freshwater lakes. Massed in schools, their elegant lines are an attractive sight in clear waters.

Florida. One of fishing's success stories, striped bass were once commercially fished to dangerously low population levels, but their worth as sporting fish was officially recognized, and a radical conservation program was introduced with great success. The numbers of these hard-fighting fish have now been restored to a sustainable level.

When the fish are running, they often come close inshore and can be caught from boats and from the shore using a variety of angling methods. They respond well to bait- and lure-fishing, while fly anglers also enjoy great success when they come within casting range.

Six to nine stripes

Pale underside

Thick-lipped grey mullet
Chelon labrosus

WEIGHT Up to 10 lb (4.5 kg).

TYPES OF WATER Coastal waters, estuaries, harbors, and rivers.

DISTRIBUTION Northeastern and eastern Atlantic Ocean; Mediterranean; Black Sea.

FISHING METHODS Bait-fishing.

Thick-lipped gray mullet grow larger than other species of mullet, and are the type of mullet most commonly targeted as sport fish. Up to 2½ ft (75 cm) long, and a uniform, dull gray, these mullet have particularly large lips. They feed mainly on small invertebrates and marine microorganisms in the mud in muddy or soft bottoms, where they leave telltale scrapes from their lips.

Notoriously wary and evasive, thick-lipped gray mullet frequent many different types of water, including estuaries, rivers, piers, harbors, marinas, and open coastal locations.

In the United Kingdom and other parts of Europe, this species is considered a fantastic light-tackle adversary. It can be hard to hook and fights hard, giving good sport. It is often described as the European bonefish.

Gray coloration

Large lips

Black seabream
Spondyliosoma cantharus

WEIGHT Up to 2¾ lb (1.25 kg).

TYPES OF WATER Mid-depth and rocky coastal waters.

DISTRIBUTION Eastern Atlantic Ocean; Mediterranean; Black Sea.

FISHING METHOD Bait-fishing.

The top of the head and body of the black seabream are dark blue to black, blending into silvery-gray flanks. There are numerous dark horizontal lines along the flanks.

Black seabream are usually found around rocky, weedy, and broken ground, often around wrecks. They feed on and near the bottom, on seaweed as well as on small fish, invertebrates, and crustaceans. Black seabream spawn from April to May and build nests, where the males protect the eggs.

Black seabream are fished mainly from boats; but in certain areas, such as the Channel Islands, they are successfully targeted from the shore. Small hooks and light rods are most often used to catch these fish on or near the bottom. Most anglers agree that squid is the most effective bait for catching black seabream.

Horizontal stripes

Pale underside

Common snook
Centropomus undecimalis

WEIGHT Up to 53 lb (24 kg).

TYPES OF WATER Warm inshore waters, lagoons, and estuaries.

DISTRIBUTION Western and southwestern Atlantic Ocean; Caribbean.

FISHING METHODS Bait-, lure-, and fly-fishing.

The common snook is the most abundant of the various snook species. This species has a long snout and a lower jaw that extends farther than the upper one. Its coloration is dark on its back, silver on its sides, and white underneath. There is a distinctive black lateral stripe that extends well into the broad, forked tail fin.

Common snook are found in inshore coastal waters, lagoons, and estuaries, usually at a depth of less than 70 ft (20 m). They do not tolerate cold water and their range is determined by the water temperature. They can tolerate freshwater and feed mainly on small fish, shrimp, and small crabs. This species responds to angling with baits, lures, and flies.

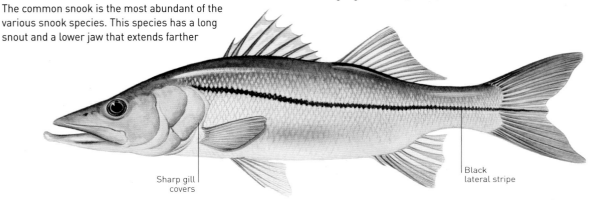

Sharp gill covers

Black lateral stripe

Permit
Trachinotus falcatus

WEIGHT Up to 80 lb (36 kg).

TYPES OF WATER Subtropical coastal shallows and reefs.

DISTRIBUTION Western Atlantic Ocean from Massachusetts Bay to southeastern Brazil, including the Bahamas and much of the Caribbean.

FISHING METHODS Fly- and bait-fishing.

Permit grow to 4 ft (1.2 m) long, and are deep-bodied, with a distinctive, crescent-shaped tail fin and an orange-yellow patch on the abdomen. They frequent shallow, coastal waters, feeding on various types of crustaceans. Famous areas for fishing this species include the Florida Keys, the Bahamas, Mexico, and Costa Rica. Fly-fishing on the flats is the classic way to catch them, although they are hard-fighting, wary, and often reluctant to take a fly. They also form schools around wrecks and reefs, where bait-fishing methods work well. Crabs are the favored bait.

INDO-PACIFIC PERMIT

Although not quite as large as its American cousin, the Indo-Pacific permit (*Trachinotus blochi*) is a popular fishing quarry in parts of northern Australia and the Indian Ocean islands, such as the Seychelles.

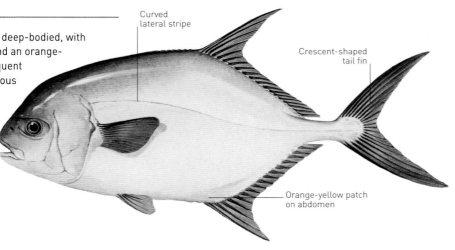

Curved lateral stripe

Crescent-shaped tail fin

Orange-yellow patch on abdomen

Goliath grouper
Epinephelus itajara

WEIGHT Up to 1,000 lb (455 kg).

TYPES OF WATER Subtropical inshore waters with mud or rock bottom; subtropical reefs and caves.

DISTRIBUTION Western, eastern, and southwestern Atlantic; eastern and southeastern Pacific.

FISHING METHOD Bait-fishing from boats.

Also known as the itajara, the goliath grouper is among the largest of the European sea bass family. This species has a broad head, small eyes, and a thick-set body that measures half as wide as it is long. Its coloration is dull green, gray, or brown, with distinctive small, dark spots on its body, head, and fins. The pectoral fins are large and rounded.

These solitary fish feed on large crustaceans, turtles, and fish. Shallow inshore waters with muddy, rocky, or coral bottoms are their favorite habitat; they also frequent wrecks, reefs, and caves. More strikingly marked juveniles can be found among mangroves and in brackish estuaries. A notoriously hard-fighting fish, the goliath grouper is often difficult to land.

Dorsal spines

Rounded tail fin

Variable brown coloration

African pompano
Alectis ciliaris

WEIGHT Up to 51 lb (23 kg).

TYPES OF WATER Warm seas and oceans to a depth of 200 ft (60 m).

DISTRIBUTION Tropical waters worldwide.

FISHING METHODS Bait-, lure-, and fly-fishing.

African pompano are found in many tropical seas around the world and are most likely to be caught in deeper water where there are reefs and rocks. This species favors water temperatures from 64–86°F (18–30°C). Small African pompano are often known as threadfish. This fish is distinguished from other threadfin species by its long and transparent anal and dorsal fins.

African pompano often come into the surf zone close to the shore, and they can turn their tall, flat bodies on one side to access such shallow water to feed. They are known for being tough fighters that, when hooked, will often head straight for snags (underwater obstructions such as rocks).

Diamond-shaped body

Bony plates

Cubera snapper
Lutjanus cyanopterus

WEIGHT Up to 125½ lb (57 kg).

TYPES OF WATER Coastal waters.

DISTRIBUTION Western central and southwestern Atlantic; Caribbean.

FISHING METHODS Bait-, lure-, and fly-fishing.

Cubera snapper are said to be the largest species of snapper. Their coloration is dark brown to gray, sometimes with a reddish tinge overall. These impressive fish have extremely strong teeth—one pair of canines is particularly large and is visible when the mouth is closed. Adult cubera snapper tend to be found offshore around rocky ledges and reefs, in depths up to about 164 ft (50 m). Young cubera snapper sometimes inhabit estuaries, areas of extensive mangroves, and grass beds. Cubera snapper feed primarily on a variety of smaller fish as well as shrimp and crabs.

AFRICAN CUBERA SNAPPERS

The African cubera snapper (see right), sometimes also known as the Guinean snapper, is reputed to grow even larger than the cubera snapper. This species is red-brown virtually all over. Adult African cubera snapper frequent a diverse range of waters, from offshore reefs to right into the surf zone and into estuaries, brackish lagoons, and mangroves. African cubera snapper targeted in the surf zone are especially susceptible to being taken on big lures.

▶▶ **Massive snapper** The vast coastal lagoons of Gabon, West Africa, hold huge stocks of massive African cubera snapper. These are targeted in the surf zone and also the calm, brackish waters of the lagoons.

Fishing for cuberas
At full moon during July and August in southern Florida, adult cubera snappers move up from deep water to depths of around 200 ft (60 m) to spawn. This is the best time to fish for big specimens. It is essential to use powerful tackle in these depths of water because they always try to head for the safety of the rocks.

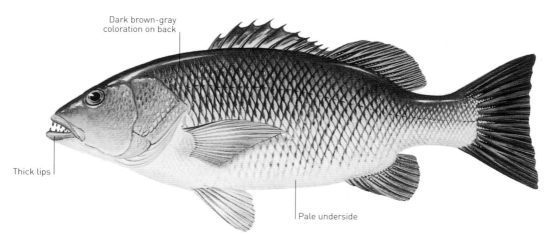

Dark brown-gray coloration on back

Thick lips

Pale underside

Mutton snapper

Lutjanus analis

WEIGHT Up to 34 lb (15.5 kg).

TYPES OF WATER Clear, rocky coastal waters; continental shelf.

DISTRIBUTION Western Atlantic Ocean; Caribbean.

FISHING METHODS Bait-, lure-, and fly-fishing.

The brightly colored mutton snapper is one of the most numerous snappers to be found anywhere in the Caribbean or the coastal waters surrounding southern Florida. Coloration on the upper sides is an olive green that blends into a whitish lower side and belly, with a slight red tinge. A black spot lies on the upper back area just above the lateral line. A pair of striking blue stripes run on each side of the cheek area of the fish. Bars on the body of the mutton snapper are prominent when the fish is resting; the body color becomes plainer when the fish is swimming.

Inshore waters

Mutton snapper are usually found inshore around grass beds, mangroves, and in tidal creeks, and sometimes larger individuals are caught offshore.

Mutton snapper are sometimes mistaken for the lane snapper (*Lutjanus synagris*), a somewhat similar species, and are often marketed as "red" snapper.

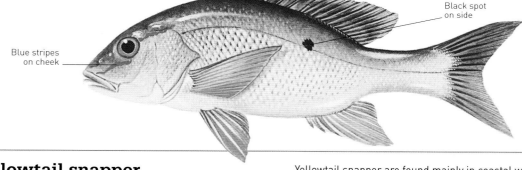

Blue stripes on cheek

Black spot on side

Yellowtail snapper

Ocyurus chrysurus

WEIGHT Up to 8¾ lb (4 kg).

TYPES OF WATER Coastal waters, coral reefs.

DISTRIBUTION Western Atlantic Ocean (Massachusetts to Brazil); Caribbean.

FISHING METHODS Bait-, lure-, and fly-fishing.

Yellowtails are fairly small among snappers. They have distinctive yellow spots on the upper side, with olive to bluish coloration, blending down to pink and yellow stripes. A broad lateral yellow stripe runs from the mouth to the tail.

Yellowtail snapper are found mainly in coastal waters where they school and spawn, mainly during summer. They are heavily fished for over grass beds and reefs, and offshore, where they frequent sandy patches that lie around reefs.

Catching yellowtails

Like various other snapper species, yellowtails respond well to baits and lures, and can also be taken by fly-fishing. A noted way to attract these snappers is to put out a net of chum (*see* p.162). They are often voracious feeders and can be easy to catch when they are feeding hard. The southeastern parts of Florida, and especially the Keys, are the best places to catch large numbers of yellowtail snappers.

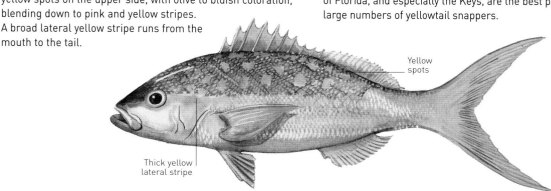

Yellow spots

Thick yellow lateral stripe

Common skate

Dipturus batis

WEIGHT Up to 214 lb (97 kg).

TYPES OF WATER Coastal waters to 656 ft (200 m).

DISTRIBUTION Northeastern and eastern Atlantic Ocean; Mediterranean.

FISHING METHODS Bottom-fishing with baits.

Also known as the blue skate, the common skate grows very large and is a hard-fighting fish that is difficult to move from the bottom. The common skate has a long snout and is olive-gray or brown in color, with pale spots on the back, while its underside is pale gray with lots of small black dots. It feeds tight to the bottom, usually over clean, hard ground, on crustaceans and many species of fish. The common skate is a slow-growing fish that is mainly found in deep coastal waters. There are other skate species found in European waters (including the long-nosed skate and the white skate), but the common skate is the primary target for anglers.

Commercial pressure

Common skate tend to spend their lives within a relatively small area and their preferred locations often leave them susceptible to overfishing, whether targeted deliberately or as a by-catch from commercial fishing operations. The anglers who target these fish for sport now always release them, often after tagging, and tagged fish are often caught many times. Although the species has been in sharp decline for a number of years due to overfishing, there is still some excellent fishing to be had on the western coasts of Ireland and Scotland.

UNDERSIDE OF A SKATE

A skate's gill slits and mouth are located on its underside. This is an adaptation for feeding on creatures that live in the sediments of the sea floor. The mouth is not much more than a narrow slit containing small teeth that are designed for crushing. The force they can apply is extremely powerful, so keep hands and fingers away when handling them.

Pale spots

Whiplike tail

Thornback ray
Raja clavata

WEIGHT Up to 39½ lb (18 kg).

TYPES OF WATER Coastal waters.

DISTRIBUTION Eastern Atlantic Ocean; Mediterranean; Black Sea.

FISHING METHODS Bottom-fishing with baits.

One of the most common ray species in European waters, the thornback ray is also somewhat confusingly known in some parts of the UK as a skate or roker. It is identifiable mainly by its mottled brown or gray coloration and distinctly right-angled "wings." The top of the thornback ray's body is prickly all over and it has a row of spines, or "thorns," that runs down its spine, often right down the tail. Large females are sometimes also prickly on the underside. This species frequents a large range of depths, from extremely shallow waters to very deep water, over rough and clean ground, and is also adept at living and feeding in estuaries. It feeds on the bottom on crustaceans and small fish. The thornback ray is usually fished for on the bottom with baits, either from boats or from the shore.

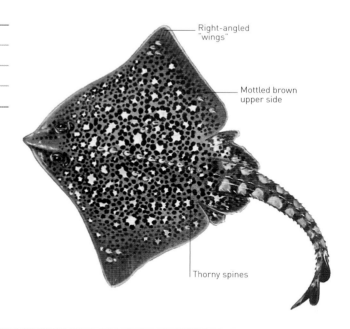

Right-angled "wings"

Mottled brown upper side

Thorny spines

Blonde ray
Raja brachyura

WEIGHT Up to 39½ lb (18 kg).

TYPES OF WATER Coastal waters.

DISTRIBUTION Eastern Atlantic Ocean.

FISHING METHODS Bottom-fishing with baits from boats or shore.

The blonde ray has a short snout and pronounced right-angled "wings." Its upper side is distinctly prickly (but not on juveniles) and its coloration is predominantly light brown to ocher, with masses of small black spots that extend right to the edge of the wings. The underside of a blonde ray is white. It is possible to mistake the much smaller spotted ray (*Raja montagui*) for a small blonde ray, but the spots on the latter stop before the edge of the wings. The blonde ray feeds mainly on crustaceans and small bottom-living fish.

Among the largest species of rays targeted by UK and Irish anglers, blonde ray are usually caught in water less than 328 ft (100 m) in depth, over clean, sandy ground. These rays are sometimes caught by shore-anglers but they are usually taken from boats. When fishing for blonde ray from the shore, powerful tackle is required.

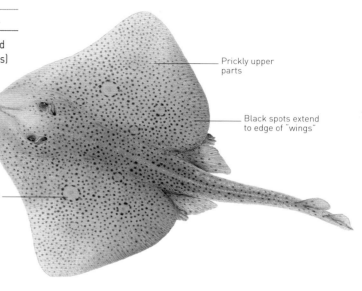

Prickly upper parts

Black spots extend to edge of "wings"

Pale brown coloration

Bluefin tuna

Thunnus thynnus

WEIGHT Up to 1,508 lb (684 kg).

TYPES OF WATER Mid-ocean to inshore waters.

DISTRIBUTION Atlantic Ocean; Mediterranean; southern Black Sea; Pacific Ocean.

FISHING METHODS Bait-, lure-, and fly-fishing from boats.

The largest of all the tuna species, gigantic bluefin tuna is among the hardest-fighting fish of all. Known for long, hard fights, its sheer size can make it an incredible adversary. Worldwide stocks of this species are continually threatened due to their extremely high worth as a food species, especially in Japan. Bluefin tuna found in the Pacific were once viewed as a separate subspecies, but now it is generally accepted that they are all *Thunnus thynnus*. The bluefin tuna has a typically tunalike shape. The lower sides and belly are silvery in color, while the upper sides and back are blue-black. Its dorsal fins are dark gray, but its anal fin is yellow.

Traveling far and deep

The bluefin tuna is a highly migratory species that travels great distances. During these long journeys, it needs to withstand a considerable range of water temperatures. It can maintain its body temperature at around 86°F (30°C) in waters as cold as 45°F (7°C). This keeps its swimming muscles warm and thus enables it to swim at considerable speeds for long periods over long distances. The bluefin tuna can swim at depths of up to 3,300 ft (1,000 m), but at times this species will also come closer inshore.

⌃ **Bluefin tuna school** Bluefin tuna form schools according to size—in general, smaller bluefins form larger schools than bigger members of the species. Schooling behavior also varies according to area.

HIGHLY PRIZED FISH

Bluefin tuna are a commercially valuable species and, as a result, stocks of these magnificent fish are declining. Around 80 percent of the world's commercially caught bluefin tuna is consumed in Japan, where it is prized as one of the prime fish for sushi and sashimi. In the markets of Tokyo, fierce bidding wars are often fought for the best bluefins. The worldwide shortage of these fish has led to numerous attempts to farm them for food purposes, but bluefin tuna are notoriously hard to raise in captivity.

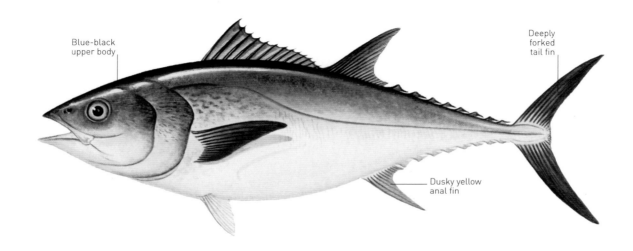

Blue-black upper body

Deeply forked tail fin

Dusky yellow anal fin

Yellowfin tuna
Thunnus albacares

WEIGHT Up to 440 lb (200 kg).

TYPES OF WATER Ocean.

DISTRIBUTION Atlantic, Indian, and Pacific oceans.

FISHING METHODS Bait-, lure-, and fly-fishing from boats.

The yellowfin tuna is dark and metallic-looking on the back, blending into yellow on the sides, and a silvery color on the belly. The dorsal and anal fins are bright yellow. This is a highly migratory species of tuna that is usually found in water no more than 328 ft (100 m) deep. It tends to congregate in large schools. Yellowfin tuna often school with other fish species of a similar size rather than specifically with members of their own species. They commonly mix with other species of tuna and, in the eastern Pacific, with dolphins. They feed mainly on fish, squid, and crustaceans.

The yellowfin is an immensely important sporting species and is known for being hard-fighting. The seas off Cape Town in South Africa are among the most famous places to chase big yellowfin. Bait- and lure-fishing are the most common fishing methods, but some anglers manage to catch large yellowfins on heavy-duty fly-fishing gear.

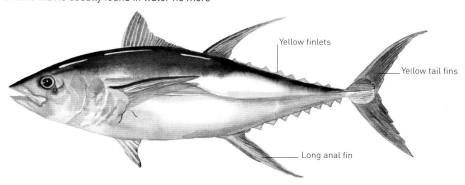

Yellow finlets

Yellow tail fins

Long anal fin

Atlantic bonito
Sarda sarda

WEIGHT Up to 24½ lb (11 kg).

TYPES OF WATER Ocean.

DISTRIBUTION Atlantic Ocean; Mediterranean; western Indian Ocean.

FISHING METHODS Bait-, lure-, and fly-fishing from boats.

The Atlantic bonito has a typical tuna shape, but differs slightly from the similar-looking Pacific bonito (*Sarda chilensis*). The side stripes of the Atlantic species run diagonally and there are 20 to 23 spines on the first dorsal fin, whereas the Pacific bonito has 17 to 19 spines on its first dorsal fin. The Atlantic bonito is primarily a deepwater fish. It requires a sea temperature of 59–72° F (15–22° C), and feeds on shrimp, small fish, and squid. It can be cannibalistic.

This species can be successfully targeted with light tackle. While trolling works well, it is also fun to cast lures and flies at them when the schools are feeding on small fish near or at the surface. It is best to position your boat upwind or uptide of the school and quietly drift down toward the fish. The bonito is known for hesitating when first hooked, but within a few seconds it is likely to charge off at high speed.

Striped upper parts

Large mouth

Bluefish
Pomatomus saltatrix

WEIGHT Up to 32 lb (14.5 kg).

TYPES OF WATER Coastal surf or moving water, near beaches and headlands.

DISTRIBUTION All oceans except the eastern and northwestern Pacific Ocean.

FISHING METHODS Bait-, lure-, and fly-fishing.

The bluefish, also known as shad or elf in southern Africa, has a greenish gray back and sides and a silvery underside. This species is highly migratory and tends to move to warmer waters during the winter and then cooler waters in summer. It is most often found behind the breakers on surf beaches, in the surf itself, and around rocky headlands where there is clean saltwater and a good supply of smaller fish for food. The bluefish has extremely sharp teeth, which makes the use of wire traces (*see* p.49) advisable when fishing for them. It is also important to be careful of the teeth when unhooking this fish.

Feeding frenzy
One of the most effective ways to find bluefish is to look for schools of their preferred prey, or baitfish, such as the mullet and menhaden found off the coast of North America. Hungry bluefish will often signal their presence by smashing into the baitfish on the surface. Schools of bluefish will often attack smaller fish in shallow water, in a feeding frenzy. The bluefish is famous for forming large schools. A huge school spotted in Narragansett Bay, Rhode Island, in 1901 was estimated to stretch 4–5 miles (6–8 km) in length.

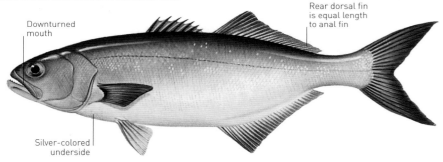

Downturned mouth

Rear dorsal fin is equal length to anal fin

Silver-colored underside

» **Fishing for bluefish** Using a long surf-fishing rod to cast a line beyond the breakers is often the best way to catch bluefish.

« **Shadow lines**
Tarpon love to lurk beneath the shadows of the huge road bridges that link the islands of the Florida Keys, where the tarpon feed on schools of smaller fish.

Tarpon
Megalops atlanticus

WEIGHT Up to 353 lb (160 kg).

TYPES OF WATER Coastal waters, estuaries, lagoons, brackish rivers.

DISTRIBUTION Eastern and western Atlantic Ocean; Gulf of Mexico; Caribbean.

FISHING METHODS Bait-, lure-, and fly-fishing.

Tarpon offer great fishing in many different areas of the world. They look somewhat like oversized herring, but tarpon are actually closely related to eels. They have distinctive upturned mouths and bright, metallic, very hard scales.

Tarpon spawn in the open sea but they school and feed in shallower water, taking small fish and crustaceans. They are usually caught in estuaries, lagoons, tidal flats, mangrove swamps, and around structures, such as road bridges.

Tarpon are successfully fished with fish and crab baits, as well as with lures in certain areas. When on tidal flats they are a popular target for accomplished fly-anglers. Hard to hook due to their bony mouths, they can grow very large and are immensely hard-fighting adversaries that may leap several times in their efforts to shed the hook.

TARPON FISHING WORLDWIDE

The Florida Keys arguably offer the most consistent big-tarpon fishing because the fish migrate through the area in spring and summer, but it is generally accepted that certain West African countries—such as Angola, Gabon, and Sierra Leone—hold the biggest tarpon in the world. The waters off the east coasts of Central and South America also offer excellent tarpon fishing. Large tarpon are highly migratory and have the ability to move into brackish waters up estuaries and even into rivers, notably those in Nicaragua.

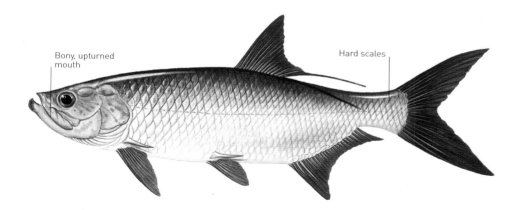

Bony, upturned mouth

Hard scales

King mackerel

Scomberomorus cavalla

WEIGHT Up to 99 lb (45 kg).

TYPES OF WATER Seas and oceans, offshore and inshore waters.

DISTRIBUTION Atlantic Ocean.

FISHING METHODS Bait-, lure-, and fly-fishing.

Also known as kingfish, the king mackerel is a hugely popular sporting fish. In the US, small king mackerel under 15 lb (6.8 kg) are often referred to as "snakes," and larger specimens over 30 lb (13.5 kg) are nicknamed "smokers" for their speed and ability to "smoke" line from a reel when hooked. The king mackerel has a blue-green back, silvery sides, and a tapered, strongly streamlined body and tail. The lateral line curves suddenly downward after the second dorsal fin. This species feeds on smaller fish, shrimp, and squid.

⏶ **Sharp teeth** The southern African king mackerel (*Scomberomorus commerson*), like its close relative *Scomberomorus cavalla*, has large, sharp teeth that demand the use of a wire trace.

Fishing approaches

In the US, slow trolling with live baits—porgie, also known as menhaden, is a popular choice—or with lures is considered the best fishing method for this species, but in other areas of the world they are also caught with flies. King mackerel are caught predominantly in offshore and inshore waters. There are numerous professional king mackerel fishing tournaments held in the US.

Anglers in southern African waters target a species known locally as king mackerel, and while they look very similar to *Scomberomorus cavalla*, they are in fact *Scomberomorus commerson*. Also known as "couta," these fish are a very important angling quarry.

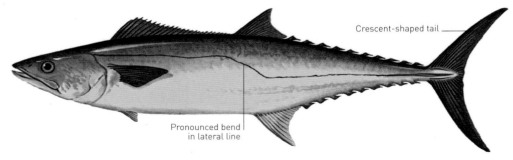

Crescent-shaped tail

Pronounced bend in lateral line

Atlantic mackerel
Scomber scombrus

WEIGHT Up to 7¾ lb (3.5 kg).

TYPES OF WATER Seas and oceans.

DISTRIBUTION North Atlantic Ocean; North Sea; Mediterranean.

FISHING METHODS Bait-, lure-, and fly-fishing.

The Atlantic mackerel is a critically important species for anglers, both as a sporting fish worth catching in its own right and as a baitfish that will attract numerous larger fish when presented in different ways. It can reach up to 2 ft (60 cm) in length and its upper parts are metallic green with 20 to 23 dark, wavy bars, while its underside is silvery.

The Atlantic mackerel is a species that forms large schools and feeds mainly on smaller fish near the surface. At times, these fish will drive

> **MACKEREL SPAWNING TIMES**
>
> Although genetically the same, the Atlantic mackerel populations in US waters follow two distinct patterns: one group spawns during April and May in the mid-Atlantic Bight, while the other group spawns during June and July in the Gulf of St. Lawrence. In the waters of the UK, there are also two distinct stocks of mackerel; one group spawns in the North Sea and the other in the Atlantic to the west of the British Isles.

small prey species to the surface in a feeding frenzy, a phenomenon that makes the sea appear to "boil". There are not many saltwater species that will not take mackerel bait, and it can even be effective when angling in freshwater—for example, when targeting pike.

Dark bars on back

Spots below lateral line

Tope
Galeorhinus galeus

WEIGHT Up to 99 lb (45 kg).

TYPES OF WATER Coastal waters, rocky headlands, steep beaches.

DISTRIBUTION Atlantic Ocean; Mediterranean; Indian Ocean; Pacific Ocean.

FISHING METHODS Bait-fishing from boats or shore.

The tope (also known as tope shark) is a prime sporting species. Up to 6 ft (190 cm) in length, with a slender body and long, pointed snout, this fish has a grayish upper body that blends into white below and a distinctively shaped, strong tail. It feeds through a large range of depths, often on the bottom and through to mid-water, on smaller fish such as whiting and pouting, squid, and crustaceans. Tope can be found over various types of sea bed, including sand and rock. It is a fast-running fish that moves with the current to provide anglers with great sporting opportunities. This fish is mostly fished for with baits on the bottom, but will pick up larger shark baits either suspended on floats or on light tackle fished from boats or the shore.

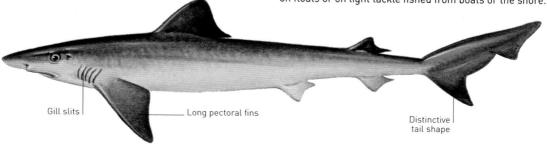

Gill slits

Long pectoral fins

Distinctive tail shape

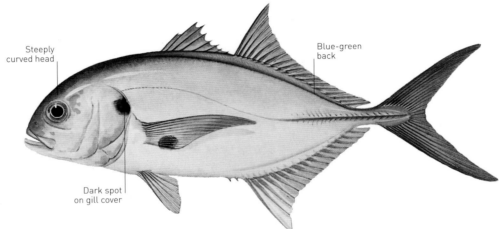

⌃ **Schooling crevalle jacks** Small crevalle jacks often gather in large, fast-moving schools. However, larger specimens are more likely to be solitary.

Steeply curved head

Blue-green back

Dark spot on gill cover

Crevalle jack

Caranx hippos

WEIGHT Up to 70 lb (32 kg).

TYPES OF WATER Warm coastal waters, brackish estuaries.

DISTRIBUTION Western and eastern Atlantic Ocean; western Mediterranean.

FISHING METHODS Bait-, lure-, and fly-fishing from boats and shore.

The crevalle jack has a distinctive, steeply curving head shape. Its coloration is a dark greenish-blue on the back, with silvery or brassy sides. Dark spots are noticeable on the edge of the gill covers, and near the pectoral fins, with sometimes a third spot farther back. This species can grow up to 4 ft (1.2 m) in length,

RUTHLESS KILLERS

Crevalle jacks are experts at working around schools of baitfish and then smashing into them. When this happens near or on the surface, it can be a spectacular sight. Waves of jacks attacking their prey sound almost like a washing machine in its spin cycle. They are voracious predators, even following commercial fishing boats for an easy meal.

although specimens found in inshore waters are much smaller. It can swim up river systems, and the young inhabit inshore areas. The crevalle jack is an aggressive fish, able to battle hard for long periods. It is often attracted to boats by chumming (*see* p.162) and makes unusual grunting sounds when caught.

Greater amberjack
Seriola dumerili

WEIGHT Up to 176 lb (80 kg).

TYPES OF WATER Warm, deep water.

DISTRIBUTION Atlantic Ocean, Indian Ocean, and Pacific Ocean; Mediterranean.

FISHING METHODS Bait-, lure-, and fly-fishing from boats.

Greater amberjacks are distinctive-looking fish, generally silvery in color, but darker on the back. There is a stripe that runs along each side. Both males and females grow at the same rate, but male amberjacks do not survive much beyond seven years old, so the largest specimens are nearly all females. Smaller amberjacks can easily be confused with other jack species.

Greater amberjacks like to spend much of their time relatively close to the surface, and they tend to swim either singly or in small groups, preferring to inhabit reefs and wrecks in warm, deep waters, where they feed on smaller fish. Amberjacks are aggressive predators that are difficult fish to land successfully. They fight hard, run savagely, and will often crash-dive repeatedly in the attempt to fight off an angler.

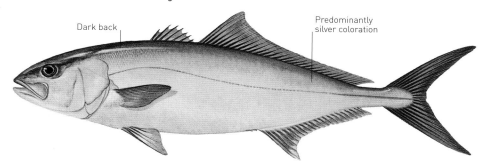

Dark back

Predominantly silver coloration

Horse-eye jack
Caranx latus

WEIGHT Up to 30 lb (13.5 kg).

TYPES OF WATER Offshore reefs; sometimes fresh or brackish water.

DISTRIBUTION Western and eastern Atlantic Ocean.

FISHING METHODS Bait-, lure-, and fly-fishing from boats and shore.

Sometimes also known as "big-eye" jacks, horse-eye jacks are similar to crevalle jacks, with which they sometimes school, but they have large eyes and do not grow as big—reaching a maximum length of about 3¼ ft (1 m). Overall, their coloration is gray to blue on the back and silver to white on the belly; the tail fin is a distinctive yellow, and the top part of the rear dorsal fin is close to black in color. What distinguishes them from crevalle jacks are the small scales on the chest area and the absence of a dark blotch on the pectoral fin. There is sometimes a small dark patch near the gill cover.

Horse-eye jacks feed mainly on other fish, shrimp, and invertebrates, and they gather in large schools. Like crevalle jacks, waves of them hitting smaller fish can often be seen from a distance.

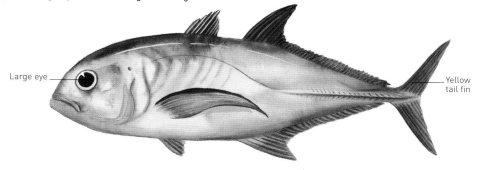

Large eye

Yellow tail fin

Dorado
Coryphaena hippurus

WEIGHT Up to 90 lb (40 kg).

TYPES OF WATER Tropical and subtropical open or coastal waters.

DISTRIBUTION Atlantic Ocean; Mediterranean; Indian Ocean; Pacific Ocean.

FISHING METHODS Bait-, lure-, and fly-fishing from boats.

FEMALE HEAD SHAPE

Female dorado (known as cows), and the young of both sexes, tend to have a more softly rounded head than the males (see below). Mature male dorado, often known as bulls, are usually larger than the females and have a square forehead with a higher and flatter shape.

Also known as mahimahi, dolphinfish, or golden mackerel, dorado are among the fastest-growing fish in the sea, reaching 6½ ft (2 m) in length and living for only about five years. Their green or electric-blue upper body, and gold sides flashed with green, seem to light up when the fish are hooked, showing off neonlike colors during highly acrobatic fights. The dorsal fin runs the length of the body. Small dorados travel in schools; large adults travel alone or in pairs. Fishing is best near floating objects such as logs, reeds, or flotsam out at sea, as well as near weed lines and buoys, where they feed on plankton, crustaceans, small fish, and squid attracted to the shelter.

Square forehead (males)

Long, concave anal fin

Wahoo
Acanthocybium solandri

WEIGHT Up to 182 lb (83 kg).

TYPES OF WATER Tropical and subtropical waters.

DISTRIBUTION Atlantic Ocean; Mediterranean; Indian Ocean; Pacific Ocean.

FISHING METHODS Trolling from boats with baits and lures; occasionally drift-fishing with livebait.

Wahoo (called queenfish in the Caribbean and ono in Hawaii) are fast, powerful fish that can swim in short bursts at up to 60 mph (100 km/h). Wahoo change direction quickly and jump repeatedly when hooked. They have a slim body shape not unlike the king mackerel, and plenty of very sharp teeth. The snout is long and tapers to a point, with the underside jaw slightly longer than the upper. The upper body is dark or electric blue with waved stripes along the flanks. Rows of small finlets lie directly behind the dorsal fins and the anal fin. Wahoo swim in waters of 70 to 86° F (21–30° C), usually preferring the waters around reefs with warm current lines and schools of baitfish, and large holes in the seabed.

Long, tapering jawline

Tail-end finlets

Blue-striped sides

Kabeljou
Argyrosomus japonicus

WEIGHT Up to 165 lb (75 kg).

TYPES OF WATER Subtropical inshore waters beyond the surf zone; brackish waters.

DISTRIBUTION Southeastern Atlantic Ocean; western and eastern Indian Ocean; northwest and western central Pacific Ocean.

FISHING METHODS Bait- and lure-fishing from boats or shore, occasionally fly-fishing.

The kabeljou (or dusky kob) is a sought-after coastal and estuarine sporting species. It is among the largest kob species and is often confused with the silver kob (*Argyrosomus inodorus*), a similar species, which is more commonly caught in colder, deeper waters.

Adult kabeljou have a blue-gray back; a darker, sometimes coppery, head; and the rest of the body being a pearly color. While juveniles often come close to the shore, adults usually remain in deeper waters beyond the surf zone. It is predominantly a schooling species and feeds mostly on shrimp, prawns, various smaller fish, squid, and sometimes even octopus. Kabeljou spawn at night, usually around inshore reef areas, and are normally caught from boats.

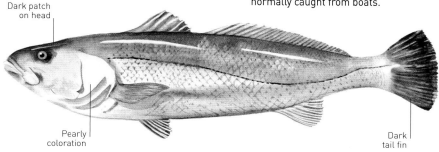

Dark patch on head

Pearly coloration

Dark tail fin

White steenbras
Lithognathus lithognathus

WEIGHT Up to 40 lb (18.5 kg).

TYPES OF WATER Subtropical waters, over sandy beaches, estuaries, lagoons, and deeper inshore waters.

DISTRIBUTION Southeastern Atlantic Ocean and western Indian Ocean.

FISHING METHODS Bottom-fishing with baits.

The white steenbras is an important coastal sport-fishing species in southern Africa, principally in Namibia and many parts of South Africa. Also known as a pignose grunter, river steenbras, or varkbek, this silvery-white fish

grows to 6½ ft (2 m) in length. It has a pointed head and up to seven distinct dark bars on the body—the smaller the fish, the darker the bars. It is sometimes possible to see the tails of white steenbras sticking out of shallow water as they blow air into crab, prawn, and worm holes to dislodge their prey.

Juvenile white steenbras come into estuaries when they reach a length of 1½ to 2 in (3–5 cm) and stay there for their first year, sometimes two or more years. Larger white steenbras of 1 to 2 ft (30–60 cm) in length prefer surf areas along sandy beaches, and this is predominantly where they are fished for. Some large specimens can be found in deeper water down to about 80 ft (25 m). This species is usually targeted with bottom-fishing tactics from surf beaches.

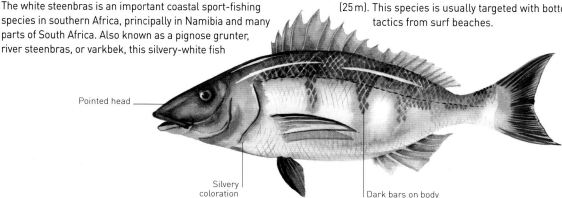

Pointed head

Silvery coloration

Dark bars on body

"THE FISH IS NOT SO MUCH YOUR QUARRY AS YOUR PARTNER."

Arnold Gingrich

Leerfish
Lichia amia

WEIGHT Up to 110 lb (50 kg).

TYPES OF WATER Coastal waters.

DISTRIBUTION Eastern Atlantic Ocean; Mediterranean; western Indian Ocean.

FISHING METHODS Bait-fishing from boats; beachcasting with surface-fished plugs; fly-fishing.

The leerfish (also known as garrick or leervis) is a sought-after species among anglers, especially in southern African waters such as the southern coastline of Angola.

Large specimens are also caught in the Mediterranean. Its coloration is generally blue- to green-gray above the distinctively curved lateral line, and silvery white below. Adult leerfish can reach 6½ ft (2 m) in length.

Leerfish are voracious predators that generally hunt in schools. Adults usually feed near the shore in clear water, from close to the surf zone out to a depth of around 160 ft (50 m). Mullet is a favorite prey, and large numbers of adult leerfish also follow the annual migration of large schools of sardine. Juveniles up to 6 in (15 cm) in length feed mainly on shrimp and small fish; they are able to open their large mouths to swallow prey that is up to 70 percent of their own size.

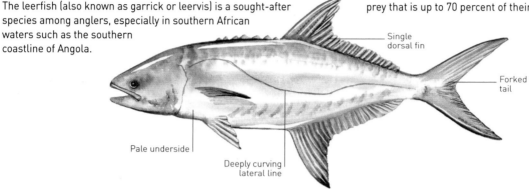

Single dorsal fin

Forked tail

Pale underside

Deeply curving lateral line

Giant African threadfin
Polydactylus quadrifilis

WEIGHT Up to 165 lb (75 kg).

TYPES OF WATER Shallow tropical waters with a sandy or muddy bottom, sometimes brackish.

DISTRIBUTION Eastern, central, and southeastern Atlantic Ocean.

FISHING METHODS Bottom-fishing, with lures and jigs; also fly-fishing.

Giant African threadfins are found predominantly on the west coast of Africa. They are powerful fighting fish that are successfully targeted in only a few places, such as Angola

(especially the Cuanza River estuary), Gabon, and Senegal. Giant African threadfins grow to 6½ ft (2 m) in length, with a distinct yellowish coloration to the belly area. The threadfins are an unusual group of fish that use the cluster of fins attached to the base of the pectorals as feelers for locating prey in surf zones and in murky estuarine waters fringed by mangroves. They are also sometimes found offshore, over sandy bottoms, at depths of up to 160 ft (50 m).

Giant African threadfins feed mainly on small fish and crustaceans. They are usually targeted with lures and jigs, but can also be taken using fly-fishing tackle.

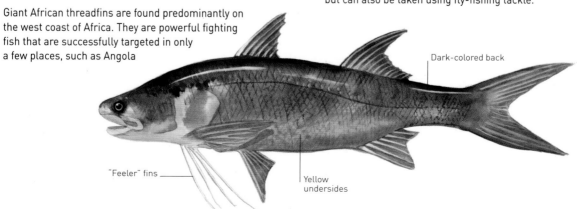

Dark-colored back

"Feeler" fins

Yellow undersides

Bonefish
Albula vulpes

WEIGHT Up to 22 lb (10 kg).

TYPES OF WATER Shallow waters with a sandy or muddy bottom.

DISTRIBUTION Worldwide in warm seas and oceans.

FISHING METHODS Fly-fishing and bait-fishing.

Arguably the most popular saltwater fly-fishing quarry, the bonefish is of little value commercially as food fish. However, this species is a highly prized sight-fishing quarry of the flats.

The bonefish is silvery gray in coloration with darker vertical bars that fade with age. The fins are darker than the body. It has a slim, elongated shape that enables it to feed close to the bottom in shallow water, where it can find shrimp and crustaceans. These fish can often be seen feeding with their tails sticking out of the water as they burrow down in the mud and sand to root out food. Anglers call this "tailing," and it is one of the classic sights of tropical fishing on saltwater flats.

Bonefish are hard-fighting fish and can run fast when hooked. Very large bonefish have been caught in the waters off southeast Africa, mainly in Mozambique. Bonefish can be taken on various baits, especially shrimp or prawns, and on small jigs. Larger specimens are usually taken on bait in deep water. However, fly-fishing on the flats is the classic method.

Dark fins

Slender, tapered body

⊻ **Bonefish on the flats** Anglers pole across the flats in the Bahamas as they sight-fish for bonefish.

Great barracuda

Sphyraena barracuda

WEIGHT Up to 110 lb (50 kg).

TYPES OF WATER Tropical waters.

DISTRIBUTION Atlantic Ocean; Indian Ocean; and Pacific Ocean.

FISHING METHODS Bait- and lure-fishing from boats or shore.

The great barracuda is a voracious predator, with plenty of razor-sharp teeth in its large mouth. Its coloration is bluish-gray on the upper body, blending into green and then silver or white on the belly, with 18 to 23 dark bars along the upper body. Distinctive black spots below the lateral line are a distinguishing feature of the great barracuda.

The great barracuda is found in most of the world's warm and tropical regions. It is often found near inshore coral reefs, sea grass, and mangroves, and even areas close to artificial

Fearsome teeth Barracuda are attracted to shiny objects. Successful lures are often those with a metallic sheen, which a barracuda will attack with its fearsome teeth.

structures, such as piers and jetties. Larger specimens also live in the open ocean, where they often remain near the surface. This species sometimes forms schools, but generally barracuda are solitary. Juveniles tend to mature near the shore amid mangroves and sea grasses, but during their second year they move to deeper water.

Feeding habits

The great barracuda is an aggressive feeder and often charges into schools of baitfish, using its large teeth to slash at its prey. The injured and dead fish are then consumed. It is recommended not to wear anything shiny when swimming in waters inhabited by great barracuda because they are attracted to this visual stimulus and have been known to attack. Anglers can target this species with lures and live baits, either from boats or the shore.

Sharp spines on dorsal fin

Pale tail fin tips

Dark spots

Sailfish

Istiophorus platypterus

WEIGHT Up to 220 lb (100 kg).

TYPES OF WATER Temperate and tropical coastal waters.

DISTRIBUTION Atlantic Ocean; Indian Ocean; and Pacific Ocean.

FISHING METHODS Trolling with baits and lures; fly-fishing.

With its long bill and a highly distinctive spotted dorsal fin that looks like a huge sail, the sailfish is unmistakable. It also has very long and narrow pelvic fins. It is blue-black on its upper parts, silvery-white on its underside, with about 20 pale blue, vertical bars along its flanks. It is a migratory, oceanic species that is found in greatest numbers close to the coast, often in large schools. Sailfish feed predominantly on smaller fish, squid, and crustaceans. Although sailfish do not grow as large as other billfish, they are exciting to catch.

Fishing methods

Sailfish can be targeted with light tackle by trolling from boats, with baits and lures. Kites are often used to spread out the lures behind the boat. Teasing fish in with live bait and then casting flies at them is also a popular technique for catching this species in some places. In the waters off Florida, where it is common practice to return all sailfish alive, anglers often fish mainly with live baits. The waters off the Florida Keys are famous for fishing sailfish, and increasingly many South American waters are visited for the large numbers of sailfish found there.

Sail-like first dorsal fin

Long bill

SAILFISH AROUND THE WORLD

Sailfish are a highly migratory species, found in many tropical and temperate waters around the world. They often follow the movement of schools of their favorite prey fish species (such as mackerel, tuna, and jacks) as these fish respond to seasonal changes in the water temperature. The sailfish populations in the Pacific migrate to spawn, and tend to be much larger than those in the Atlantic, which reach only about 128 lb (58 kg). For this reason, some authorities divide sailfish into two species: the Indo-Pacific sailfish (*Istiophorus platypterus*) and the Atlantic sailfish (*Istiophorus albicans*).

« Landing a sailfish
Bringing a sailfish on board is easier with two people. The fish can be safely held by the bill and sail.

◀◀ **Good sport** Black marlin stay deep through a fight, but will often jump spectacularly when first hooked. With these strong fish, the fight may be long.

Black marlin

Makaira indica

WEIGHT Up to 1,653 lb (750 kg).

TYPES OF WATER Warm surface waters, near shores and reefs.

DISTRIBUTION East-central Atlantic Ocean; Mediterranean; Indian Ocean; Pacific Ocean.

FISHING METHODS Trolling with lures or rigged baitfish; also fly-fishing.

The black marlin is among the largest of billfish, capable of growing to well over 1,000 lb (454 kg)—fish of this size are known as "granders" by sport anglers. Like all marlins, the black marlin has a distinctive bill. If viewed in cross section, the bill is rounded. This species has two dorsal fins, and pelvic fins that can be tucked back efficiently into a groove on its underside. The black marlin is dark blue on the upper body and silver-gray on its underside, with no distinctive markings. It tends to be found in the surface waters near islands and reef systems, and feeds mostly on fish (especially small tuna when they are plentiful), but also on cuttlefish and squid. This fast, powerful fish often uses its bill to slash at prey.

Catching black marlin

The black marlin is a popular target species for big-game anglers. The most common method of fishing is by trolling brightly colored lures or rigged baitfish behind fast-moving boats, but some adventurous fly-anglers take smaller black marlin on heavy fly gear. If caught, most black marlin are tagged and released to conserve stocks.

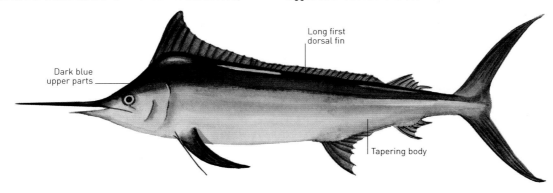

Long first
dorsal fin

Dark blue
upper parts

Tapering body

Striped marlin
Tetrapturus audax

WEIGHT Up to 970 lb (440 kg).

TYPES OF WATER Deep oceanic waters.

DISTRIBUTION Southeastern Atlantic Ocean;
Indian Ocean; Pacific Ocean.

FISHING METHODS Trolling with lures or livebait.

Striped marlin are fished for extensively by sport-anglers in
the Pacific and Indian oceans, notably off the coasts of New
Zealand. They are smaller than blue or black marlin, and
their coloration is dark blue on the back, with bright blue
or lavender-colored stripes. The dark upper body fades down
to a silvery white on its underside. The first dorsal fin is the
same height as the body depth at that point, and it stretches
almost as far back as the tiny second dorsal fin. The pectoral
fins fold against the body, and they are usually straight in
profile with a slight curve at the bottom.

Striped marlin tolerate colder water than black and blue
marlin, and occur most frequently a long way from land in
very deep water. They are known for long migrations, and
have been recorded as swimming over 3,000 miles (4,800 km)
in three months. Striped marlin tend to be solitary fish, apart
from during the breeding season.

MARLIN IN MEXICO

Mexican waters are famous grounds in which to chase
striped marlin. They are found all along the Pacific coast of
the beautiful Baja California peninsula, and on the eastern
side as far up as the Midriff Islands region of the Sea of
Cortez. They are found when the water temperature is
between 68 and 77° F (20–25° C). The popular Los Cabos
area at the southern tip of the peninsula offers very
consistent striped marlin fishing.

Striped marlin feed on fish, squid, and crustaceans. They are
normally fished for by trolling lures through waters they
are known to frequent, but if the fish can be seen (rarer than
with other marlins), then live baits will often work. The stripes
tend to vary with the location of the fish.

⬆ **Feeding on sardines** Striped marlin are often aggressive
feeders and, along with other species, will work schools of
small baitfish, such as sardines, into a ball. This bait ball
then makes an easy feeding target.

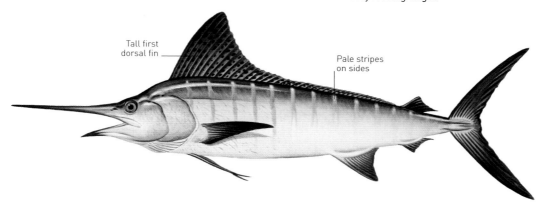

Tall first
dorsal fin

Pale stripes
on sides

Giant trevally

Caranx ignobilis

WEIGHT Up to 176 lb (80 kg).

TYPES OF WATER Coastal waters in clear lagoons, shallows, and over reefs.

DISTRIBUTION Indian Ocean and Pacific Ocean, from the Red Sea and eastern coast of Africa to Hawaii.

FISHING METHODS Lure- and fly-fishing on the flats or from boats.

From deep water to shallow sand flats, the various trevally species offer some of the most brutal, arm-wrenching fights in saltwater fishing. The giant trevally, sometimes known as the GT, is the largest. It has a steeply profiled head and a downturned mouth, and can grow up to 5½ ft (1.7 m) in length. The coloration of this species can vary from silver to near-black. Adult giant trevally are solitary fish that tend to inhabit clear-water lagoons, flats, and reefs, and can often be seen cruising around the edges of tropical reefs. In some areas this species is found on the flats, where it swims with stingrays, which are thought to act as cover for its hunting. The giant trevally feeds on smaller fish and crustaceans. It can also be caught over deep-water reefs.

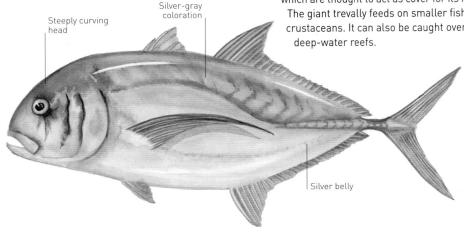

Steeply curving head

Silver-gray coloration

Silver belly

Bluefin trevally
Caranx melampygus

WEIGHT Up to 94 lb (43 kg).

TYPES OF WATER Warm, coastal waters over deep-water reefs; inshore lagoons and channels.

DISTRIBUTION Indian Ocean and Pacific Ocean.

FISHING METHODS Lure- and fly-fishing from boats and shore.

These striking-looking fish grow up to 4 ft (1.2 m) in length. The vibrant blue markings around the tail area are unmistakable. Bluefin trevally are aggressive fish, voracious predators, and very strong swimmers. Often seen in the same waters as giant trevally (opposite), bluefin trevally are found throughout the Indian Ocean region. They need a water temperature of 70 to 86° F (21–30° C) and frequent a range of depths, from deep waters, around reefs and rocky islands, to shallow, inshore lagoons and channels.

Although often solitary fish, bluefin trevally also form small schools in both deep-ocean locations and inshore shallows. Anglers target them with lures and flies from boats and from the shore. These are strong, fighting fish—their instinct tends to be to charge for the nearest obstruction.

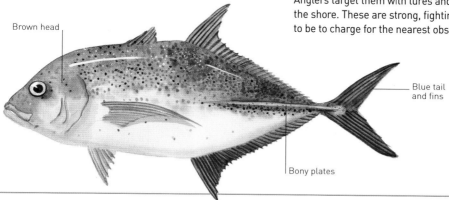

Brown head

Blue tail and fins

Bony plates

Big-eye trevally
Caranx sexfasciatus

WEIGHT Up to 40 lb (18 kg).

TYPES OF WATER Inshore reefs in warm waters; estuaries.

DISTRIBUTION Indian Ocean and Pacific Ocean, from the Red Sea and eastern coast of Africa to Hawaii.

FISHING METHODS Bait-, lure-, and fly-fishing from boats.

Big-eye trevally have a glowing, blue-green upper-body coloring, and are silver below. They have the distinctive, steeply curving head of all trevally species, and large eyes. The dorsal and anal fins have white tips. The tail fin is yellowish to black. Big-eye trevally inhabit mainly inshore reef areas, and are most active at dusk or at night. They often form large schools that move slowly around the reefs during the day, and then disperse at night to feed on smaller fish and crustaceans. Their preferred water temperature range is 77 to 84°F (25–29°C).

Juvenile big-eye trevally often live among the tentacles of jellyfish, and will sometimes come into estuaries. Adults tend to prefer deeper water, and often feed by burrowing through the sand to hunt for invertebrates. The Cabo Pulmo reef in Mexico is well known as a place where huge schools of big-eye trevally congregate, attracting predators, such as sea lions. Fish of this species are hard fighters, and will change direction frequently when hooked.

White dorsal fin tip

Large eyes

White anal fin tip

Barramundi
Lates calcarifer

WEIGHT Up to 132 lb (60 kg).

TYPES OF WATER Tropical, slow-moving creeks and estuaries.

DISTRIBUTION Western and eastern Indian Ocean; northwestern and Pacific Ocean.

FISHING METHODS Bait-, lure-, and fly-fishing.

Reaching up to 6½ ft (2 m) in length, barramundi have large mouths with distinctly protruding lower jaws. They are mostly dark, greenish-gray on the upper part of the body, blending into silver-colored underparts. They are found primarily in river creeks and estuaries in clear to turbid water, especially in larger rivers that have a slow, continuous flow and average water temperature above 68°F (20°C). They are predatory and feed on smaller fish and crustaceans.

Young males, old females

All barramundi start their lives as males and reach maturity at three to four years old. When around five years old, they change gender to female. This means that small barramundi are almost always male fish, and larger ones are female.

Adult barramundi tend to move downstream to estuaries and coastal waters to spawn, often during flooding. From an angling point of view, they are a cunning fish that often hides around snaggy areas such as mangrove roots and rocky outcrops. They can be caught with baits, lures, and flies.

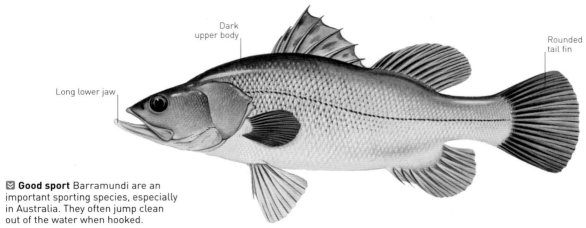

Dark upper body

Rounded tail fin

Long lower jaw

☑ **Good sport** Barramundi are an important sporting species, especially in Australia. They often jump clean out of the water when hooked.

⌃ **Schooling cobia** Although usually a solitary fish, at times cobia have been observed in large schools, especially when in pursuit of prey.

Membrane-free dorsal fin

Prominent lateral stripe

Large anal fin

Cobia
Rachycentron canadum

WEIGHT Up to 150 lb (68 kg).

TYPES OF WATER Warm, coastal waters.

DISTRIBUTION Atlantic Ocean; Indian Ocean; Pacific Ocean.

FISHING METHODS Bait- and lure-fishing, from boats.

A cobia has a long, slim body with a broad, slightly depressed head, and a protruding lower jaw. Its overall coloration is dark brown with a strong dark lateral stripe that runs from the eye to the tail. The distinctive first dorsal fin has seven to nine spines that do not have any membrane connecting them. The cobia is a powerful fish that can grow up to 6½ ft (2 m) in length, and is highly migratory, preferring warm water. Often this species can be seen traveling in shallow water, around buoys, anchored boats, and navigation markers. They feed on small fish and crustaceans.

Sight-fishing in Florida
The cobia is a hugely popular sporting species, especially in the waters off Florida. Large numbers spend the winter months on Florida's Atlantic coast around the reefs and wrecks. Sight-fishing for them is exciting. The angler must cast lures in front of a moving cobia and then retrieve it across its path. Cobia are famous for accompanying other large fish, especially rays, and many anglers will look for these when targeting cobia.

» **Ultimate catch on the fly** From a distance it is possible to mistake milkfish for huge bonefish, but their large tails and feeding patterns soon give them away. They are perhaps the ultimate species to fly-fish for on the flats.

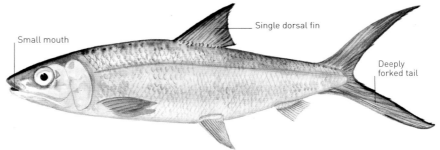

Small mouth

Single dorsal fin

Deeply forked tail

Milkfish
Chanos chanos

WEIGHT Up to 40 lb (18 kg).

TYPES OF WATER Tropical, shallow, coastal waters, sometimes brackish estuaries.

DISTRIBUTION Southeastern Atlantic Ocean; Indian Ocean; Pacific Ocean.

FISHING METHODS Fly-fishing.

One of the most sought-after species among adventurous fly-anglers, the milkfish has a long, silver body, darker on the back, and a huge, forked tail. It may reach 6 ft (1.8 m) in length. The milkfish has a small mouth with no teeth and soft lips, designed for feeding on algae. Adult milkfish gather in schools around coasts and in shallow water areas, and move on to the flats for feeding. This species frequently enters estuaries, and sometimes even penetrates farther inland into freshwater streams. In addition to algae, it sometimes feeds on larvae and small bottom-dwelling invertebrates.

Catching the uncatchable
A wary, spooky species, milkfish were for years believed to be virtually impossible to catch on the fly. However, anglers have effectively caught them on the flats, and sometimes in open water, using special flies that imitate algae. One of the hardest-fighting saltwater flats fish, milkfish take off at amazing speed once hooked. Many anglers consider the remote Indian Ocean atolls of the Seychelles to be the best location for catching large milkfish on the fly.

California yellowtail
Seriola lalandi

WEIGHT Up to 215 lb (97 kg).

TYPES OF WATER Warmish waters near the shore or beyond the continental shelf.

DISTRIBUTION Southwestern and southeastern Atlantic Ocean; Indian Ocean; Pacific Ocean.

FISHING METHODS Lure- and bait-fishing, from boats or shore.

Sometimes also known as yellowtail amberjack, or yellowtail kingfish, California yellowtails are powerful fish, inhabiting the upper waters of the open sea by nature. They grow up to 8 ft (2.5 m) in length. Overall coloration can vary between individuals, but usually they are dark green or blue on the back, shading down to a metallic blue-green on the sides and silver or white on the belly. The tail is bright yellow, and there is a noticeable gold or yellow stripe that runs along the flank. Small yellowtails often form large schools close to coasts, but larger fish tend to form much smaller groups around deepwater reefs and offshore islands. They prefer clean water with a temperature of more than 64°F (18°C). Yellowtails are fished for mainly with lures and baits.

YELLOWTAIL JIGGING

Yellowtails respond well to jigging in water up to about 200 ft (60 m) deep. It is best to drop the jig to the bottom, and then retrieve quickly—this method is known as butterfly or vertical jigging (*see* pp.164–165). Wind as fast as you can because a yellowtail will hit the jig with ease if it chooses to. When yellowtails are feeding on squid, they do so exclusively and will touch nothing else. Live squid is obviously the perfect bait in this situation.

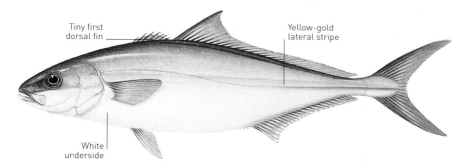

Tiny first dorsal fin

Yellow-gold lateral stripe

White underside

☑ **Yellowtails among kelp** When California yellowtails gather in schools near kelp, one of the favored ways to attract them is by chumming, and then targeting them with live baits.

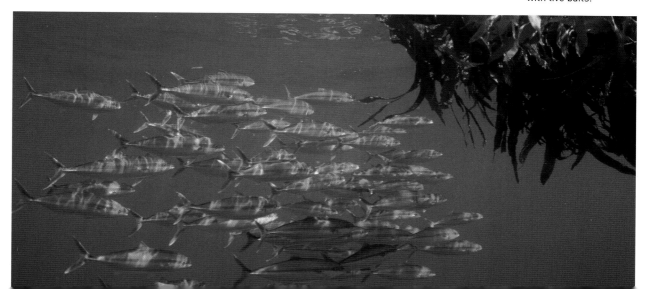

Blue shark

Prionace glauca

WEIGHT Up to 454 lb (206 kg).

TYPES OF WATER Temperate and tropical seas and oceans.

DISTRIBUTION Atlantic Ocean; Mediterranean; Pacific Ocean.

FISHING METHOD Boat-fishing with bait.

The blue shark is distinctively sleek and graceful, with an unmistakable blue coloration on its upper parts, and a pale underside. While not by any means the largest shark species, the blue shark can grow to an impressive size: up to 13 ft (4 m) in length. Generally this species is found in deep water and does not usually come very close to land, but in areas where the

⌃ **Oceanic wanderer** The blue shark, seen here feeding among a school of mackerel, is famed for roaming over great distances. Tagged sharks have often been recovered hundreds of miles from where they were initially caught.

continental shelf narrows, it may come inshore. The blue shark feeds mainly on fish, squid, and certain types of crustaceans.

Blue sharks are almost always caught from boats. Usually, they are attracted by chumming with chopped-up fish and oils (*see* p.162). Like all sharks, the blue shark has an astonishingly well-developed and highly sensitive sense of smell, and can home in on this kind of bait from a great distance.

Among anglers, the blue shark is known for making long, powerful runs when hooked. Strong wire traces are essential for all shark fishing, because of the sharp and very efficient teeth of this group of fish.

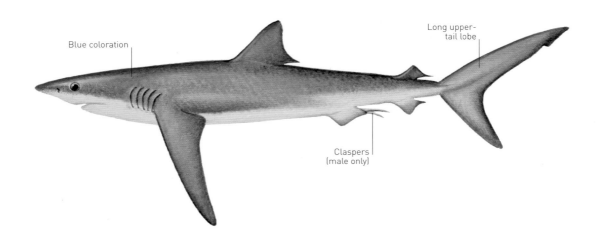

Blue coloration

Long upper-tail lobe

Claspers (male only)

Shortfin mako shark

Isurus oxyrinchus

WEIGHT Up to 1,120 lb (506 kg).

TYPES OF WATER Temperate and tropical seas and oceans.

DISTRIBUTION Atlantic Ocean; Indian Ocean; Pacific Ocean.

FISHING METHOD Boat-fishing with bait.

The shortfin mako shark, commonly known simply as the mako shark, is distinguished by its large black eyes and hooked teeth. It is dark blue above and white below, and has tiny dorsal and anal fins. It is usually found in coastal waters down to about 500 ft (150 m). An oceanic shark that can come close inshore at times, the mako tends to feed near the surface on other fish—including other sharks—and shellfish. Larger makos may sometimes even take large billfish (such as marlins) and cetaceans (whales and dolphins). It is believed that mako sharks have seasonal migratory patterns.

Speed and aggression

The shortfin mako is reputed to be the fastest-swimming shark in the ocean, and is therefore a highly prized species for anglers. It is also capable of leaping clear of the water when hooked. It can be aggressive and has been known to attack swimmers and even boats.

The waters off southern California are now recognized as being a very important breeding area for this species and it is believed that adults remain in these waters throughout the year. The mako shark is viviparous (gives birth to live young). The female produces a brood of around 5 to 10 young. Well-developed mako shark young have been known to eat less mature members of the same brood in the uterus.

Fly-fishing for mako

There are ever-growing numbers of forward-thinking fishing guides and anglers who are successfully targeting mako sharks on the fly, especially in the waters off southern California. In these breeding grounds there are plenty of small mako sharks, which are easier to manage on light tackle and are therefore suitable targets for fly-fishing.

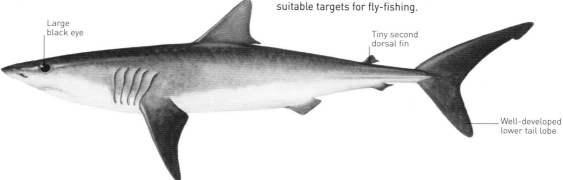

Large black eye

Tiny second dorsal fin

Well-developed lower tail lobe

◀◀ Knifelike teeth
Typically, the smooth-edged teeth of the shortfin mako shark are narrow and pointed. However, the teeth of exceptionally large individuals are usually more wedge-shaped.

Lemon shark

Negaprion brevirostris

WEIGHT Up to 406 lb (184 kg).

TYPES OF WATER Shallow subtropical waters.

DISTRIBUTION Western Atlantic Ocean (northern US to southern Brazil, including Caribbean); eastern Atlantic Ocean; eastern Pacific Ocean (Baja, California, to Ecuador).

FISHING METHODS Float- or bottom-fishing from boats; fly-fishing.

Lemon sharks are sleek and fast-moving predators, adept at coming into very shallow water for feeding purposes. These sharks are targeted by anglers in many parts of the world.

Lemon sharks are recognizable by a yellowish tinge to the overall brown color, and a second dorsal fin that is nearly as large as the first. Their distinctly triangular teeth have a slight curve to them, and a young lemon shark loses and replaces a

Mother lemon shark A warm, shallow Caribbean lagoon with a sandy bottom is the ideal birthing ground for lemon sharks. The young sharks are born about 2 ft (60 cm) long, in litters of 4 to 17 pups.

whole set of teeth, one at a time, every week or so. Although they may migrate in the open ocean, lemon sharks inhabit sand flats, creeks, docks, and cays (low islands, banks, or coral reefs), and are therefore highly accessible to inshore anglers. They feed mainly on small fish, but also eat some crustaceans and mollusks. Adults mate in relatively shallow waters during the spring. Following a gestation period of 10 to 12 months, the females return to shallow nursery areas between April and September to give birth.

Fishing is mainly from boats, using chum (fish and other natural baits in nets hung from the boat) to attract them to float- or bottom-fished baits. They may be caught on big flies when very close.

Yellow-brown coloration

Large second dorsal fin

Bronze whaler shark
Carcharhinus brachyurus

WEIGHT Up to 672 lb (305 kg).

TYPES OF WATER Tropical and temperate inshore and offshore waters.

DISTRIBUTION Atlantic Ocean; Mediterranean; Indian Ocean; Pacific Ocean.

FISHING METHODS Float- or bottom-fished baits, from the beach or boats.

The bronze whaler (or copper) shark is a large, gray- to bronze-colored shark, white below the lateral line, with a broad snout. A wide-ranging species of shark, it is well adapted to both offshore and inshore waters. This shark is found in temperate and tropical waters throughout the world. In the northern part of its range it is migratory, moving northward in spring and south in fall. The bronze whaler feeds on various upper-water species of fish, but is just as effective at coming in close to shore to feed on bottom-feeding fish, rays, and smaller sharks. This shark is also very comfortable feeding in the surf zone. The bronze whaler shark is famous for following the annual sardine migration that takes place off the southern African coast from May to July.

Fishing for bronze whaler sharks is one of the most challenging forms of beach-fishing. It is increasingly popular, especially in Namibia, where large numbers of these sharks come close to the shoreline, and also in South Africa and southern Angola. Bronze whalers are also targeted from boats.

Dark bronze coloration

Broad snout

⌄ **Bronzed hunter**
Bronze whaler sharks follow schools of migrating small fish for easy feeding.

World of
Fishing

Fishing is, without doubt, one of the best reasons for visiting new places. Some of the locations in this section are explored only by sport-fishing enthusiasts. Whether exotic or local, it does not matter—each time you visit somewhere different, your fishing will be cherished.

If you are thinking about heading somewhere different for your fishing, how do you choose where to go? The destinations in this section include some of the world's best fishing, in some of the most special places on the planet. Use these recommendations as a useful guide, and then spend time researching your choices.

You will find information on the types of fishing, the species to discover, the locations, other points of interest, and what to think about when you go. Specialty fishing-vacation operators can guide you on where to go, what to fish for, and how to get there, but remember that in some locations, you can do things yourself. If you are going to fish somewhere new and for species you have never encountered, nothing can beat hiring a good, local guide. Just as you may know your home waters like the back of your hand, your guide will know his or her local waters inside out.

⌃ **Destination fishing** Hot or cold weather, saltwater or freshwater—fishing in foreign waters provides a vast spectrum of wonderful adventures.

Some of the fishing destinations described are more popular and accessible than others. But remember that no destination is better than another—what to one angler may seem exotic, might well be everyday fishing to another. An angler who fishes the wild and remote saltwaters of southern Angola might dream of fishing an English chalk stream. However, an English chalk-stream angler might dream of chasing milkfish on a remote saltwater flat, far from a cell-phone signal or Internet access. Who knows what other anglers dream of?

Fishing new waters for new species will always give you a new, heightened sense of perspective on your own, more regular fishing. Fishing new places can be such a thrill that it can be hard to return to normality—some anglers fall in love with a different destination or species and relocate permanently. The destinations featured in this section have been selected to excite, enthuse, and inform in equal measure. The possibilities are virtually endless—it is up to you where you go.

◄◄ **The thrill of the chase** Catching different fish all around the world is such a big part of what makes fishing so special.

British Columbia

WESTERN CANADA, NORTH AMERICA

The Canadian province of British Columbia offers some staggeringly diverse fishing in beautiful, unspoiled countryside. Stretching for 740 miles (1,190 km) down the west coast of Canada, it is the most varied area of the country.

There is great sea and freshwater fishing for numerous species, but to the fly-angler, British Columbia is known as the home of steelhead fishing. These sea-run rainbow trout are a prized catch. The huge Chinook (or king) salmon are also a major draw, as are other species of Pacific salmon and halibut.

British Columbia has more than 6,000 coastal islands, 12,000 miles (19,300 km) of fjords, shoreline, and coastal straits, as well as more than 24,000 lakes and rivers, all with individual charms and attractions. Grizzly and black bears are found in many parts of British Columbia, and the central coast is the only place where you can see Kermode (spirit) bears while on your fishing trip. British Columbia is also one of the best places for watching killer whales (orca) and humpback whales.

Fishing infrastructure

There is a well-organized network of fishing guides, specialty tour operators, and charter boats that offer fishing opportunities. Some

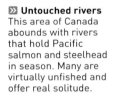

》 Untouched rivers
This area of Canada abounds with rivers that hold Pacific salmon and steelhead in season. Many are virtually unfished and offer real solitude.

of the wildest, most out of the way fly-fishing is accessed with helicopters, and is known as heli-fishing.

Although steelhead are a popular target for visiting fly-anglers, the Fraser River is renowned throughout the world for the chance to catch large sturgeon, always carefully released afterward. It is rare to find a fishery that is actually improving, but strenuous conservation methods ensure that these large freshwater fish are now flourishing.

Coasts, lakes, and rivers

The massive number of islands and long coastline mean that the saltwater fishing opportunities are endless. Not only are the main Pacific salmon species caught at sea, but also huge halibut, and various rockfish species. The many lakes and rivers offer plentiful freshwater fishing, including strong yearly runs of Pacific salmon. Many nonanglers

also come to watch the annual spawning of Pacific salmon in the rivers, through late summer and early fall—a time that can be good for bear-watching as they feast on the plentiful fish supplies. What you see and do when visiting British Columbia depends upon which part you visit.

Prize catch Chinook salmon can grow to huge sizes, and some awesome fish are caught both at sea and in the rivers of British Columbia.

ESSENTIAL INFORMATION

Climate Coastal areas are generally mild with lots of rain. The climate is more extreme farther north. Temperatures inland in southern British Columbia range between 82 and 90° F (28–32° C) in July.

When to fish Steelhead fishing is best from August to late October; for Chinook salmon, visit in June and July.

Key species Steelhead, Chinook salmon, halibut, rockfish, and sturgeon.

Hot spots The entire Skeena River system is very good for steelhead.

Don't forget Dress according to the season. Waders, thermals, wading boots, and waterproofs are essential. You will need a license appropriate for whatever fishing you do in British Columbia.

Alaska

UNITED STATES, NORTH AMERICA

ALASKA

Anchorage Kenai
 Peninsula
 Kodiak
 Island

Pacific Ocean

Alaska is the largest peninsula in the western hemisphere, with more than three million lakes, 3,000 rivers, and numerous fishing streams. It offers fishing for a number of species, including Pacific salmon, halibut, and rainbow trout.

Varied fishing

Each region of the huge state of Alaska offers different kinds of fishing in a variety of surroundings. The famous Chinook (or king) salmon runs offer spectacular fishing that draws anglers from all over the world. It is possible to fish in complete solitude in Alaska, with many fishing lodges organizing fishing tours on which visiting anglers are taken by floatplanes and helicopters into the unspoiled wild country of Alaska.

The Kodiak Island archipelago lies 30 miles (48 km) off the coast, and is considered to be one of the finest all-around destinations for fishing. Fishing for large halibut and Chinook salmon can be particularly successful here.

Travel and tourism are among Alaska's fastest-growing industries and there is a great infrastructure for visitors. There is a wealth of activities to enjoy alongside fishing, including wildlife observation, hiking, and other outdoor recreational activities.

ESSENTIAL INFORMATION

Climate This is a region of huge climatic variation. Anchorage has a generally warm summer and a mild winter. Kodiak is similar, but expect rain at any time. The yearly temperatures average 32 to 63° F (0–17° C).

When to fish Halibut are around most of the year; Chinook salmon are best in June and July in the rivers, and from June to September in saltwater.

Key species Chinook salmon, rainbow trout, halibut, Dolly Varden, and steelhead.

Hot spots The Kenai Peninsula teems with fish. Kodiak Island is another remote area with abundant and varied fish stocks.

Don't forget Take layered clothing for varying temperatures and rain, and prepare for mosquitoes. You will need fishing licenses.

» Wilderness fishing
Karluk River, Kodiak Island, offers some truly wild adventure fishing, especially for coho salmon and steelheads. Prepare for genuine solitude here.

Ontario

CANADA, NORTH AMERICA

CANADA
Lake Superior
Ontario
USA
Toronto
Lake Erie

Ontario is considered to be a sport-fishing paradise. The Great Lakes include the biggest lake in the world, Lake Superior, and there is some excellent fishing for walleye, lake trout, steelhead, brown trout, and smallmouth bass.

Great Lakes fishing

With more than 400,000 lakes, rivers, and streams in Ontario, the choice of fishing is wide. There are wonderful fishing opportunities in Northern Ontario in remote locations with pristine waters that are especially good for muskellunge, or "muskie." Lake Erie is known as the most productive of the Great Lakes, especially for walleye, which can be fished for virtually all year. Ice-fishing in the depths of winter is a much-loved way of catching fish; anglers put up small, heated huts, and cut holes in the ice in order to fish for their favorite species.

River-fishing opportunities

There are numerous trout-fishing streams and rivers in Ontario to attract visiting fly-anglers. Some of the best places for river fishing are the Albany and Ogoki River systems. The annual

ESSENTIAL INFORMATION

Climate The summers are hot, and winters cold, with temperatures ranging between 9 and 73° F (–13–23° C).

When to fish Winter months for ice-fishing on Lake Erie; walleye fishing is good from June to October.

Key species Walleye, steelhead, lake trout, brown trout, and muskellunge.

Hot spots Lake Erie.

Don't forget You will need layered clothing, and waterproofs. Remember sun protection and insect repellent in summer.

Maumee River walleye run is anticipated with pleasure by countless anglers. This is the period when vast schools of walleye migrate up the Maumee River for spawning; it begins around early March and continues through to early May. It offers stunning scenery, plenty of wildlife, and lots of anglers all trying for a 11-lb (5-kg) walleye.

» **Erie tranquillity** Lake Erie is the smallest and shallowest of the Great Lakes. Its waters warm quickly in summer and freeze over in winter.

Montana

UNITED STATES, NORTH AMERICA

Wild brown, rainbow, and cutthroat trout abound in numerous rivers and lakes in Montana, and the state manages these wonderful natural resources well. Anglers from all over the world travel to fish the "Treasure State."

Fishing in national parks

The most famous fishing destinations in Montana are the Yellowstone and Glacier national parks. Supremely well managed and truly wild in many places, Glacier National Park has large fishing lakes and big mountains. Yellowstone National Park, which spreads into parts of Montana and Wyoming, is known for spectacular fly-fishing, fantastic scenery, wildlife, and thermal geysers. Fishing methods employed, which vary with the seasons, include fly-fishing, spinning, and bait-fishing, but most visitors come for the fly-fishing, especially using dry flies. Wading is common, but many rivers can also be accessed by float boats, and motorboats are allowed on most waters.

Protected habitats

Guiding services for anglers are available throughout Montana. Regulations that govern fishing in the state include strong catch-and-release regulations, and measures to protect the natural habitat for all visitors to enjoy. It is truly one of the most spectacular areas to go fly-fishing for wild trout. Most anglers need to obtain both a conservation license and a fishing license.

ESSENTIAL INFORMATION

Climate The western part of Montana has a warmer climate than the east, which has harsh winters. Temperatures average 84° F (29° C) in July, and 28° F (−2° C) in January. Extreme temperatures are possible.

When to fish Some parts can be fished all year, but most are affected by seasonal regulations and water conditions. Fly-fishing is best from June to October.

Key species Wild brown, rainbow, and cutthroat trout.

Hot spots Yellowstone National Park and Bighorn River.

Don't forget Take layered clothing, waders, and wading boots.

» Montana river fishing The clear rivers of Montana offer some great boat-fishing. Rivers are accessible to visitors, but take care to respect private land.

Long Island, New York

UNITED STATES, NORTH AMERICA

Fishing for striped bass on Long Island can be fantastic at various times of the year, from the beaches, jetties, and piers, and from boats. There is also excellent fishing for bluefish, bonito, false albacore, and winter flounder.

Striped-bass angling

The US striped-bass fishery is a world-famous conservation success story, and commercial fishing is tightly regulated. This means that there is plenty of good striped-bass fishing for visiting and local anglers to enjoy each year, with strict size and bag limits imposed.

Long Island is nearly 120 miles (193 km) long, and stretches from 12 to 20 miles (19 to 32 km) in width. The western end is part of New York City's harbor, and is very built-up, but the quieter, eastern end is still partly rural and has plenty of long, sandy beaches that are good for striped-bass fishing.

Varied habitats

The many jetties and piers on Long Island offer a variety of fishing opportunities. All kinds of techniques are used, including surfcasting, trolling, fly-fishing, and chumming. The south shore of Long Island is one of the most diverse habitats in New York State, and the striped bass come close inshore to feed, making them easily accessible to anglers. Good numbers of bluefish and false albacore migrate along the coast, and will enter the numerous inlets during peak season. Long Island is a good vacation location, and offers a wealth of activities to enjoy alongside your fishing.

ESSENTIAL INFORMATION

Climate Summers are warm, and winters cold. The western end of Long Island is usually warmer than the east. Summer temperatures average 72° F (22° C)

When to fish There are various spring, summer, and fall runs of striped bass, but fall is considered best for big fish.

Key species Striped bass, bonito, bluefish, and false albacore.

Hot spots Montauk Point and the Shinnecock Inlet.

Don't forget Early- and late-season fishing requires layered clothing and waterproofs. Buy fishing licenses from local tackle shops.

⊠ Sharing the shore
Anglers shore-fish a Long Island beach, as couples stroll by in the evening light. This is a deservedly popular weekend-break location.

South Carolina

UNITED STATES, NORTH AMERICA

Fishing in South Carolina is centered on the state capital of Charleston, which stands at the mouth of the estuary of the Ashley and Cooper rivers. This beautiful city guards a magnificent natural harbor and a large area of intracoastal waterways.

Tidal flats, harbors, and lakes

South Carolina provides varied fishing throughout the year. Spring brings large tides that enable redfish to feed in the creeks of the Isle of Palms and the extensive spartina-grass salt marshes, and these greater depths allow boat access. Some anglers also like to wade at this time of year. The wonderful fishing possibilities can continue right into fall, and late summer usually sees a good

run of aggressive crevalle jack in Charleston Harbor. At various times it is also possible to catch speckled trout, tarpon, bluefish, and black drum. As winter approaches and the water cools, the abundant redfish gather into huge schools that produce excellent sight-fishing results. Winter is also good for trout fishing in these waters. There are also plenty of lakes in South Carolina that hold good stocks of largemouth bass and catfish, and good trout fishing exists in the hills.

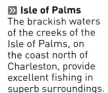 **Redfish** Also known as red drum, spottail bass, and channel bass, the impressive redfish is the prime target species of the South Carolina salt flats.

Isle of Palms The brackish waters of the creeks of the Isle of Palms, on the coast north of Charleston, provide excellent fishing in superb surroundings.

ESSENTIAL INFORMATION

Climate Subtropical conditions mean high humidity in summer and temperatures on the coast of 90° F (32° C) or more. Short, mild winters average 68° F (20° C) on the coast.

When to fish All year, but winter and spring are particularly good for sight-fishing for redfish and speckled trout.

Key species Redfish, black drum, jacks, speckled trout, bluefish, tarpon.

Hot spots Charleston Harbor and the surrounding flats give prime fishing.

Don't forget A fishing license is required.

Bahamas

WESTERN ATLANTIC OCEAN

The islands of the Bahamas have wonderful ocean wildlife. Many islands are surrounded by extensive saltwater flats—home to bonefish, sharks, barracuda, tarpon, permit, and snook—while plenty of big-game species swim farther offshore.

Flats and bluewater angling

The approximately 700 islands that make up the Bahamas are famous as an angling destination. The islands of Bimini, Andros, and Abaco, as well as Acklins and Crooked Island, all offer excellent guided flats fishing, most often from fast boats that access the shallow waters. Various big game-fishing operations offer blue-water (ocean) fishing, and there are angling tournaments throughout the year.

Many anglers do not realize that, in addition to busy tourist resorts, the Bahamas offer numerous quiet waters where bonefish are rarely fished for. These out-of-the-way locations are accessible via a network of interisland flights. The Inagua Islands offer some truly marvelous bonefish angling. In addition, Great Inagua has a vast inland lagoon that holds abundant tarpon and snook. A vast

area of flats surrounds this big island, creating some wild saltwater fly-fishing, notably for permit and bonefish. There are virtually no tourist facilities on Greater Inagua, but the visiting angler can find these on the neighboring island of Mayaguana.

✉ **Island climate** The coastal flats of these subtropical islands may be warm, but they are windswept. Be ready for changeable conditions.

Florida Keys

FLORIDA, UNITED STATES, NORTH AMERICA

FLORIDA
The Everglades
Loggerhead • Miami
Key
Islamorada
• Key West
Atlantic Ocean

The Florida Keys are a chain of limestone and coral islands that stretch 220 miles (350 km) south of Miami Beach to Loggerhead Key in the Gulf of Mexico. The region offers a vast array of saltwater fishing opportunities.

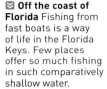

⊠ Off the coast of Florida Fishing from fast boats is a way of life in the Florida Keys. Few places offer so much fishing in such comparatively shallow water.

Fishing choices

The Florida Keys include several very well-known fishing areas, including the Everglades, Islamorada, Marathon, Big Pine, and Key West. There are plenty of places to stay, from well-appointed campsites to classy hotels and lodges. The whole Keys culture is based on fishing and diving, so visiting anglers are welcome everywhere, and there are fishing guides to suit all fishing methods and species.

Florida's famous backcountry flats network is where big bonefish, tarpon, permit, and snook roam. The bridges that link the many islands hold enormous stocks of big, migratory tarpon. Farther out to sea, other species, such as marlin, sailfish, shark, tuna, cobia, and dorado, are found in abundance.

Saltwater fly-fishing for bonefish, tarpon, and permit is extremely popular. In fact, it is one of the few places where a legitimate "Grand Slam" can be achieved—catching a bonefish, a permit, and a tarpon in a single day on fly-fishing tackle.

Fishing for big fish

The Florida Keys has, without doubt, the finest tarpon fishing in the world. Every year huge schools of big specimens migrate through the islands and feed on the abundance of smaller fish. During periods of warm weather in February,

March, and April, tarpon begin to arrive in this area, but they are most prevalent from May until mid-July. These hard-fighting fish are famous for their spectacular jumps and their ability to throw hooks and break lines.

There are also plenty of shark species that swim on the flats (shallow inshore waters) in this area, and these are becoming increasingly popular targets for fishing. Indeed, some anglers specialize in taking big sharks on fly-fishing tackle.

The diving in Florida is excellent with warm, clear waters full of many different species. It is also possible to see the famous manatees (sea cows).

Inland fishing

Throughout eastern North America and especially in the warm southern states, largemouth and smallmouth black bass are among the most popular freshwater species. Florida has many big lakes where there are large numbers of largemouth bass. Much of the fishing is with live baits or lures and there are also professional bass-fishing tournaments.

◄ **Unhooking a tarpon**
A notoriously difficult fish to hook and play, tarpon are usually unhooked at the side of the boat and released unharmed.

ESSENTIAL INFORMATION

Climate Tropical. Rain can occur from late May through the hurricane season of mid-August to mid-October. Summer temperatures average around 86° F (30° C).

When to fish Different species provide good fishing all year, but the best months for big migratory tarpon are from April to July.

Key species Tarpon, bonefish, permit, sailfish, sharks, marlin, cobia, snook.

Hot spots Islamorada, commonly referred to as "The Sport Fishing Capital of the World." Key West is also an excellent base.

Don't forget Take tropical fishing clothing, plenty of sunscreen, and a light, waterproof jacket. Be sure to buy the correct fishing licenses, available at the many tackle shops.

Yucatan Peninsula

MEXICO, CENTRAL AMERICA

The Yucatan Peninsula is at the southeastern tip of Mexico, between the Gulf of Mexico and the Caribbean Sea. It is a mix of bustling, modern vacation resorts, ancient ruins, beaches, colonial cities, and stunning natural environments.

Gulf Stream influences

The Yucatan is a large peninsula, covering around 76,300 square miles (198,000 sq km). Alongside the ruins of the ancient Mayan civilization, and modern beach resorts, there is a wealth of classic flats-style fishing. Species such as bonefish, tarpon, snook, and permit draw many visiting fly-anglers to these shallow waters.

There is a big, deepwater channel between the Yucatan coast and the island of Cozumel that in effect "squeezes" the Gulf Stream as it passes by the popular resort of Cancún. This natural upwelling brings about an abundance of fish, and this area offers some outstanding boat-fishing for sailfish. Around Cozumel itself there is excellent marlin fishing.

World heritage site

The 1.3-million-acre (5,260-square-km) Sian Ka'an Biosphere Reserve, which includes Ascension Bay, is a protected marine area of outstanding biodiversity. The area contains excellent fishing on the flats and abundant wildlife. These waters also offer consistent permit and tarpon fishing. There are many fishing lodges that offer light-tackle saltwater fishing to visitors, and it is easy to escape the crowds and fish in wild solitude, with excellent guides.

» **Crystal-water wading** Clear waters and brilliant sunshine make fly-fishing the flats a particular delight.

Coasts of Costa Rica

COSTA RICA, CENTRAL AMERICA

Costa Rica is in the narrow neck of Central America, with Nicaragua on its northern border and Panama to the south. A slender country, with both Atlantic and Pacific coastlines, at its narrowest point only 74 miles (100 km) separate the oceans.

Caribbean coast

The sheer variety of waters of the Caribbean coast means that this is some of the most exciting and varied saltwater fishing possible, but the majority of visiting anglers come for the marlin and sailfish that can often be found close to shore. There is also excellent tarpon fishing in various tidal river areas on the Caribbean side, especially in the Río Colorado, Parismina, and in the Tortuguero National Park. A mass of varied inshore waters also offer fantastic fishing for species such as roosterfish, cubera snapper, snook, and barracuda.

Pacific coast

The Osa Peninsula in the southwest corner of Costa Rica is a great place to fish and visit. This peninsula is considered to be one of the most biodiverse areas in the world. The visiting angler has a wide choice of species to fish and types of fishing in which to participate.

ESSENTIAL INFORMATION

Climate Tropical. The annual temperature ranges between 70 and 80° F (21–27° C). The rainy season is from May to December.

When to fish The largest black marlin are caught in July and August. The best blue marlin and sailfish fishing is from November to March; big tuna are also most frequently caught in these months.

Key species Marlin, sailfish, roosterfish, dorado, wahoo, cubera snapper, and permit.

Hot spots Rio Colorado, Osa Peninsula.

Don't forget Take tropical fishing clothing, a lightweight rain jacket, and plenty of sun protection.

Most tourist lodges offer a selection of eco-tours to a diverse range of habitats, including rain forests, beaches (there is some excellent surfing), extensive mangrove swamps, and volcanoes. Costa Rica is also an unmissable destination for people interested in environmental conservation projects.

» **Rain-forest fishing** Shallow-draft boats provide a steady platform for tarpon fishing among tropical vegetation on the Rio Colorado in the northeastern part of the country.

Los Roques

VENEZUELA, SOUTH AMERICA

Caribbean Sea
Los Roques

• Caracas

VENEZUELA

The unspoiled Los Roques archipelago that lies 90 miles (145 km) north of Caracas, the capital of Venezuela, is a great bonefishing destination. The "pancake" flats are unique, and the climate provides an unusually long fishing season.

Exceptional marine ecosystem

The Los Roques archipelago is a national park area of lagoons, white sands, coral reefs, mangroves, and sea-grass beds. While there are hundreds of conventional bonefish flats dotted around the 40–50 major islands that make up the archipelago, what makes Los Roques really famous are localized "pancake" flats. These are small, flat-topped hills of ½–3 acres (0.2–1.2 hectares) in area, which rise from deeper water and are covered with very shallow, crystal-clear, tropical waters. Some 300 of these pancake flats exist. There is also big-game fishing in the deeper waters.

Bonefish are normally fished for with flies that fish on the bottom, but because these fish sometimes attack the huge schools of minnows that swarm around the islands, fly-anglers can also take bonefish using surface fly-fishing techniques. It is even possible to successfully target huge bonefish from the pier as they try to dislodge minnows from the beaks of diving pelicans.

ESSENTIAL INFORMATION

Climate There are cooling trade winds that blow for most of the year, and very little rain. Temperatures throughout the year range from 79 to 84° F (26–29° C).

When to fish The long fishing season is best from January to October.

Key species Bonefish, tarpon.

Hot spots The hard-bottomed pancake flats of Los Roques are unmissable places to fly-fish for bonefish.

Don't forget Take tropical fishing clothing, flats boots, and sun protection.

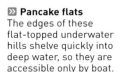

» Pancake flats
The edges of these flat-topped underwater hills shelve quickly into deep water, so they are accessible only by boat.

Tierra del Fuego

ARGENTINA, SOUTH AMERICA

ARGENTINA
Atlantic Ocean
CHILE
Rio Grande
Ushuaia •
Lake Fagnano
• Tierra del Fuego

Tierra del Fuego is part of the group of islands at the southern tip of South America, bounded on one side by the Pacific Ocean, and on the other by the Atlantic. The Argentinian part of the area contains the southernmost national park in the world.

Chilly fishing

This remote, subpolar region is known for cool weather, and mostly strong winds. The climate, however, does not affect the tremendous fishing—Tierra del Fuego offers arguably the finest fly-fishing for big sea trout in the world, and in season the runs of fish in the Rio Grande are very consistent.

Most fly-fishing in these remote rivers is done with floating lines and relatively small flies, often for sea trout averaging more than 10 lb (4.5 kg), with fish of more than 30 lb (13.5 kg) being recorded. Most of the rivers are highly regulated and well maintained, and most lodges and guides adhere to a strict catch-and-release policy. Prices charged reflect both the remoteness of the area, and the quality of the fishing. The capital of Tierra del

ESSENTIAL INFORMATION

Climate The region is cold and windy. Summer (December to March) temperatures range from 43 to 54° F (6–12° C); spring and fall (September to December and March to June) are often closer to 32° F (0° C).

When to fish The Rio Grande season is from October to April; peak times are January, February, March, and April.

Key species Sea trout, brown trout.

Hot spots Rio Grande.

Don't forget Take layered clothing, to deal with wind and cold. A good wading jacket, waders, and wading boots are essential.

Fuego, Ushuaia, is the southernmost city in the world. There is a large national park, which includes part of Lake Fagnano. Other parts of the southern tip of South America, especially the mountainous areas of southern Chile, also offer good, unspoiled brown- and rainbow-trout fishing.

» Waterfalls and rapids Tierra del Fuego's national park is one of the region's main attractions and includes several spectacular rivers within its boundaries.

Southern England

UNITED KINGDOM, WESTERN EUROPE

The history of fly-fishing is bound up with the famous chalk streams of Wiltshire and Hampshire. In addition to these exclusive waters, southern England offers fishing in lesser-known rivers, as well as saltwater fishing in the English Channel.

highly prized quarry is the wild brown trout, but there are also plenty of grayling, and stocked brown and rainbow trout. What makes these rivers so special are the unique characteristics of chalk streams: consistent flows and water temperatures, a fantastic clarity (this type of fishing is based on sight-fishing), and beautifully unspoiled scenery. Most fishing in these areas is done from the bank.

Chalk-stream fishing

Rivers such as the Test, Kennet, Itchen, and the Hampshire Avon are world-famous fishing venues and for several centuries have been extensively managed, principally for sport-fishing purposes. The accepted methods in these waters are almost exclusively upstream dry-fly fishing, and the most

Other forms of freshwater fishing

Southern England also offers excellent freshwater fishing for species such as pike, perch, barbel, roach, and carp. The Kennet River is most famous for its fly-fishing. However, much of the river is also open to freshwater anglers who choose to use other methods of fishing.

WRECK FISHING

There is some excellent boat-fishing all along the southern coast of England that attracts many visiting anglers. The numerous wrecks that litter the bed of the English Channel—a testament to the high volume of sea traffic in one of the world's busiest waterways—provide a particularly rich fishing environment. Many charter boats with experienced skippers offer anglers the opportunity to fish in these waters for species such as big conger eels, cod, ling, and pollack.

▶ **Catching a conger eel while wreck fishing**

Coastal fishing

The Isle of Wight, which lies off the coast of southern England in the English Channel, has many miles of beach and estuary fishing. Big European sea bass and conger eels are among the saltwater species regularly caught in these waters, and this is about the only place in the United Kingdom where it is feasible to boat-fish for thresher sharks. However, they are not a common catch. It is also possible to catch big undulate and blonde rays. Overall, southern England offers a wide variety of fishing to suit all kinds of anglers and budgets.

ESSENTIAL INFORMATION

Climate Temperate. The annual average temperature is around 63° F (17° C), but summer temperatures can reach over 86° F (30° C). Rainfall is frequent.

When to fish The trout season is from April 1 to October 15. Many anglers like to fish what is known as "Duffers' Fortnight," when the mayflies hatch (late May to early June).

Key species Brown and rainbow trout, and grayling.

Hot spots The Test River, especially around Stockbridge, is the most sought-after location.

Don't forget It is essential to purchase the correct tickets and daily passes for the stretch of water you intend to fish, since most are tightly controlled.

◀ **Peaceful fishing** The tranquil chalk streams of southern England are considered by many to be the place where the art of fly-fishing was developed.

Scotland

UNITED KINGDOM, NORTHERN EUROPE

Scotland is a world-famous destination for anglers wanting to catch Atlantic salmon, wild brown trout, and sea trout—indeed, the major salmon rivers of this extraordinary country are often considered to be the birthplace of the sport of salmon fishing.

Diverse opportunities

The highly regarded Tay, Tweed, Spey, and Dee Rivers can be exclusive and expensive to fish, but Scotland is a very diverse country and it has many other salmon rivers that provide worthwhile fishing. There are also numerous lochs and rivers where it is possible to catch wild brown trout, and there are sea-trout runs in rivers to the south and east.

Salmon fishing tends to be done with a hired guide, known as a gillie, and takes place from a boat or the bank, as well as via wading. The salmon are not as abundant as they once were, but there is still excellent fishing to be enjoyed, and many visitors make annual trips to their favorite stretch, or beat, of the river.

River, loch, coast, and sea

While the bigger salmon rivers are found on the east coast, on Scotland's west coast there are hundreds of small spate rivers, streams, and lochs. In these waters, there is plenty of freshwater fishing available, and much of it is free. The legendary lochs, including Lomond, Awe, and Ken, are revisited time after time by pike enthusiasts. The beautiful Caithness and Sutherland regions farther north also provide anglers with a variety of rivers, lochs, and streams.

Off the coast of Scotland there is excellent sea fishing for species such as the giant common skate, shark, cod, pollack, and porbeagle sharks. In addition, the many Scottish islands, such as those of the Inner and Outer Hebrides, offer wild fishing in awe-inspiring surroundings. The staggeringly beautiful, unspoiled, and truly wild highlands are a wonderful place to visit, especially for enthusiastic walkers and climbers. Scotland is also famous for its golf, and is often called the "home of golf," and visiting anglers may enjoy a visit to one of its world-famous courses, such as St. Andrews, Carnoustie, or Royal Troon.

⊗ **Highland waters** The Spey River has given its name to a major fly-casting technique, which is a reflection of the importance of Scotland to the sport of fly-fishing.

ESSENTIAL INFORMATION

Climate Generally cool and damp, the weather is extremely changeable and unpredictable, with regional variations. Average temperatures in winter range from 41 to 45°F (5–7°C), and those in July and August average 66°F (19°C).

When to fish The salmon season is usually early February until late October, but check for local variations. Brown trout are fished for from March 15 to October 6.

Key species Atlantic salmon and wild brown trout, sea trout.

Hot spots The Tay, Spey, Tweed, and Dee Rivers are renowned for salmon fishing.

Don't forget Scotland has an extremely variable climate and the wise angler is prepared to experience every season in one day. Good waterproofs are essential.

Tweed River A fly-angler casts a line into the clear waters of the Ravenswood beat of this famous Scottish river.

County Clare

SOUTHWEST IRELAND, WESTERN EUROPE

The west coast of Ireland has a spectacular coastline. County Clare offers true rock-edge fishing, as well as fishing from beaches, harbors, and the banks of the huge Shannon estuary. There is also lots of good boat-fishing.

Rocks and beaches

Along the desolate and virtually deserted Loop Head, in the southern part of the county, there are plenty of good rock-edge fishing spots for species such as European sea bass, pollack, and wrasse. On some days the huge Atlantic swells that crash into the coast make it too rough for rock-edge fishing, so it is wise to head inland and fish the more sheltered Shannon estuary for a variety of species, including rays, bull huss, mullet, and tope. There is also some good European sea bass fishing from the west-facing beaches of the estuary. The largest fish tend to arrive in the middle of winter. The visiting angler should expect to have to cope with plenty of wind and rain, but the peace and quiet of the region more than compensate. Arguably Clare's most famous tourist attraction are the Cliffs of Moher, in the northern part of the county. These stretch along the coast for almost 5 miles (8 km) and at times rise to nearly 700 ft (200 m) above the sea.

Rock fishing
Fishing directly into deep water from the rocks on the rugged coast of County Clare is a great way to catch a wide variety of species.

ESSENTIAL INFORMATION

Climate Generally mild and wet. Average temperatures range from 48° F (9° C) in winter to 70° F (21° C) in summer.

When to fish The best rock-edge and estuary fishing is from May to September. Beach-fishing for European sea bass is best in midwinter.

Key species Pollack, wrasse, bull huss, ray, European sea bass, mullet, and tope. Blue sharks are sometimes caught from boats.

Hot spots The coastline around Kilkee and the Shannon estuary.

Don't forget Good waterproofs are essential for fishing in Ireland. When fishing on these coasts, keep a close eye on changing sea conditions.

Freshwater possibilities

There is also plenty of freshwater fishing in County Clare. Indeed, some of the waters are among the most productive in Ireland. There is also excellent salmon and pike fishing on various tributaries of the Shannon.

Wexford coast
SOUTHEAST IRELAND, WESTERN EUROPE

The coast of County Wexford in the southeast of Ireland offers some marvelous European sea bass fishing. There are also great fishing spots for many other sea species. For the fly-angler, there is also good salmon, sea-trout, and brown-trout fishing.

» European sea bass County Wexford provides ideal opportunities for catching this highly prized fish.

European sea bass fishing
The Wexford coastline is far gentler than that of Ireland's west coast. For the bass angler there is very good fishing with baits from the many beaches, estuary mouths, and areas of rough ground. It also offers extensive areas of shallow water over broken ground that are excellent for lure- and fly-fishing. Some of the south- and west-facing beaches also produce good runs of cod during the winter. There are also lots of mullet and flounder in the estuaries. Near the ferry port of Rosslare it is possible to catch tope and smooth hound off the shore during summer.

» Rough ground, shallow water Many parts of the coast of southeast Ireland offer shallow water with rocky edges and plenty of seaweed, which is perfect for European sea bass fishing.

ESSENTIAL INFORMATION

Climate Ireland has a mild and wet climate. Temperatures in Wexford average around 46°F (8°C) in winter and 64°F (18°C) in summer.

When to fish European sea bass fishing is best from April to December. The close season is from May 15 to June 15. Other species can be caught all year, but winter is best for cod.

Key species European sea bass, mullet, flounder, cod, wrasse, tope, smooth hound.

Hot spots Kilmore Quay offers excellent boat- and shore-fishing. Rosslare Strand can provide good bait-fishing for European sea bass.

Don't forget Anglers may take only two European sea bass in any 24-hour period and these must be more than 16 in (40 cm) in length.

There is also some good boat-fishing over wrecks, reefs, and sandbanks from the charter boats that run out of Kilmore Quay, and the shore-fishing around this area can be excellent. There is also plenty to do for nonanglers, and there are numerous hotels, guesthouses, and restaurants, as well as many pubs in which locals and visitors gather to socialize and share fishing stories.

Norwegian Sea

NORTHERN NORWAY, NORTHERN EUROPE

Norwegian Sea
Lofoten
•Tromsø
Røst
Bodø NORWAY
Arctic Circle

Many anglers seeking some of the biggest cod in the world head to the Norwegian Sea above the Arctic Circle. These waters also provide the opportunity to catch very big coalfish. In certain areas the halibut is still a viable fish to try for.

Abundant cod and coalfish

There are very few places left where it is still possible to catch large numbers of big cod; overfishing has led to the decimation of stocks in many waters of the world. Norway works hard to protect its fish stocks, and the best fishing is in the remotest areas, deep within the Arctic Circle. The 52,000-mile (83,000-km) coastline is indented by numerous deep-water fjords and there are more than 50,000 islands along the coast.

Cod of up to 100 lb (45 kg) have been caught commercially in the waters off Norway. Less well known is the outstanding fishing for big coalfish, especially around the southern Lofoten Islands.

⬇ **Arctic fishing**
Fishing in the icy waters of the Arctic Circle demands the right equipment for the job.

Big coalfish are renowned fighters and offer excellent sport. There is also shallow-water fishing for large halibut and the strange-looking wolf fish, a favored fish to eat.

⬆ **Monster cod**
Few sights in fishing surpass a large cod breaking the surface after being hooked in deep water.

Northwest Norway

NORWAY, NORTHERN EUROPE

The river systems above the Arctic Circle in Norway offer superb Atlantic salmon fishing. There is a real chance of hooking very big fish with the added bonus of being surrounded by some of the most stunning scenery imaginable.

Freshwater challenges

There are more than 450 productive salmon-fishing rivers in Norway, and it is one of the most important spawning grounds in the world for wild Atlantic salmon. Approximately 200,000 salmon are caught by visiting anglers each year, some weighing more than 40 lb (18 kg).

Many of the most famous salmon rivers of Norway are in the region above the Arctic Circle. These rivers also offer excellent fishing for brown trout, grayling, and Arctic char. Modern fly-fishing methods and tackle have opened up many areas that were previously considered unfishable.

Powerful river
Some of the Norwegian salmon rivers are large and powerful bodies of water that demand a steady footing, but the rewards can be wonderful.

Short season

The fishing season within the Arctic Circle is short and intense, and the best rivers and guides need to be booked well in advance. Many visiting salmon fishermen book through special fishing-tour operators that have access to the best waters at the most popular times.

ESSENTIAL INFORMATION

Climate The weather can be changeable. Summer temperatures in the north average 57° F (14° C) in July, but then drop swiftly as fall approaches.

When to fish The salmon season in Norway is normally June 1 to August 31, but there are some regional variations.

Key species Atlantic salmon, brown trout, Arctic char, and grayling.

Hot spots The Alta River consistently produces salmon averaging around 25 lb (11 kg), and fish over 50 lb (22 kg) are occasionally caught.

Don't forget Even in summer, you will need clothing to deal with extreme shifts in temperature within the course of a day. It is advisable to wear layers.

Western Baltic coast

DENMARK AND GERMANY, NORTHERN EUROPE

The western Baltic offers excellent sea fishing in some scenic locations, including more than 230 miles (370 km) of unspoiled shoreline along Germany's north coast. There are plenty of fishing villages and islands that provide convenient bases for the angler.

Varied fishing

All along the western Baltic coastline there is great shore-fishing for various flatfish species, as well as cod, mullet, European sea bass, and mackerel. Fly-fishing for sea trout, in particular, is becoming ever more popular. Plenty of anglers like to use spinning tackle as well.

Along this coast, facing the historic town of Stralsund on the mainland, lies Germany's largest island, Rügen, which has some wonderful sandy beaches and imposing white chalk cliffs. The brackish waters of the many lagoons (known as Bodden) in the area provide superb pike fishing from small boats, which are available for rent.

Danish waters

The North Jutland area of Denmark provides access to the extensive Yellow Reef system. This lies many miles offshore and is reached

mainly by boats fishing out of Hirtshals. Big cod, coalfish, ling, and pollack are the main attraction for visiting anglers. Denmark is also famous for the quality of its freshwater fishing. The Jutland area has numerous lakes and rivers that have plentiful stocks of trout, pike, perch, roach, bream, and carp. Huge catches of fish are taken in freshwater matches.

ESSENTIAL INFORMATION

Climate Yearly average temperatures are around 46° F (8° C); in summer, temperatures reach more than 68° F (20° C).

When to fish Sea fishing is done all year; the summer months are best for most freshwater species; the best pike fishing is in fall.

Key species Cod, coalfish, pollack, sea trout, pike, zander.

Hot spots Yellow Reef system; Fyn Island; Rügen Island.

Don't forget You will need licenses for fishing in both Denmark and Germany.

» **Remote shores**
The famous chalk cliffs of the shores of the Jasmund National Park in the northern part of the island of Rügen face waters that offer great cod-fishing possibilities.

Kalmar region

SOUTHEASTERN SWEDEN, NORTHERN EUROPE

Sweden's Baltic coastline is home to some fine pike fishing. In the area of Vastervik is an archipelago of more than 4,000 islands, where the pike are content to feed in both fresh and brackish water on prey species such as roach, perch, and even herring.

Pike country

In the southeast of Sweden there are a number of lakes that hold big stocks of salmon, and an increasing number of fly-anglers fish for them from boats. However, without doubt, the pike is the most sought-after target species, and Sweden is rightly famous for the quality of its pike fishing.

Visiting anglers usually choose to fly into Stockholm and rent a car for the drive south, passing through spectacular scenery. Plenty of fishing camps and guides are located throughout the archipelago. Most pike fishing is done with light tackle and a selection of hard and soft lures, and fly-fishing for pike is becoming increasingly popular. Bait-fishing tends to work well in summer when the pike are lying deeper down.

Sea fishing

Offshore there is also the opportunity to fish for significant numbers of big Atlantic salmon. These are generally caught by trolling lures. Sea trout are also common in the waters surrounding the outer islands of the archipelago.

ESSENTIAL INFORMATION

Climate Swedish winters are severe, especially in the north, but summers are generally warm and pleasant. Temperatures in southern Sweden average around 63° F (17° C) in July.

When to fish April and May are good months to fish for pike, when they have entered shallow bays for spawning. June and July are good for open-water fishing when the pike are out feeding.

Key species Pike, Atlantic salmon, and sea trout.

Hot spots The Vastervik area.

Don't forget Bring layered clothing to deal with temperature fluctuations; use sun protection in summer. If you rent a boat, be careful not to fish in private bays—check access and ownership before you set out.

» In pursuit of pike
Sweden is full of pike-fishing opportunities, and there are plenty of guides to help you find the best lakes and advise on the most effective strategies.

Andalucía

SPAIN, SOUTHERN EUROPE

SPAIN
Sierra Morena
Andalucía
• Andújar
Rio • Málaga
Grande
Mediterranean
Sea

Many traveling freshwater anglers are unaware of the unspoiled and wild barbel fishing that is available in Andalucía. One of the most varied regions in Spain, it is better known for its coastal tourism, historic cities, and white villages than its fishing.

From mountain to coastline

Andalucía stretches from the Sierra Morena mountains in the north to the dry, desertlike areas of the southeast, including Almería and the extensive Mediterranean coastline along the south. This beautiful part of Spain contains many quiet rivers where anglers can enjoy fishing using traditional freshwater methods, including fly-fishing. Various species of barbel are widely caught. For example, there is often plenty of the striking Andalucian barbel (also known as gypsy barbel), while in the western and northwestern areas it is possible to catch the huge Comizo barbel.

There are also a number of natural and artificial lakes that hold good stocks of black bass, and these can be fished for with flies and lures. The famous town of Rio Frio lies between Granada and Málaga and is famous for the quality of its trout fishing. Indeed, records indicate that people have fished for trout here as far back as 1664. Huge trout—some of which reach a weight of more than 10 lb (4.5 kg)—have been caught.

Year-round fishing

Enjoying mainly mild, rainy winters and dry, hot summers, this is a wonderful place to visit for fishing. However, river flows vary accordingly and, because the barbel prefer a decent depth of running, oxygenated water, you should bear these factors in mind as you decide on your fishing destination.

Some of the fishing on the rivers is free and the methods can be kept simple, but you must purchase a fishing license (*permiso de pesca*) and always check carefully for relevant local permit requirements.

⏏ **A perfect barbel river** The moderately shallow, warm, clear water of this steady-flowing Andalucian river is ideal for barbel.

ESSENTIAL INFORMATION

Climate July and August are hot, up to 104° F (40° C). The best times to visit are March to June and September to November.

When to fish Barbel fishing is best in late spring and early summer.

Key species Various barbel species, carp, and black bass.

Hot spots The rivers around Andújar are particularly wonderful.

Don't forget It can get extremely hot in Spain. Take plenty of sun protection and tropical fishing clothing, plus a light rain jacket. Drink plenty of water in the heat.

Ebro River
SPAIN, SOUTHERN EUROPE

The Ebro River in northern Spain is without doubt the most famous place in Europe for fishing for big wels catfish. Huge specimens are caught regularly and there are plenty of specialty tour operators that cater to all the needs of the visiting angler.

An introduced species
One of Spain's major rivers, the Ebro flows into the sea on the Mediterranean coast between Barcelona and Valencia in the Tarragona region. Most of the fishing takes place between the Ebro delta and the city of Tortosa, where the river is most easily navigable.

The wels catfish are not native to the area and it is believed that they were introduced to the Ebro many years ago by some visiting anglers. They are voracious predators and grow quickly on a diet of local species, such as carp and mullet. Specimens weighing more than 200 lb (90 kg) have been caught and released. There are also plenty of big carp to be caught, and in the hills, one can find good fly-fishing.

The mighty Ebro The longest river in Spain, the Ebro finally enters the Mediterranean near Tortosa. The Ebro delta spans 124 square miles (320 sq km).

Sea fishing
Just off the coast of this part of Spain there is some good saltwater fly-fishing for species such as bonito and false albacore. There is also the chance of catching leerfish and bluefish in the waters of the Ebro delta. Bluefish in this area will often form schools and attack schools of their preferred baitfish in large numbers.

ESSENTIAL INFORMATION

Climate Typically Mediterranean with summer averages of 90° F (32° C) inland and 79° F (26° C) on the coast.

When to fish March to June and September to November. Midsummer can be good.

Key species Wels catfish, carp (freshwater); bonito, false albacore, bluefish (saltwater).

Hot spots Around Tortosa, but each guide company has its favored stretches of river.

Don't forget In summer, dress for hot weather and take plenty of sun protection.

Limousin region

FRANCE, EUROPE

Generally pleasant weather, plenty of lakes well-stocked with huge carp, and a range of specialty accommodations designed to suit visiting anglers make Limousin a particular favorite with many dedicated carp anglers.

Carp fishing

The stunning but relatively quiet Limousin region of central France is famous for its carp-fishing lakes. Many companies specialize in affordable carp-fishing packages. Most carp-lake owners cater fully to the needs of the anglers, and offer accommodations right next to the fishing area. While many visiting anglers choose to bring their own bait and fishing gear, many specialist carp lakes in the region also offer bait and tackle for sale to those anglers who do not want to travel with their own.

The region also contains many miles of rivers that hold stocks of trout and salmon, but do make sure to get the relevant fishing permit (*carte de peche*) before you start to fish. The season for fishing in the first (*première*) category lakes and rivers

(those that contain mainly trout and salmon) is mid-March through to the end of September. Second (*deuxième*) category waters, containing a variety of freshwater species, are often open all year. Apart from carp, salmon, and trout, other species available are pike, perch, and zander. The Vienne River holds stocks of large catfish as well.

⌃ **Carp-filled waters** Visiting anglers can look forward to long hours on the banks of the carp-filled lakes of the Limousin.

⌃ **Worthy of respect** The ultimate prize for many freshwater anglers, big carp in superb condition abound in the lakes of the Limousin region. Many anglers travel long distances to fish these waters. A catch such as this is treated with great respect and is always safely returned.

ESSENTIAL INFORMATION

Climate Summer temperatures may exceed 86° F (30° C), but generally Limousin has a milder and wetter climate than neighboring regions of France.

When to fish Most visiting anglers favor spring, summer, and early fall fishing.

Key species Carp, trout, salmon, pike, perch, zander, and catfish.

Hot spots Chapel Lake and Paradise Lakes consistently produce big carp.

Don't forget Wet-weather gear in spring and fall; sun protection is necessary in the summer months.

Switzerland

SWITZERLAND, EUROPE

Switzerland is a relatively small country with a mass of rivers and lakes amid its mountainous terrain. The mixture of German, French, and Italian influences appeals to a huge number of visitors, and there is some excellent fishing.

Alpine lakes and rivers

There are more than 20,000 miles (32,000 km) of rivers, and more than 520 square miles (1,350 sq km) of lakes, at a variety of altitudes in Switzerland, so visiting anglers need to be adaptable. The Swiss Alps offer some fantastic fishing for wild brown trout, brook trout, char, and grayling, in beautiful rivers in a landscape that contains a wonderful mixture of mountains, forests, and glaciers. There are plenty of lakes that hold stocks of large lake trout and northern pike, as well. It is possible to fish in many wild areas.

Switzerland is also excellent as an area for hiking, especially after the snow melts in the Alps and the skiers leave for the season. Anglers who are physically fit and prepared to walk a reasonable distance to reach the best fishing spots will find this an advantage.

ESSENTIAL INFORMATION

Climate Expect temperatures of 77 to 82° F (25–28° C) in summer, though higher parts of the Alps may be much cooler.

When to fish Mid-March to the end of September for trout, and from September to December for grayling.

Key species Trout, grayling, lake trout, pike, perch, and char.

Hot spots The Swiss Alps are packed with rivers and lakes that provide good fishing.

Don't forget Take layered clothing to deal with temperature fluctuations, plus sun protection. Breathable waders are essential for most river-fishing.

High-altitude fishing The calm of the Little Schottensee, a lake on the Flüela mountain pass near Davos, offers fishing in unrivaled tranquillity.

Northern Italy

SOUTHERN EUROPE

Some excellent fishing, particularly fly-fishing, is to be had in northern Italy. The waters range from fast-running rivers in the southern Alps to the tranquil streams that flow through the gentle hills of Tuscany. There are also some well-stocked lakes.

Fly-fishing in Italy

Italy's many fine rivers for fly-fishing are less well known outside the country than they deserve, but gradually these waters are being discovered by traveling fly-anglers. The rivers and small streams of the Apennine region of Tuscany offer some fantastic light-tackle fly-fishing opportunities for excellent trout and grayling. These waters have the great advantage of being easily accessible from Florence, enabling visitors to combine a fishing trip with a foray into the cultural treasure trove of this historic city.

There is also some wonderful fly-fishing in the alpine regions of Italy, but the rivers tend to be very affected by snowmelt from the mountains. It is worth seeking out good local guides who will be able to organize guided trips when the rivers are at their best. Fish species in these areas include trout and grayling. Waders are essential in these cold waters, and take extra care with powerful currents. The Alpine lakes offer good stillwater fishing during spring and summer, and the Alto Adige region also offers plenty of good fishing waters.

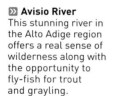

» **Avisio River**
This stunning river in the Alto Adige region offers a real sense of wilderness along with the opportunity to fly-fish for trout and grayling.

Austria
CENTRAL EUROPE

Austria is perhaps best known for its wonderful winter skiing, but this relatively small and mainly mountainous European country is packed with lakes and streams, and has some superb fly-fishing on its numerous clear, fast-flowing rivers.

Fishing in Alpine waters

Fishing in Austria's mountain rivers is often at its best when the winter snows have melted and the rivers are crystal clear. In these waters the abundant wild brown trout and grayling are not very hard to catch because there is little pressure on fish stocks from sport-fishing. A lot of the river fishing requires wading in relatively fast-flowing, cold water. There is a real chance of catching huge grayling and trout using dry-fly and nymphing techniques. The eastern Tyrol region of Austria, between the Alps and the Dolomite mountains, provides particularly excellent fly-fishing for trout and char in the cold waters. Not nearly as famous for trout fishing in North America and New Zealand, Austria is nevertheless a stunning place to fly-fish. There is so much water around that if one river is in poor fishing condition due to low water levels, you can always find another that will fish well within easy access. An angler who is prepared to walk will find great fishing in Austria.

There are also numerous lakes to fish. In the mountains, these usually contain trout. Lakes at lower altitudes are stocked with species such as carp, pike, and char.

⌂ **Scenic waters** Regarded as one of the prettiest rivers in Europe, the Salza River offers superb clear waters and a wide variety of fishing opportunities.

ESSENTIAL INFORMATION

Climate Summers tend to be warm, often above 72° F (22° C) in the daytime.

When to fish Most rivers open to fishing between March and May and the season usually closes in October.

Key species Trout and grayling.

Hot spots Rivers such as the Drau, Gmundner Traun, Salza, Mur, and Isel.

Don't forget Waders and felt-soled wading boots are usually essential. Bring layered clothing to deal with temperature fluctuations, and sun protection in summer.

» **Grayling** One of the foremost fly-fishing quarries throughout Europe, the grayling offers a real challenge to traveling anglers. Their large dorsal fin is distinctive.

Kola Peninsula

RUSSIA, EUROPE

Barents Sea
Murmansk
Kola Peninsula — Ponoi River
RUSSIA

The remote Kola Peninsula, in the Murmansk province of Russia, has abundant Atlantic salmon in many of its big rivers. A huge wilderness with few roads and a tiny population, most of the land lies above the Arctic Circle.

Remote camps

Lodges and camps have been built for visiting anglers, and some are so remote that visitors are flown in by helicopter from Murmansk; others are accessible by tour bus (albeit a long ride). This is true wilderness fishing, and all activities are based around the lodges. Most anglers fish all day, perhaps have lunch on the river bank, and then return to camp for the evening meal. Trout and char are caught, as well as salmon.

"White nights" fishing

The season is long, from the thaws of late May through to the October freeze. Midsummer can be exciting, with 24-hour fishing through the "white nights" of Arctic daylight, and plenty of fish. Fall offers the chance of catching 30-lb (13.5-kg) Atlantic salmon.

The salmon are fished for exclusively with fly-fishing tackle. Much fishing is carried out by wading the rivers with a guide; in some locations it is possible to take salmon on dry flies, but wet-fly techniques are more usual.

« Fishing the Ponoi River The longest river on the peninsula runs through a nature reserve just north of the Arctic Circle. Water levels are stable, and wildlife is plentiful.

ESSENTIAL INFORMATION

Climate An average temperature of 50°F (10°C) in July does not adequately convey the fluctuations possible, ranging from 32 to 86°F (0–30°C) through the long season.

When to fish The largest number of salmon of all sizes are caught at the start of the season. The biggest fish tend to run from early August onward.

Key species Atlantic salmon, sea trout, brown trout, and char.

Hot spots The Ponoi River offers a consistent level of salmon fishing throughout the season.

Don't forget You need layered clothing, breathable waders, and wading boots. You should also take clothing for wet weather. Be sure to protect yourself against the large numbers of mosquitoes prevalent from the end of June to mid-August.

Kamchatka

RUSSIA, ASIA

The volcanic peninsula of Kamchatka, in eastern Russia, is the remotest of remote areas. It was closed to foreigners until 1991. Now anglers and scientists work together to protect one of the world's great areas for salmon, steelhead, char, and trout.

Tough conditions

Visiting anglers to this remote part of the world pay top prices for wild fishing, with few domestic comforts, and the money helps support scientific research. The 1994 Kamchatka Steelhead Project works to protect the various fish species and their ecosystems. Nearly a quarter of the world's wild Pacific salmon are produced within this 800-mile- (1,290-km-) long peninsula, and Kamchatka is home to Russia's only steelhead run.

Conditions vary widely on the peninsula, with volcanic mountain ridges, hot geysers, and mineral springs, as well as long and spectacular rivers. The area freezes over completely in winter. Anglers also visit to catch big rainbow trout, and kundzha—large, seagoing, whitespotted char that can grow to more than 20 lb (9 kg) in weight. The best way to fish and explore this wilderness is with the organizations that offer float trips down various rivers. Anglers might see bears, moose, caribou, foxes, and abundant birdlife, including Steller's sea eagles. This is true wilderness fly-fishing.

ESSENTIAL INFORMATION

Climate Temperatures vary depending on what part of the peninsula you are fishing. Summer can reach 77° F (25° C) in places. But be aware that temperatures can fluctuate enormously within a single day.

When to fish Fishing activities are concentrated in summer.

Key species Steelhead, rainbow trout, Pacific salmon, kundzha, and grayling.

Hot spots Zhupanova River has islands, side streams, and rapids for varied fishing.

Don't forget You will need layered clothing to cope with daily temperature fluctuations. Take breathable waders and wading boots.

» Icy waters, hot springs The rivers of Kamchatka freeze over in winter, except where hot springs surface, and the water is still extremely cold in summer.

Mongolia
CENTRAL ASIA

RUSSIA

Hovsgol

Lake Baikal

• Ulaanbaatar

MONGOLIA

Fishing in Mongolia is a chance to visit a totally wild, exotic country that is virtually unchanged by human habitation. The principal quarry is the taimen—a species of nonmigratory landlocked salmon, which grow extremely large.

Local-style camps

Most Mongolian angling trips provide accommodations in rustic camps along the river banks, consisting of traditional Mongolian tents, known as gers. Some operations use

special float boats to cover as much river as possible. The farther from human influence, the better the taimen fishing. Known as the "river wolf" by the Mongolians, these famously aggressive fish often take small ducks and mice off the surface—one of the most successful dry-fly patterns imitates a mouse. Taimen will also hit lures. They can live for 50 years and may reach more than 75 lb (34 kg) in weight.

Fishing visitors usually arrive via the capital, Ulaanbaatar, and it is worth spending a day or two there, either going out or coming back. The Winter and Summer Palaces and the Gandan Hiid Buddhist Monastery are highlights. There is also excellent rafting, hiking, and horseback riding for anglers with a taste for other activities.

« **Pristine waters** Much of the fishing in Mongolia is with dry flies on clear rivers surrounded by spectacular scenery, many miles from any kind of civilization.

ESSENTIAL INFORMATION

Climate Winters are extremely cold, summers relatively warm, but many different conditions are possible on one day. The average summer temperature is 68° F (20° C); in winter the average is –4° F (–20° C).

When to fish Mid-May to mid-July, and then mid-August until the end of September, are the best times to fish for taimen.

Key species Taimen, lennok trout, and grayling.

Hot spots The northern Hovsgol region offers great taimen fishing on a variety of scenic rivers.

Don't forget Clothing to deal with a wide range of temperatures. Take spare rods and reels to allow for breakages, as replacing tackle is difficult in these remote regions.

Japan

EASTERN ASIA

Japan lies in the western Pacific Ocean and consists of many islands, but four main ones make up the greater part of the mountainous and rugged landmass—Hokkaido, Shikoku, Honshu, and Kyushu. The capital, Tokyo, is on Honshu.

Targeting suzuki

In Japanese waters, one of the most popular species to target is the Japanese sea bass, called the suzuki. Fished for predominantly with lures and baits on light tackle, these fish inhabit mostly estuaries and inshore waters.

There is also extensive big-game fishing around some of the islands, principally for species such as bluefin tuna, large black and blue marlin, giant trevally, dogtooth tuna, grouper, and amberjack. There are numerous big-game fishing boats to rent, which fish around areas such as the Tsushima Strait, and the Izu, Ogasawara, Okinawa, and Tokara Islands. There is no need to purchase a license to go sea fishing in Japanese waters.

Freshwater fishing

Two of the favorite freshwater species in Japan are the native trout, called the Iwana (also known as the Japanese char), and Yamame trout. However, anybody intending to go freshwater fishing must

Sukuji Beach
The calm waters of the beautiful Sukuji Beach, Ishigaki, Okinawa, offer fine saltwater boat-fishing relatively close to the shore.

ESSENTIAL INFORMATION

Climate The climate is essentially temperate, but summer temperatures can reach as high as 104° F (40° C).

When to fish Fish spring to fall for suzuki, March to October for marlin, July to February for big bluefin tuna. The main trout-fishing season runs from March 1 to September 30, with local variations.

Key species Suzuki, buri (yellowtail), marlin, tuna, salmon, and giant trevally.

Hot spots Niigita is known for suzuki, Yonaguni Island for big-game fishing.

Don't forget Freshwater fishing requires various licenses and tickets; check with local fishing tackle shops and convenience stores.

buy the relevant fishing tickets, which are available from local tackle shops and some convenience stores. Ticket prices vary from area to area.

It is generally accepted that some fishing tackle technology is highly advanced in Japan, especially for lure-fishing. Anglers visiting the country often enjoy the opportunity to add innovative items of tackle to their kit.

Kaveri River

KARNATAKA, SOUTHERN INDIA

There is little in angling to compare with fishing for mahseer in the fast-running Kaveri (Cauvery) River of southern India. Savagely hot temperatures, hard-fighting fish, and spectacular wildlife and scenery contribute to a great experience.

Mahseer fishing

While the mahseer can be found all over India, especially in the Himalayan rivers, it is in the southern part of the country where the largest specimens tend to be found. The principal species that is caught is the golden mahseer, but sometimes the rarer silver and black mahseer can be taken as well. All fishing is now performed on a catch-and-release basis to help protect the fisheries. Most of the fishing on the Kaveri River takes place in deep, rocky river valleys surrounded by forest.

The mahseer is principally fished for using baits (local ragi paste, freshwater crabs, and fish live baits) and your local guide will help you to place them in exactly the right positions, often in the middle of the fastest-running water. Some more steady-footed anglers choose to wander the banks and cast big lures for the mahseer, but it is also possible to take smaller specimens on fly-fishing tackle. These huge freshwater fish are perfectly adept at living in brutal terrain and often seem to treat anglers with a degree of contempt. They have certainly earned a reputation for their fighting abilities. The first run you have to deal with, often through the nearest rapids, is like no other fishing experience.

Tourist facilities

There are a few basic but comfortable fishing camps along the Kaveri River that are designed to cater for visiting anglers. Usually two anglers are allocated to one experienced local guide, who is well acquainted with the best fishing locations. The guide will advise on exactly where to cast for the best chance of catching fish in such an inhospitable terrain. There are opportunities to see local wildlife, including elephants, monkeys, and many species of bird.

The mighty mahseer
These distinctive fish of the Indian rivers are truly worthy adversaries. A power-packed body that enables it to live in these rugged conditions also means hard fights for any angler.

ESSENTIAL INFORMATION

Climate India has a pronounced monsoon climate and during the wet season (June to September) the waters of the Kaveri River rise so high that it becomes unfishable. During the dry season (March to May) temperatures can reach over 104°F (40°C).

When to fish Mahseer fishing is best from December to March.

Key species Golden mahseer is the principal quarry, but silver, black, and even pink mahseer, as well as various local carp and catfish species, can be caught.

Hot spots The Mekedatu ("Goat's Leap") Gorge is only for the most intrepid angler, but it holds some huge fish.

Don't forget Essentials include tropical clothing and good walking shoes to provide a firm grip in the rough terrain. Anti-malaria medication is advised. Remember to drink plenty of water.

<< **Brutal terrain**
The rocky course of the
Kaveri River contains
stretches of rapids in
which mahseer can
give the angler a
memorable fight.

Iguela Lagoon

GABON, WEST AFRICA

Gabon lies astride the equator and is thus blessed with warm temperatures all year round and high humidity. Its low population density and long, virtually deserted Atlantic coastline provide generally unspoiled sea fishing.

Ecotourism

Only recently has the fishing world begun to awaken to the fantastic sport-fishing potential of some of the countries of West Africa. In recent years, Gabon has set aside vast tracts of land for national parks. The huge Iguela Lagoon system of southern Gabon lies within the Petit Loango National Park and is home to many different fish species, including what are believed to be the largest cubera snapper in the world, tarpon, giant African threadfin, Guinean barracuda, and various jacks, rays, and sharks. Fishing tends to take place either within the sheltered, tannin-stained waters of the lagoon, mostly for cubera snapper, or around the lagoon mouth and nearby sandy beaches for tarpon, threadfin, barracuda, and jacks.

This is about the only place in the world where you have the opportunity to see hippos "surfing" in the sea as they emerge from the jungle. Visitors should also expect to see forest elephants, buffalo, sitatunga, red river hogs, and possibly even leopards. Within some of Gabon's other national parks, you might also be lucky enough to catch sight of chimpanzees and gorillas.

Variety of techniques

Fishing in Iguela Lagoon tends to be based on the use of lures and baits, but the adventurous fly-angler can often have real success here. These locations provide a chance to fish in waters that are on the whole unaffected by human activity and where the small amount of subsistence fishing carried out by the local inhabitants does not adversely affect the fish populations.

In the surf The warm waters of the coast of Gabon invite the adventurous angler to get into the waves, while keeping a careful eye out for sharks.

ESSENTIAL INFORMATION

Climate Tropical. Temperatures average around 81° F (27° C) all year. The wet season is between October and May.

When to fish Peak season for all species is from October to March.

Key species Tarpon, cubera snapper, giant African threadfin, longfin jack, crevelle jack, Guinean barracuda.

Hot spots The lagoon mouth is best for many of the big predatory fish. It is also fun to fish around the mangrove edges.

Don't forget Antimalaria medication. Visitors must have proof of yellow fever immunization.

Southern Angolan coast

ANGOLA, SOUTHWEST AFRICA

Angola is an unexpected tourist destination, but its largely unspoiled coastline offers some marvelous saltwater fishing for the adventurous traveler. Fishing here is a serious proposition for anglers who like wild coastlines, no crowds, and big fish.

Varied coastline

The coastline south of the capital Luanda is hugely varied, from the lush vegetated landscape close to the capital to huge sandstone cliffs and deserted beaches farther south near the Cunene River (the Namibia-Angola border). The cold Benguela current influences fishing in the southern part of Angola and there is a mix of species, including bronze whaler sharks, kob, cubera snapper, and big leerfish. The waters off central West Africa are reputed to have the largest tarpon in the world and the mouth of the Cuanza River south of Luanda is a famous place to fish for them, along with giant African threadfin, cubera snapper, very big jacks, and various rays. The beaches surrounding the river

⊠ Fishing from the beach The virtually untouched waters of the Angolan coast provide some incredible fishing. Powerful tackle is often needed in Angola to deal with potentially huge fish.

⌃ Catching a sand shark Also known as a guitarfish or shovelnose ray, this powerful species is plentiful off the Angolan beaches. They come in close to the shore to feed.

mouth offer unmissable opportunities for visiting anglers to fish for these giant tarpon from the shore.

There are a number of big-game boats situated in Luanda, where they head offshore to fish for marlin, tuna, and big dorado that are attracted by floating vegetation flowing out of the Cuanza River. Be aware, there is little tourist infrastructure in Angola, but there are a few lodges for visitors that are geared toward anglers and angling.

ESSENTIAL INFORMATION

Climate Tropical, but increasingly desertlike in the south. Temperatures rarely rise above 81° F (27° C) and the dry, cooler season is from June until late September.

When to fish The best time for fishing for tarpon and leerfish is during the summer.

Key species Tarpon, leerfish, kob, cubera snapper, sharks, jacks.

Hot spots The mouth of the Cunene River is famous for big kob; the mouth of the Cuanza River for big tarpon; the coast south of Namibe for leerfish.

Don't forget Antimalaria medication and protective clothing for tropical fishing.

"FISH COME AND GO.... IT IS THE MEMORIES OF THE AFTERNOONS ON THE STREAM THAT ENDURE."

E. Donnall Thomas

Skeleton Coast

NAMIBIA, SOUTHWEST AFRICA

The wild and windswept Atlantic coast of Namibia is home to some of the finest shore-fishing in the world, and in particular, beach-based shark fishing. In season, visitors can also participate in excellent fishing for kob and steenbras.

The Benguela current

This part of Namibia's coastline is known as the Skeleton Coast primarily because of the numerous shipwrecks littered along the shoreline. The native people of the country's interior refer to the wonderfully bleak coastline as "The Land God Made in Anger." The cold Benguela current, which flows down the length of this coast, carries large stocks of many Atlantic fish species, providing fantastic fishing for visiting anglers as well as for the local people.

Beach-fishing for sharks

These rich, cold waters are home to large numbers of predatory bronze whaler (copper) sharks, which often feed within casting range of the beaches. The fact that so many big sharks are regularly caught off the beaches is one of the key attractions of the area for visiting anglers. There are plenty of highly competent guides, who take visitors to fish the desolate beaches for shark and other species. When the sought-after edible fish species, such as the kob, are running, you can expect to see plenty of local fishermen on the beaches, fishing for the table rather than for sport. It is the visiting anglers who tend to concentrate on catching sharks.

>> **Wild beaches**
Accessible only by four-wheel-drive vehicle, the remote, deserted beaches of Namibia offer fantastic shore-fishing.

Vaal and Orange Rivers

SOUTH AFRICA, SOUTHERN AFRICA

SOUTH AFRICA

Johannesburg
Standerton
Orange
River | Vaal
River
Cape Town
Gansbaai

South Africa offers the visiting angler plenty of great fishing, both saltwater- and freshwater-based. Arguably, the most famous freshwater species are the smallmouth and largemouth yellowfish of the Vaal and Orange River systems.

ESSENTIAL INFORMATION

Climate Temperatures in summer range from 68 to 90° F (20–32° C), and in winter from 50 to 77° F (10–25° C).

When to fish The summer months (from September to April) are best for both species of yellowfish.

Key species Smallmouth and largemouth yellowfish.

Hot spots Both rivers provide good fishing, especially the Vaal near Standerton. Seek local advice on the precise places to fish.

Don't forget Tropical fishing clothing, sun protection, felt-soled wading boots, and neoprene gravel guards.

Yellowfish on the fly

The attraction of fishing the warm waters of the Vaal River and upstream nymphing (see pp.176–177) with an African sky overhead is a great reason to make the journey to South Africa. The smallmouth and largemouth yellowfish, which are the prime targets in these waters, are hard-fighting species that are perfect to catch on fly-fishing tackle. Yellowfish inhabit only the Vaal and Orange River systems, but South Africa has many hundreds of miles of fishable waters that are easily accessible and generally full of fish. Many lakes (often created by dams) also offer the visitor great trout fishing. It is common to catch trout up to 10 lb (4.5 kg) with an occasional catch of up to 14 lb (6 kg). Most fishing is done using floating lines, imitation nymphs, and dry flies.

From fly-fishing to cage-diving

South Africa has much to offer apart from the fishing, including wildlife safaris, and a wealth of marine-based activities (notably cage-diving with great white sharks around Gansbaai).

▽ **Wet-wading in the rocky shallows** The rocky bottom of the Vaal River provides a perfect habitat for yellowfish. Wading is a good way for the angler to access these waters.

Bazaruto Archipelago

MOZAMBIQUE, EAST AFRICA

Santa Carolina
Bazaruto
Indian Ocean
Magaruque
Benguerra
Vilanculos
Banque

MOZAMBIQUE

The Bazaruto Archipelago lies 15 miles (24 km) off the coast of mainland Mozambique. The archipelago has been a national park since 1971 and sustains a diverse range of wildlife, including a wide variety of saltwater fish species.

Diversity of species

The clear waters surrounding the islands offer spectacular saltwater fishing of many kinds. There is excellent big-game fishing for black and blue marlin, tuna, and sailfish in the deeper waters surrounding the islands, and closer inshore there is boat-fishing for king mackerel, giant trevally, job fish, several species of shark, dorado, and wahoo. These waters are perfect for bait-, lure-, and fly-fishing. Some forward-thinking fly-fishing guides have pioneered ultra-deepwater fly-fishing techniques over the many reef systems of the archipelago.

The island of Bazaruto also offers great shore-fishing. It is possible to cast big lures off the reefs for giant trevally. Huge deepwater bonefish may also be caught on baits. Sharks, rays, and even king mackerel can be caught off the sand spit on the northern end of the island.

Tourist access

The archipelago is a true tropical island paradise for tourists. There are lodges to cater to most budgets, but do not expect cheap, mass-market tourism. Visitors usually fly in or take boats from Vilanculos on the mainland. There is also great diving all around the Bazaruto Archipelago, and many of the tourist lodges have good facilities for this activity. Visitors may be lucky enough to see humpback whales, dolphins, whale sharks, manta rays, and dugongs (a rare sea mammal related to manatees), which are all natives of these waters.

ESSENTIAL INFORMATION

Climate Temperatures along the coast average 81°F (27°C). There is a rainy season from October to March.

When to fish Black marlin are best fished for from October to November, sailfish from June to September. Shore-fishing is good all year.

Key species Marlin (black and blue), sailfish, wahoo, giant trevally, job fish, sharks, tuna, and dorado.

Hot spots The rocky reefs on the western side of Bazaruto island offer the best chance for catching big giant trevally off the shore.

Don't forget Antimalaria medication, tropical fishing clothing, and sun protection. Polarized sunglasses are essential.

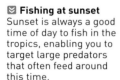

Fishing at sunset
Sunset is always a good time of day to fish in the tropics, enabling you to target large predators that often feed around this time.

Caprivi Strip

NAMIBIA, CENTRAL AFRICA

The Caprivi Strip is in Namibia, bordering Zambia, Botswana, and Zimbabwe. The region's rivers are filled with the famously aggressive tiger fish. These have been caught traditionally with lures and baits, but now are increasingly taken on fly-fishing tackle.

The Chobe meets the Zambezi

The Chobe River runs through the Caprivi Strip and drains into the mighty Zambezi River system. The predatory tiger fish take full advantage of large numbers of small fish attracted by the nutrient-rich waters. They appear predominantly during the cooler months of June and July, when local river levels are at their highest. In the hotter months later in the year, anglers usually head farther up the Zambezi. Guides assess the most productive waters for fishing each day, based on local knowledge.

Small, fast boats are used to access the best waters for fishing, and often the visiting angler is treated to sightings of many different wild animals that congregate on the river banks. These may include elephants, hippopotamuses, crocodiles, giraffes, various species of antelope, buffalo, and even lions.

>> **Tiger-fish teeth** One of Africa's most striking-looking freshwater species, the tiger fish has sharp teeth and a bony mouth that makes setting the hook difficult.

>> **Boat-fishing near the river bank** Fishing with a local guide is wise on these waters. Many large animals wander the river banks, providing a spectacular setting for your sport.

ESSENTIAL INFORMATION

Climate The average daytime temperature is around 79° F (26° C) from May to early October, but the mornings and evenings can be surprisingly cold.

When to fish June and July.

Key species Tiger fish. A local bream species called the nembwe is also fun to fly-fish for.

Hot spots Near the river banks where flood waters trickle into the river. Take advice from a local guide.

Don't forget Antimalaria medication; sun protection; some warm outer layers. Watch out for crocodiles and hippos at all times; they can be dangerous.

Murchison Falls

UGANDA, EAST AFRICA

The impressive Murchison Falls are located above Lake Albert. Here, the waters of the Victoria Nile explode through a narrow gap and cascade 400 ft (122 m) down the rocks. Nile perch, among the world's largest freshwater fish, swim below the falls.

Big fish, wild waters

Most visiting anglers camp either at the top of Murchison Falls (also known as the Kabalega Falls) or stay in one of a number of tourist lodges that are within the Murchison Falls National Park (the largest in Uganda). The best spots to fish are a long, steep walk down a path to the river's edge below the falls, but it is worth the effort to be able to fish around such wild water for a fish as formidable as the Nile perch. They are voracious predators that grow to an enormous size; indeed, the largest specimen landed at Murchison is believed to be more than 200 lb (90 kg). Fishing is mainly from the river bank, but it is possible to rent a boat. Strong tackle is needed to land such big fish in strong river currents, and most anglers use big lures and baits. Fly-fishing is also possible. It is strongly advised to keep an eye on the water at all times; there are plenty of large crocodiles and hippopotamuses in the area.

≪ **Fishing at the falls** Standing precariously beneath these mighty falls is only for the most adventurous anglers, but the rewards can be immense.

ESSENTIAL INFORMATION

Climate Temperatures range from 70 to 86° F (21–30° C). The dry seasons are from mid-December to mid-February, and June to July.

When to fish Big Nile perch can be caught all year, but the best fishing is from January to April and July to August.

Key species Nile perch.

Hot spots The Devil's Cauldron, the pool at the base of the falls, but it requires steady feet and a degree of bravery to fish here.

Don't forget You need to take antimalaria medication. Good-quality walking shoes are needed for the descent and for a secure foothold on the rocks and grass at the water's edge. Be sure to take a spare fishing rod and tackle in case of breakages and/or loss.

Kenyan coast

KENYA, EAST AFRICA

Kenya has a long Indian Ocean coast, with some of the best tourist beaches in Africa. There is a long history of good big-game fishing for marlin, sailfish, swordfish, and tuna, as well as lighter-tackle fishing for giant trevally, king mackerel, and wahoo.

Sailfish on the fly

Most fishing that takes place on the coast of Kenya is from boats, usually trolling offshore waters for the large migratory species such as marlin and tuna, but increasingly these Indian Ocean waters are becoming known for the chance to catch big sailfish on fly-fishing tackle. Over deepwater reefs it is also possible to catch giant trevally and amberjack.

Big-game fishing in Kenya starts around mid-July, but the seas tend to be quite rough then. By mid-August the season is in full swing, and the seas are calmer. In addition, the main species are migrating through the local waters. The Pemba Channel has the most numbers of tuna around September and October.

When not fishing, visitors can also enjoy the wealth of safari locations that are available in Kenya, such as the famous Masai Mara game reserve and the Amboseli National Park, with its spectacular views of Mount Kilimanjaro.

ESSENTIAL INFORMATION

Climate Humidity is high on the coast, and the temperature averages 82° F (28° C). It rarely drops below 70° F (21° C), and peaks at about 90° F (32° C) from December to March.

When to fish Fishing is available all year, but warmer and calmer seas are better; these tend to be from November to March.

Key species Marlin, sailfish, swordfish, giant trevally, wahoo, yellowfin tuna, dorado.

Hot spots Watamu; Manda Bay is gaining a reputation for excellent fly-fishing for sailfish.

Don't forget Antimalaria medication is essential. Take advice about other immunizations that may be necessary. You need tropical fishing clothing, plus plenty of sun protection.

Fishing at Watamu An ancient coral reef has been eroded into craggy outcrops in the sea. A number of big-game fishing operations are based in Watamu.

Seychelles

EAST AFRICA, INDIAN OCEAN

Mahé ——
SEYCHELLES
Alphonse —— *Indian*
Island *Ocean*
Cosmoledo —— Providence
—— Farquhar
Group
—— Astove

The tropical islands of the Seychelles are one of the world's great tourist destinations. Located in the Indian Ocean about 1,000 miles (1,600 km) east of the coast of Kenya, countless fish species abound in the warm waters of these enchanting islands.

Remote atolls

Few visitors to the Seychelles realize that far from the luxury hotels, beaches, and lodges lie some of the most unspoiled waters in the Indian Ocean. Uninhabited atolls situated hundreds of miles to the southwest of the main islands provide some of the best fishing in the world, especially saltwater fly-fishing. Access to these remote atolls is generally by means of private charter flights from the capital Mahé to the landing strips on the islands of Alphonse or Farquhar. From these points, groups of anglers can board a "mother ship" that will carry them to the principal atolls that are fished, such as Cosmoledo, Astove, and Providence. The mother ship is home for the trip duration, and each morning the anglers are ferried onto the flats (coastal shallows) on tender boats. There is no infrastructure on these atolls, so everything is carried on board. It is important to choose a specialty travel company with care, making sure they have environmental credentials and can provide the facilities (such as guides and accommodations) that fishing these waters requires.

Fish of the flats and deep waters

Seas that are virtually untouched by humans always offer the best fishing. The remote atolls of the Seychelles provide the opportunity for flats-fishing on pristine sand, coral, and turtle-grass, allowing sight-fishing for giant trevally, bonefish, milkfish, triggerfish, and other species such as the huge bumphead parrot fish and Napoleon wrasse. The waters surrounding these atolls are also home to many other ocean species. These include sailfish, tuna, and wahoo.

✉ **Vast sand flats**
The atolls are known for remote flats that are rich in giant trevally, bonefish, and milkfish, but visiting anglers are still relatively rare.

<< **Beautiful bonefish** Large specimens of this superb tropical fish feed on these remote flats and offer the adventurous angler some of the best saltwater fly-fishing to be found anywhere in the world.

Although Cosmoledo is generally accepted as being one of the world's prime locations for sight-casting significant numbers of large giant trevally, it is fished by very few people each year. The lesser-known atolls of Astove and Providence have been visited by only a handful of anglers.

Green turtles are among the varied marine life of the waters around the Seychelles, and on the atoll of Astove you stand a good chance of seeing a giant tortoise. When fishing these waters, always keep an eye out for marauding sharks, which can suddenly appear in the shallows. This is truly wild fishing.

ESSENTIAL INFORMATION

Climate Throughout the year temperatures average 86° F (30° C).

When to fish November to early April.

Key species Giant trevally, bonefish, milkfish, triggerfish, sailfish, tuna, wahoo, bluefin trevally.

Hot spots The waters around Cosmoledo and Astove are famous for large numbers of giant trevally.

Don't forget Take high-SPF sunscreen and tropical fishing clothing. In particular, you will need special flats boots to protect your feet on the coral and rocks.

Northern Territory

AUSTRALIA

Arafura Sea
Darwin — Shady Camp
Mary River
Daly River
Kakadu National Park

AUSTRALIA

The massive Northern Territory region of Australia is known for its great fishing. A mostly flat coastline with a mass of mangrove swamps offers an ideal habitat for one of Australia's best known and most popular fish, the barramundi.

Environmental management

The area around Darwin is renowned for the quality of its barramundi fishing. The most notable destinations are the nearby Kakadu National Park, the Mary River, Daly River, and Shady Camp. Rigorously enforced conservation management ensures that a consistent level of sport-fishing is available to visiting anglers, who sometimes are able to catch "trophy barra," which are barramundi weighing more than 40 lb (18 kg). Plenty of big fish are caught by trolling lures behind a boat, but many anglers consider the most enjoyable type of fishing to be casting lures directly next to or even into snags (underwater obstructions, such as sunken trees) and experiencing the arm-wrenching hit from one of these superb fish. Other species that inhabit these waters include giant trevally and marlin. There is an extensive network of professional fishing guides who can help visitors find the best fishing locations. Anglers seeking

an even bigger adventure can travel to more remote destinations, including some of the offshore islands.

More than fish

The waters in these areas are also home to saltwater crocodiles, and the forests, billabongs, and lagoons support extensive bird life. The Kakadu National Park also has an important cultural heritage.

ESSENTIAL INFORMATION

Climate Typically tropical. Most rainfall is from November to April; the dry season is from May to October. The temperature range is 75 to 90° F (24–32° C).

When to fish March to June is the best season for barramundi.

Key species Barramundi, plus various bluewater species, including king mackerel, tuna, marlin, and giant trevally.

Hot spots The Daly and Mary River systems.

Don't forget Take tropical fishing clothing and plenty of sun protection.

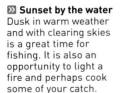

» **Sunset by the water**
Dusk in warm weather and with clearing skies is a great time for fishing. It is also an opportunity to light a fire and perhaps cook some of your catch.

Cairns

QUEENSLAND, AUSTRALIA

For many years, the area around Cairns on Australia's Queensland coast has been recognized as one of the world's main centers for big-game fishing, with arguably the finest and most consistent run of giant black marlin every year.

Big black marlin

In early September each year, big female black marlin arrive to spawn along the long stretch of the Great Barrier Reef near Cairns. These magnificent fish attract huge numbers of visiting anglers. The Cairns black-marlin fishery became renowned following the capture in 1966 of a 1,064-lb (480-kg) black marlin off Euston Reef. This single fish put Cairns on the world big-game fishing map, where it has remained ever since. The aim for anglers in these waters is to catch a black marlin that is more than 1,000 lb (454 kg), known as a "grander."

Light-tackle fishing

While Cairns is viewed principally as a big-game fishing destination, the fish-rich waters also offer a wealth of light-tackle sporting opportunities. A huge variety of Pacific game species frequent the Cairns waters, including tuna, wahoo, dorado, sailfish, and Spanish mackerel. There are plenty of charter boats that provide trolling and lure-fishing. The large, tropical North Queensland area is fast becoming one of the hottest saltwater fly-fishing destinations, for species such as golden and giant trevally, barramundi, marlin, and various tuna species. The remote Cape York peninsula, north of Cairns, is one of the best places for this type of fishing.

ESSENTIAL INFORMATION

Climate Tropical. The rainy season is from November to May. Temperatures reach above 86° F (30° C) from November to March. June and July are often relatively cool.

When to fish The best fishing for black marlin is from September until late December.

Key species Black and blue marlin, barramundi, dogtooth tuna, giant trevally, sailfish, yellowfin tuna, and wahoo.

Hot spots Cairns for all-around boat-fishing, Cape York for fly- and light-tackle fishing.

Don't forget You will need tropical fishing clothing, plenty of sun protection, and polarized sunglasses.

» Marlin jumping
One of the most exciting sights of big-game fishing is that of a hooked marlin jumping clear of the water in a bid for freedom.

Tasmania

AUSTRALIA

The island of Tasmania lies about 150 miles (240 km) south of the Australian mainland. This mountainous island, with more than 3,000 rivers, streams, and lakes, is famous for trout fishing. There is also excellent saltwater fishing around its coasts.

Inland and coastal fishing

Brown trout were introduced to Tasmania during the 19th century and, after they became established, rainbow trout from North America were brought in. These two species, together with small pockets of brook trout and limited stocks of Atlantic salmon, now account for much of Tasmania's international fishing appeal. Trout fishing in the varied and spectacular scenery of Tasmania is becoming increasingly popular among fly-anglers from mainland Australia and many other parts of the world.

In Tasmania you can see the unusual sight of trout tailing in extremely shallow water, like bonefish on tropical flats. While there are many well-known lakes—such as Arthur Lake and Great Lake—as well as rivers such as the Meander, St. Patrick's River, and Brumby's Creek, there are also opportunities to fish for good trout in out-of-the-way places. Various big-game charter fleets fish the coastal waters for marlin, sharks, and tuna. St. Helens is a good marlin-fishing area, and tuna fishing is best offshore around Maria

Trout fishing
Glorious scenery and beautiful trout rivers, coupled with mild weather, make fishing in Tasmania a pleasure in every season.

Island, which lies off the Tasman Peninsula. Various other species, such as the Australian salmon, flathead, yellowtail, and snapper, can also be caught off the coast.

A wildlife haven

Tasmania is a largely unspoiled and relatively underpopulated state that boasts 19 national parks. For fishing, the best-known parks are Ben Lomond, Mount William, Tasman, and Savage River, all with diverse and distinct landscapes and ecosystems. Few places offer such diversity and consistent fishing.

An extensive area of southeast Tasmania is classed as a World Heritage Area, together with Macquarie Island. Large numbers of sea birds return to this island each year to breed, and there are healthy populations of marine animals, such as elephant seals and fur seals—indicators of abundant fish stocks.

◀ **Lake-fishing in Tasmania** Many of the lakes in Tasmania offer world-class trout fishing in unspoiled, clear waters. A high vantage point provides good fish-spotting opportunities.

ESSENTIAL INFORMATION

Climate Extremes of temperature are rare. The west coast is the wettest region; the east is drier and milder. Rain is possible throughout the year. The average summer temperature is 70° F (21° C); in winter the average is 54° F (12° C).

When to fish The trout season is August to April. Saltwater fishing is good year-round.

Key species Brown and rainbow trout; marlin, tuna, shark, and Australian salmon.

Hot spots Arthur Lake is the most popular trout fishery. The north of Tasmania is known for its trout-fishing rivers. St. Helens is a key center for big-game fishing.

Don't forget Take layered clothing. Breathable waders are great for river fishing.

New Zealand

SOUTHWESTERN PACIFIC

The stunningly beautiful islands of New Zealand offer plenty of fishing. Huge brown trout, rainbow trout, and salmon frequent the rivers and lakes, while the extensive and varied coastline provides a wide range of sea fishing for many different species.

North Island

The North Island is the main area for rainbow-trout fishing, with Lake Taupo and the famous Rotorua lakes being extremely popular places to fish. Big rainbow trout, which travel up the Tongariro River from May to September to spawn, attract many anglers. There is also some good brown-trout fishing on the North Island, especially on the central plateau close to Lake Taupo.

During the summer, fishing for striped marlin around the north coast of the island is as good as anywhere in the world. Many world records have been achieved in these waters. From February to late May, large numbers of striped marlin congregate to feed on the abundance of baitfish that are drawn to the current upwellings in and around the beautiful Bay of Plenty and Three Kings Islands. There are also increasing numbers of blue marlin being caught.

A famous New Zealand saltwater species is the yellowtail kingfish (known locally as the "kingie"). The biggest specimens in the world are caught in these waters, especially around the Bay of Plenty, Three Kings Islands, White Island, and the Ranfurly Bank.

South Island

The staggeringly beautiful South Island is world famous for the quality of its brown-trout fishing. Most rivers and lakes hold good stocks of very big fish, and much of the fly-fishing involves heading into the remote back-country and stalking individual fish in crystal-clear waters. The whole of the South Island offers good trout fishing, but the best areas are in the west: Southland, Otago, and Fiordland. Salmon run in the Rakaia, Waimakariri, Hurunui, and Waiau Rivers from November to March.

New Zealand is known for its amazing scenery and relaxed lifestyle. It has an outdoors-based culture that attracts all kinds of visitors, many of whom seek exciting outdoor activities, for which there are numerous options.

☒ Lake Taupo
New Zealand's North Island provides anglers with superb fishing at locations such as Lake Taupo, on the central plateau.

ESSENTIAL INFORMATION

Climate Northern New Zealand has a subtropical climate, whereas the south is temperate. Summer temperatures range from 68 to 86°F (20–30°C), and in winter from 50 to 59°F (10–15°C).

When to fish Brown-trout fishing is best in summer and marlin fishing from February to May. Other species are good to fish all year.

Key species Brown and rainbow trout, marlin (striped, black, and blue), yellowtail kingfish.

Hot spots Lake Taupo for rainbow trout; South Island for brown trout. The Bay of Plenty offers the most exciting sea fishing.

Don't forget Take layered clothing to deal with temperature fluctuations.

◄◄ **Trout fishing**
Clear waters and breathtaking scenery make New Zealand a major destination for fly-fishing. The tranquillity is unparalleled, and many of the fish grow to huge sizes.

Hawaii

UNITED STATES, PACIFIC OCEAN

The volcanic islands of the state of Hawaii, located in the central Pacific, are home to outstanding fishing. There are eight main islands and many more smaller ones spread over 1,500 miles (2,400 km) from the west to the east of the ocean state.

Big-game species

Many of the islands of Hawaii have substantial big-game charter-boat fleets that fish all year for various saltwater species, including blue, black, and striped marlin, as well as tuna species (skipjack and yellowfin), spearfish, wahoo, and dorado (also known as mahimahi or dolphinfish). There are also large sharks, and plenty of bottom-feeding fish such as snapper and grouper. A lot of the best big-game fishing takes place over deep water, where the boats troll lures and baits. Many of the islands have extremely deep waters close to the shore; the leeward side of the islands, in the shelter of the mountains, offers the calmest water.

Hawaiian waters are known as one of the prime locations in the world to try to catch "grander" marlin, as those more than 1,000 lb (454 kg) are termed. The numerous big fishing tournaments throughout the islands include the World Cup, the Lanai Rendezvous, the Lahaina Jackpot Tournament, and the Hawaiian International Billfish Tournament. The latter has been conducted from Kona, on the island of Hawai'i, for nearly 50 years, and is fished according to the rules of the International Game Fish Association (IGFA).

Fishing from the shore

The Hawaiian islands are among the few places in the world where very large giant trevally are specifically targeted from the shore. Known locally as "ulua," numerous large specimens

Coastal fishing
Bait- or lure-fishing from the rocky shores and reefs of Maui is exhilarating, as the great waves surf past. Trevally and snapper are among the species caught.

《 Game fishing
A fleet of game-fishing boats in the Hawaiian International Billfish Tournament leave Kona Harbor past an interisland cruise ship.

of this hard-fighting fish have been caught by using long, powerful shore rods, with big conventional reels, and heavy lines and weights, to put live baits down into deep, rocky ground. Increasing numbers of shore-anglers in Hawaii are also turning to smaller species, such as the stunning bluefin trevally and barracuda, which can be caught on light tackle from the

extensive reefs and sandy channels. Fly-fishing for bonefish is also becoming increasingly popular.

Supreme surfing

In addition to angling, Hawaii provides the most outstanding big-wave surfing in the world; breaks such as Pipeline and Waimea on Oahu are legendary.

ESSENTIAL INFORMATION

Climate Hawaii is warm all year, with temperatures ranging from 68 to 82° F (20–28° C). The rainy season is from December to March.

When to fish Marlin can be caught all year, but July and August are the prime months for big blue marlin. Many other species are fished for throughout the year.

Key species Marlin, tuna, giant trevally (ulua), bluefin trevally, barracuda, snapper, wahoo, dorado, shark, and amberjack.

Hot spots Most islands offer good big-game fishing. The southeast shore of Oahu is a famous area for fishing for giant trevally from the shore.

Don't forget You will need tropical fishing clothes and sun protection. The best big-game boats are heavily booked well in advance, so be sure to plan ahead.

Glossary

Adipose fin Small fin, between the *dorsal fin* and the *caudal fin*.

AFTMA/AFTM The American Fishing Tackle Manufacturers' Association, commonly known as the AFTM. The AFTM number is the code by which fly rods and fly lines are matched. The AFTM scale, recognized throughout the world, is based on the weight of the first 30 ft (9.1 m) of the fly line. Rods are then matched by the manufacturer to the weight of line that they can cast effectively. Reels are often described as being suitable for certain AFTM code numbers.

Algae Simple plants that do not have roots and constitute a food source for many fish and small aquatic animals.

Anadromous Fish species that are born in freshwater, migrate to saltwater, and then migrate back to freshwater to spawn.

Anal fin The fin located behind the anus.

Back-cast The part of the cast when both the rod and line are behind the person casting.

Backing Thin line that is put on a reel (usually a fly reel) to increase the diameter of the *spool*.

Bait Any natural or processed food (including *dead bait* and *live bait*) that is put on a hook to attract fish.

Bait-casting reel A reel that has a *revolving spool*, which multiplies leverage on the line as it is winched in. Also known as a *conventional reel*.

Bait clip A clip that secures the baited hook during the *cast*.

Baitfish Any small fish used for *bait*.

Bale arm The part of a *spinning reel* that guides the line on to the *spool*.

Barbel (1) A fish species. (2) A barbule, or slender spine or bristle, located around the mouth or head of a fish.

Blood knot The most common knot for connecting lines to hooks, flies, and *lures*, and for connecting two lines together.

Blue water The deep waters of open oceans.

Bottom-fishing To fish on the bottom with baits.

Brackish water Slightly salty water, such as the water in areas where the freshwater from rivers runs into the saltwater of the sea.

Braid Low-diameter, low-stretch fishing line, made by braiding strands of synthetic fiber.

Breaking strain The amount of dead weight it takes to break a line, usually quoted in pounds (lb) or kilograms (kg).

Butt pad A protective pad with a fitting that holds the butt of a fishing rod while fighting a fish, generally worn around the groin or lower stomach area.

Caddis fly An important order of aquatic insects that the flies used by fly-anglers are designed to imitate.

Cast To put a *lure*, *bait*, or imitation fly out onto the water, using a rod and reel.

Casting arc The path that a fly rod travels during the cast. Fly-fishing instructors often describe the parts of the casting arc in terms of an analog clock face.

Caudal fin Tail fin.

Chum Chopped fish, and other attractors, such as fish oil, put overboard to attract fish, when sea-fishing from boats. Also known as "rubby dubby."

Clutch The *drag* system on a reel.

Conventional reel A reel that has a revolving spool, which multiplies leverage on the line as it is winched in. Also known as a *baitcasting reel*.

Dead bait Any dead fish or creature that is used for fishing *bait*.

Dead drift To fish a fly so that it drifts freely in the water, and travels at the same speed as the current.

Dorsal fin The fin located on the back of a fish, in front of the *adipose fin*.

Double-haul A fly-fishing technique that is used to increase line speed.

Downrigger A device fixed to a boat that uses a cable and a heavy weight to *troll baits* and lures at a set depth, eliminating the need for a weight on the fishing line.

Drag The pressure applied internally to the *spool* of a reel, to make it harder work and more tiring for a fish to take line when running.

Drogue A device dragged behind a boat to reduce speed, commonly a canvas, cone-shaped bag.

Dropoff A sudden drop in depth, from shallow to deep water.

Dry fly Any fly that floats on top of the water when fished.

Ebb tide The outgoing, or falling, *tide*.

Eddy (back eddy) A water current, or drift, that is moving in the opposite direction of the main current or flow.

Flasher board A reflective or colored board tied in front of a *bait* or *lure* to impart movement to the lure and to act as a visual attractor.

Flats Shallow, generally tidal, inshore saltwater areas that are waded by anglers.

Floating fly line A fly line made of material that floats on the surface of the water.

Flood tide The incoming, or rising, *tide*.

Forward cast The part of the *cast* when the line is in front of the person casting.

Fry A fish in an early stage of development, especially salmon or trout species.

Game fish Sometimes also referred to as *sport fish*, any freshwater and saltwater species of fish that is governed by *sport-fishing* laws.

Gills Vascular organs on a fish, used for aquatic respiration.

Gravel guard Either a separate neoprene wrap worn around the ankles, or the part of a pair of *waders* that clips on to the wading boot, to stop gravel from getting into boots.

Grilse A young Atlantic salmon that has returned to the river from the sea, to *spawn* for the first time.

Gully A (usually small) channel that has been formed by moving water.

Hooklength The line that is attached to the hook, often known as a *leader*. A hooklength and hook together form a *trace*.

IGFA International Game Fish Association. This organization, based in Florida, sets standards for fishing tackle and maintains a list of record fish.

Indicator A means by which the angler can visually detect a fish bite—often a float or a small, visible, floating object secured to the end of the fly line.

Jig A fishing *lure* that is jerked (or jigged) to appeal to fish.

Kelt A salmon or steelhead that has spawned recently, and, for this reason, is unlikely to be in the best condition.

Lateral line A visible line found running along the body of many fish, formed by a series of sensory pores.

Leader The length of line between the *main line* and the hook, lure, or fly.

Lever drag A form of *drag* system on a fishing reel, adjusted by moving a lever on the side of the reel.

Lie A generally quiet spot in the water where a fish will hide, rest, or feed.

Live bait Any *bait* that is used live.

Loading/compressing the rod Putting a bend in a rod when casting, to create the impetus for the *cast*.

Loop The shape formed in a fly line as it unfurls during the *forward* and the *back-casts*.

Lure An object attached to the end of the fishing line designed to entice fish.

Main line The principal fishing line on the fishing reel.

Mending A way of creating less *drag* on the fly line after it lands on the water.

Migrate To move from one area to another. In fishing, this applies to large, seasonal movements of fish from one area to another, usually in search of food, or to reproduce.

Monofilament Fishing line made from a single strand of nylon filament.

Neap tide *Tide* with the least difference between levels of high and low water, occurring during the first and last quarters of the moon.

Nymph The immature form of many insects, often imitated by fly patterns.

Outrigger A pole that extends from a boat, to allow several lines to be fished at the same time without tangling.

Panfish Members of the Centrarchidae family. Also used to describe, especially in North America, any small, edible freshwater fish.

Pectoral fins The front pair of fins on a fish, usually located on either side, behind the *gills*.

Pelagic Relating to the open ocean. Pelagic fish are those that spend the majority of their lives in the upper parts of the ocean.

Playing Fighting a hooked fish, in order to tire out the fish so that it can be brought to hand for unhooking.

Plug A fishing *lure*, usually designed to be *cast*.

Point fly The last fly in a team of flies, farthest from the main fly line.

Popper A surface *lure* with a concave face that splashes water, or "pops," when retrieved.

Presentation The art of casting the fly onto, or into, the water, and presenting it to the fish in the most natural way possible.

Reel seat The fixture that holds a reel in place on the fishing rod.

Retrieve To bring the fly, *lure*, or *bait* back toward the angler after the cast, either by hand (fly-fishing) or by turning the reel handle (lure- and bait-fishing).

Rig The end gear, or *terminal tackle*, the elements of which are assembled together and attached to the line.

Rise The act of a fish breaking the surface of the water to take an insect.

Run (1) The rapid movement away from the angler made by a hooked fish. (2) A fast-flowing stretch of a river.

Running line The thin section of a fly line, lying behind the head section of a fly line.

Sandbank A bank or plateau of sand that is usually submerged, but can be uncovered at low *tide*.

Scales The protective plates that cover the skin of some fish.

Setting the hook Securing the hook in the fish's mouth. Also known as *striking*.

Sight-casting/sight-fishing Fishing for, or casting to, fish that you can see.

Sinking fly line A fly line made from material that sinks completely beneath the surface.

Sink-tip A floating fly line that has a sinking section at the end, varying in length.

Slack tide The brief period between the *ebb* and the *flood tides*, when the current is at its weakest.

Smolt A young salmon that is ready to migrate to sea. At this stage the fish has the silvery color of an adult.

Snag (1) Rocky or foul ground that can trap *lures*, hooks, and weights. (2) To catch a hook, lure, or weight on an underwater obstruction such as a rock or fallen tree.

Spawn (1) The eggs produced by fish. (2) The act of a fish producing or depositing eggs.

Spin To fish with *spinners* or *lures*.

Spinner A fishing *lure* that often revolves when retrieved. The term is also used more generally to refer to a wide range of *lures*.

Spinning reel A fishing reel that incorporates a nonrotating spool.

Spool The part of the reel around which the line is wound.

Sport fish A fish that is sought by anglers.

Sport fishing The pursuit and catching of any species of fish by any method, for sporting or recreational purposes.

Spring tide A *tide* with the largest difference between the levels of high and low water, which occurs around the time of the new and full moon.

Strike/striking To sweep the rod back to secure the hook when a fish bites.

Stripping basket A perforated "basket" that attaches around the angler's waist, to store the excess fly line produced when *stripping*, prior to winding it back on to the reel.

Stripping/strip retrieve To retrieve fly line by using your hands to pull it in.

Swim The section of water fished by an angler.

Swim bladder The internal organ that enables a fish to control its buoyancy.

Tag/tag end The short section of redundant line that has been trimmed down after a knot has been tied.

Take The action of a fish taking a bait or hitting a *lure*.

Taper The part of the fly line that gradually decreases in diameter toward the hook.

Tapered leader A *leader* that tapers from thicker to thinner line, with the thinner end being attached to the fly or *lure*.

Terminal tackle Also known as the "end gear," items such as hooks, *lures*, weights, and swivels that are attached to the end of the line.

Tide The regular variation in the level of the ocean surface caused by the gravitational pull of the moon and sun.

Tippet The thin, end section of the *leader* to which a fly is tied.

Trace Part of a *rig*, consisting of a line and hook that are attached together.

Troll To pull *lures* or *baits* on a line behind a moving boat.

Vent The anus of a fish.

Waders Waterproof hip- or chest-length overalls, often incorporating boots, worn by anglers.

Weight-forward (WF) fly line A fly line in which most of the weight is in the forward section of the line, and which is therefore easier to *cast*.

Wet fly Any fly that fishes (sinks) below the surface of the water.

Wet wading Wading without *waders*, usually in tropical waters, wearing appropriate footwear.

Wind knot A knot that can appear in the leader or *main line* when casting, generally with *braid* or fly line, which weakens the line.

Index

Page numbers in **bold** refer to main entries.

Acknowledgments

Picture credits

The publisher would like to thank the following for their kind permission to reproduce their photographs:

(Picture Key: a = above; b = below/bottom; c = centre; f = far; l = left; r = right; t = top)

Adam Tavender: 6-7, 62-63, 72-73, 168bl; Alamy Stock Photo: The History Collection 233b; Arco Images 221t; blickwinkel 307b; Feargus Cooney 308b; Reinhard Dirscherl 219t; Javier Etcheverry 299b; David Fleetham 242t; David Gowans 302bl; Jeff Greenberg 22bl; D. Hurst 340-341b; Images&Stories 208bl, 217tr; Jeff Morgan tourism and leisure 222tr; David Kleyn 210–211b; Detail Nottingham 75fcrb; M. Timothy O'Keefe 260t; 297f; f1 online 315tr; Photo Network 20fbl; Wolfgang Polzer 208t, 227t, 228b; Dave Porter

213b; CuboImages srl 314b; Stephen Frink Collection 267b, 269fbr; Scottish Viewpoint 303c; Chris Wilson 319b; Andrew Woodley 341t; **Ardea:** Pat Morris 239t; **BDAA:** 10b, 22cl, 25br, 52b; **Barry and Cathy Beck:** 19tr; **Ben Matthews Photography:** 4-5, 168-169c; **Dreamstime.com:** Kondratova 25cra (laptop screen); **Faceless Fly Fishing:** 16-17, 78-79c, 100, 284-285; **Fly Odyssey UK:** Gilly Bate 98-99; **George Gunn:** 18-19c; **Getty Images / iStock:** Peopleimages / E+ 25cra, PerfectStills 209tr; **John Bailey:** 318bl; **William E. Blair (The Best Of Kamchatka, www.thebestofkamchatka.com):** 317b; **Dean Butler:** 167cl, 334b, 335b; **Corbis:** Blaine Harrington III 292ca; Arno Balzarini 313b; Chinch Gryniewicz 331b; Kit Kittle 291b; Karl Weatherly 20bl; **Peter Gathercole:** 190br, 191br, 191t; **Getty Images:** Jack Hanrahan 289b; **Henry Gilbey:** 2, 8-9tr, 9br, 10-11tc, 12-13b, 13tc, 14-15, 18a, 18bl, 22-23b, 24t, 25tl, 26tl, 26bl, 27c,

28tl, 28-29b, 29tr, 30tl, 30bl, 31tr, 32b, 33tc, 33tr, 38ca, 40cra, 54tl, 54bl, 54cra, 55l, 55tr, 57tr, 58tr, 69b, 69cla, 75t, 78tl, 78bl, 80br, 81cla, 81ca, 81cra, 81clb, 81crb, 82bl, 82ca, 82br, 83b, 83tl, 83tr, 84bl, 84br, 84ca, 85bl, 85br, 85tl, 85tr, 86bl, 86br, 86ca, 87bc, 87bl, 87br, 87t, 88bl, 88br, 88ca, 89b, 89cla, 89cra, 89t, 90ca, 91b, 91crb, 92cla, 92b, 93tr, 93bl, 96fl, 97br, 97cr, 101c, 102tl, 102-103c, 103tr, 106br, 107bl, 107cl, 107t, 108-109, 110b, 111bl, 111br, 111tl, 111tr, 123tr, 124br, 124ca, 125b, 125ca, 126tl, 126bl, 126-127c, 127tr, 128b, 129bl, 129br, 129c, 129tl, 132cra, 132bl, 133tl, 133cl, 134-135b, 135crb, 135tl, 135tr, 136br, 137b, 137cra, 137tl, 138b, 139bl, 139c, 139tr, 140-141c, 141br, 141cr, 141tl, 141tr, 142-143b, 143tl, 143cra, 144br, 145tl, 145cla, 145cr, 145bl, 146cra, 146br, 147tl, 147bl, 147tr, 148br, 149tl, 149cra, 149bl, 151tl, 151clb, 151crb, 152br, 153tl, 153tr, 153br, 154bl, 155clb, 155tt, 156cr, 157br, 157ca, 158br, 159tl, 159tr, 159clb, 159br, 160bl, 160cr, 161cl, 161tr, 162bl, 162br, 163bl, 163br, 163t,

164bc, 165tr, 165clb, 165crb, 168tl, 169tr, 170b, 170cra, 171bl, 171br, 171t, 172-173b, 173br, 173tl, 173tr, 174b, 175br, 175c, 175tr, 176br, 176-177t, 177bl, 177br, 179br, 180br, 181bl, 181cr, 181br, 181t, 182br, 182cra, 183bl, 183br, 183t, 184-185b, 185br, 185cl, 185cr, 186bl, 186-187b, 187br, 188b, 188cra, 189br, 189c, 190bl, 192br, 193bl, 193br, 193t, 194bl, 194cra, 194-195b, 195br, 195ca, 196b, 197b, 197t, 200b, 201bl, 201t, 202b, 202cra, 203br, 203t, 204-205, 207ca, 208-209c, 218b, 226b, 230b, 231t, 232b, 234tl, 234bl, 234-235c, 235tr, 238b, 250tr, 257t, 258t, 268t, 272t, 276t, 282-283, 285ca, 286-287b, 287tr, 293b, 294-295b, 295tr, 298b, 300-301b, 301tr, 304b, 305b, 305cl, 306bl, 306br, 309b, 315bl, 322bl, 326b, 327b, 328b, 329br, 329cra, 330r, 332-333b, 310tr, 311b, 320bl, 321c, 323bl, 323tr, 324-325, 333t; **Sander Boer Fotografie**: 30-31c, 104cra, 104br, 105tl, 105tr, 105cl, 105br; **Svendsen Sport A/S**: 20cra, 40cl, 40c, 40bl, 40bc, 41c, 41cr, 42br, 43cra, 56crb, 56bc, 57clb, 57cb, 57bc, 58bc, 58br, 59tl, 59cla, 59clb, 59bl, 59br, 106ca, 112cra, 118cra, 120cra, 122cra, 128cra, 130cla, 134cra, 138cra, 142cra, 143br, 144cra, 148cra, 150cra, 158cra, 164cra; **Ole Wisler**: Ole Wisler 130bl, 130-131b, 131tl, 131tr, Malthe Wisler 133br; **Brad Harris**: 178br, 179t, 336-337b, 337tr, 339c; **Nick Helleur**: 312br, 312cra; **David Johnson**: 116ra, 116crb, 116b, 117br, 117cl, 117t; **Lax-A Club**: 316bl; **David Lewis**: 150br, 166crb, 167br, 167t; **Masterline International**: 40br; **Cathy Meeus**: 121br; **Brian O'Keefe**: 79tr, 198bl, 198-199b, 199cla, 206c, 215t, 264-265c, 288b, 290b, 292b, 296b; **OSF**: photolibrary.com 216b, 236b, 252br, 254tr, 271tr, 278t, 279bl, 280t, 281b; **Sea Pics**: Mark Conlin 275t; Alistair McGlashan 270a; Doug Olander 274b; Sea Pics 246t, 277b; **Shimano UK Ltd**: 8cla, 20cra, 39br, 41cl, 110cra, 152cra, 154cra, 160cra, 162cra; **Richard Stewart**: 222-223b; **Still Pictures**: Ed Reschke 256b

Cover images: *Front and Back Background*: **Getty Images**: Peter Dazeley; **Getty Images/ iStock**: MichaelJay; *Front*: **Hardy & Greys**: Daniel Hansens: ca; **Henry Gilbey**: fcra, fcrb; *Back*: **BDAA**: fcla; **Ben Matthews Photography**: c; **Corbis**: AlaskaStock clb, Image Source cb; **Henry Gilbey**: ca, crb, fclb, fcrb; *Spine*: **Hardy & Greys**: Daniel Hansens

Maps on pages 284–338 are Mountain High Maps ® copyright © 1993 Digital Wisdom, Inc.

Every effort has been made to trace the copyright holders. The publisher apologizes for any unintentional omissions and would be pleased in such cases to place an acknowledgment in future editions of this book.

All other images © Dorling Kindersley
For further information see: **www.dkimages.com.**

Henry Gilbey

Utterly consumed by fishing since the age of seven, for more than 20 years Henry Gilbey has successfully managed to avoid having to grow up and get a "real job." Instead he is involved in all types of fish-related things, such as writing, photography, TV appearances, consulting, or guiding. Henry currently freelances for various fishing magazines; runs a regularly updated blog and website at www.henry-gilbey. com; guides anglers on bass-fishing holidays in the southwestern part of Ireland; and does an increasing amount of bass-fishing-related consulting for the international lure-fishing tackle company Savage Gear.

Author's acknowledgments

I have been fishing now for 40 years, and as a complete fishing addict, I am here to tell you that the addiction only gets stronger. I love fishing and working in fishing more than ever, and I simply cannot do what I do within the world of fishing without my incredible family and the love and support they give me. This book is for my three girls, who are not themselves into fishing, but who I think understand why I am so consumed by it all: my wife, Islay, who is my best friend and is the best person I have ever known; and my two teenage daughters, Isabel and Molly. As their dad, I am obviously biased, but my girls are awesome, and as a father, it is beyond rewarding to watch them grow up and develop their own passions. I have to mention my ever-faithful sheepdog Storm, who is into fishing mainly because so much of my own day-to-day fishing requires lots of walking around the Cornish coastline, and as a sheepdog, she thrives on it. A special thanks goes to my parents and my two brothers. Family is everything.

There are far too many fishing-related people to try to thank individually here, but anglers all around the world are some of the finest people you could ever hope to meet, and I remain eternally grateful to a large number of them. Fishing is a very small world, and all of us who fish are connected in some way. I have fished and worked with so many incredibly kind and generous people over the years, and I am lucky enough to call a lot of them my friends. My work in fishing has taken me all over the world, to some of the most special places you could ever hope to see, but my heart lies here in Cornwall where I live, and also over in Ireland, where I feel so at home with the people and the places and the fishing.

It may be my name on the front cover of this book, but that doesn't tell nearly enough of the story. As with fishing and the process of trying to outwit nature, books are a hugely collaborative process—a huge thank you to Stephanie Farrow and Jill Andrews for so much hard work and patience and understanding.

Publisher's acknowledgments

For this edition, Dorling Kindersley would like to thank Nikolaj Korsholm of Svedsen Sport (www. svendsen-sport.com) for his generous support, and also Terry Moseley, founder of the British Disabled Angling Association (https://bdaa.co.uk). Thanks to Ankita Gupta for editorial assistance; DTP Designers Mohd Rizwan and Rakesh Kumar; Jacket Designer Tanya Mehrotra; Jackets Editorial Coordinator Priyanka Sharma; Managing Jackets Editor Saloni Singh; Helen Peters for the index; and to Sarah Smithies and Deepak Negi for picture research.

For their assistance on earlier editions, Dorling Kindersley and Schermuly Design Co. would like to thank the following for their invaluable help with this book: Tony Phipps, Sophie Argyris, Silke Spingies, Aparna Sharma, Ashita Murgai, Saloni Talwar, Rajnish Kashyap, Pooja Pipil, Neha Gupta, Akanksha Gupta, Diya Kapur, Neetika Vilash, Pallavi Singh, Garima Sharma, Harish Aggarwal, Mohd. Usman, Dheeraj Arora, Becky Alexander, John Bailey, Nick Helleur, Simon Peters, and Helen Schermuly. We would also like to thank all the manufacturers who generously supplied fishing tackle and equipment for photography: Delkim, Drennan, The Friendly Fisherman, Gardner Tackle, Hardy Greys, Korda, Masterline, Rok-Max, Sportfish, and Veals.

Dorling Kindersley would like to thank the following individuals for their work on *Eyewitness Companions—Fishing*: Henry Gilbey and Nick Hart for text; Andy Steer, Sally Pinhey, and Colin Newman for illustrations; Mike Good and Gerard Brown for photography; Richard Gilbert, Cathy Meeus (Schermuly Design), Gill Edden, and Jo Weeks for editorial; Susan St. Louis, Hugh Schermuly (Schermuly Design), and Steve Woosnam-Savage for design.